VALLEY OF DARKNESS

The Japanese People
and World War Two

VALLEY OF DARKNESS

The Japanese People and World War Two

Thomas R.H. Havens

UNIVERSITY
PRESS OF
AMERICA

LANHAM • NEW YORK • LONDON

Copyright © 1986 by

University Press of America,® Inc.

4720 Boston Way
Lanham, MD 20706

3 Henrietta Street
London WC2E 8LU England

Copyright © 1978 by W.W. Norton & Company, Inc.

Library of Congress Cataloging in Publication Data

Havens, Thomas R. H.
  Valley of darkness.

  Reprint. Originally published: New York : Norton,
© 1978.
  Bibliography: p.
  Includes index.
  1. World War, 1939-1945—Japan.   2. Japan—Social
life and customs—1912-1945.   I. Title.
[D767.2.H29   1986]   940.53'52   86-13189
ISBN 0-8191-5495-4 (pbk. : alk. paper)

All University Press of America books are produced on acid-free
paper which exceeds the minimum standards set by the National
Historical Publications and Records Commission.

By the same author

Nishi Amane and Modern Japanese Thought
  (*Princeton University Press, 1970*)

Farm and Nation in Modern Japan: Agrarian
Nationalism, 1870–1940
  (*Princeton University Press, 1974*)

Contents

A Note of Thanks

Long after dark on a Tuesday evening in August 1945, I
marched, a puzzled but delighted five-year-old, up and down
the narrow beach of Lake Mokoma in northern Pennsylvania,
beating a sauce pan with a wooden spoon and singing the
"Star-Spangled Banner" as the older kids set off fireworks to
celebrate the end of World War Two. At about the same
hour, as Americans heard the newsflash, it was noon,
Wednesday, August 15, in Tokyo, and the emperor of Japan
was telling his people in a prerecorded radio message to give
up the fight. Like the instant Kennedy was shot or Armstrong
and Aldrin walked on the moon, it was one of those days
when you never forget where you were or what you were
doing. The surrender of Japan was an electric moment in

time, when the age of European fascism, Japanese militarism, and total war suddenly expired. I hope this book helps to explain why that epochal day is even more unforgettable for any Japanese old enough to remember the war.

In preparing this account of wartime life in Japan, I am grateful for the help of many friends whose queries, insights, and encouragements have been a great benefit. I am particularly indebted to Kawahara Hiroshi for friendly counsel and generous hospitality during 1976–1977 when I was a visiting fellow at Waseda University. I am also grateful to these colleagues in Japan for help with my studies: Akimoto Ritsuo, Isamu and Kazuko Amemiya, Frank Baldwin, Nobuya M. Bamba, Kenneth E. Heim, Kano Masanao, Katō Taizō, Katsumura Shigeru, Kazue Kyōichi, Kimura Tokio, Mori Jōji, Motoyama Yukihiko, Okada Hiroaki, and Tanegashima Tokiyasu.

For advice about my work I am grateful to Gordon M. Berger, Delmer M. Brown, Ed Drea, Peter Duus, Miles Fletcher, Marius B. Jansen, Anne S. Johnson, Christopher E. Lewis, Barbara Molony, Leila Rupp, Ben-Ami Shillony, Richard J. Smethurst, Henry DeW. Smith II, and Valdo H. Viglielmo.

I am indebted to the directors and staffs of the following libraries for help with the materials used for this book: National Diet Library, Tokyo; Waseda University Library; the collection of the Shakai Kagaku Kenkyūjo (Institute of Social Sciences), Waseda University; East Asiatic Library, University of California, Berkeley; Harvard-Yenching Library; Connecticut College Library, especially Helen Aitner.

I am grateful to the editors of *The American Historical Review* for permission to reprint portions of my article, "Women and War in Japan, 1937–45" [*The American Historical Review* 80, no. 4 (October 1975): 913–34].

Funds from the United States Education Commission in Japan (Fulbright Commission), John Simon Guggenheim Memorial Foundation, the Joint Committee on Japanese Studies of the American Council of Learned Societies and the Social Science Research Council, and Connecticut College speeded my studies, and I am grateful to each of these sources for generous assistance. Edwin Barber, Fred Bidgood, and the staff of W. W. Norton & Company provided their customary expert editorial and production care.

Finally, I acknowledge the indulgence of readers in accepting a few stylistic conventions. Japanese and Chinese surnames precede personal names, except for Western-language publications written by Japanese authors. Notes containing complete source information are gathered following the last chapter, with citations by page and line number. Unless otherwise indicated, English translations are my own.

Ogikubo, May 1977

VALLEY OF DARKNESS

The Japanese People
and World War Two

1

The War at Home

Japan's eight-year encounter with total war began in obscurity late on the night of July 7, 1937. Hardly anyone in the home islands paid much heed when a company of Japanese soldiers, posted in China under the Boxer protocol of 1901, tangled with a Chinese patrol that evening near Marco Polo Bridge southwest of Peking. The episode, which even today is cloaked in mystery, began with rifle fire of unknown origin. Noticing that one of his troops was missing and presumably hit (as it turned out, the man was relieving himself), the commander attacked the Chinese with an entire battalion. In this haphazard manner Japan was plunged into a war that eventually cost three million of its citizens their lives.

It was not surprising that civilians back home disregarded this newest clash. Ten years of continental adventures by the

Japanese military had made the army infamous around the world. There was little reason to think that this fresh skirmish would be any different from the ones before it. Almost no one imagined that the shots at Marco Polo Bridge would dilate into a war too big to be won but too tantalizing to be abandoned. In 1928 the Japanese Kwantung Army had murdered Chang Tso-lin, the warlord of Manchuria, and three years later it seized the province from his unexpectedly intractable son and successor, Chang Hsüeh-liang. Friction was chronic thereafter with any Chinese troops who opposed the Japanese army's dream of dominating north China. But there was a difference between 1931 and 1937. Now that the fighting had spread to China proper, Japan found that it could not define its objectives and thus could not limit the crisis. Unsure what they sought, the Japanese had no way of knowing when they had attained it. The war ballooned, then bogged down, they finally pulled Japan into conflict with several of the world's most powerful nations.

Security and Social Stability

The events in China jolted Japanese society less sharply than had the Manchurian affair, not only because citizens were inured by now to unruly military exploits but also because Japan was far more prosperous and equable a country in 1937 than six years earlier. Industrial production had recovered quickly from the depression and was now 83 percent higher than in 1931, lifting both workers' wages and the number of strikes. Farmers also benefited from better times. Wholesale prices for their products were up 58 percent, raising farm income much faster than the overall rate of inflation. Sports headlines were dominated by the sumo champion Futabayama, who attracted millions of followers with an unbroken series of wrestling victories dating back to the spring 1936 tournament—a streak that eventually reached sixty-nine before he was defeated by Akinoumi in January 1939.

The nation also felt more secure with its larger army and navy, whose budgets had undergone an eight-fold rise and now accounted for 70 percent of national expenditures, compared with less than 30 percent in 1931. A strong military meant stability abroad and order at home, the latter especially welcome after five years of feckless but disturbing political terrorism in Tokyo. Japan had been an anxious country in diplomacy as well. With the naval agreements reached at London in 1930 due to expire after six years, the nation felt relief after joining Germany and Italy in an anticommunist alliance, effective 1936, that provided a measure of international security. All in all, the Japanese thought themselves relatively safe and reasonably well off. The fighting near Peking seemed like little more than a ruffle to most of them in July 1937.

Their feelings of well-being were based on a very stable social order. Since earliest times Japan has been an uncommonly coherent nation. Its people have lived together isolated by geography from other peoples, sharing a relatively constant gene pool, a single language, and common beliefs in the Shinto agrarian gods. They have carried on cooperative rice farming based on village units, lived together under political institutions legitimized by a single sacerdotal throne, and perpetuated a strongly hereditary method of family organization. Total war was one of the very few historical phenomena weighty enough to menace, let alone upset, the equipoise of so enduring a community.

It is possible, of course, to exaggerate the cohesiveness of the Japanese people, particularly in premodern centuries. As in most countries, politically ambitious rulers habitually spun out myths of even greater homogeneity than really existed, in order to centralize their power. Sharp mountains and steep valleys cut up the country into distinct regions, and long periods without external enemies doubtless invited internal warfare that divided the people rather than uniting them. Nevertheless the ministers, regents, generals, and priests who continually fought one another for control almost never threatened the stability of society at large.

The organizational forms used to carry out ordinary tasks varied with time, but the underlying structural principle of

Japanese social units, patterned after the family, persisted to modern times without much change. The group nature of social relations, based on tangible associations of persons in close contact with one another, produced a great emphasis on such qualities as loyalty, harmony, teamwork, and competence. Naturally, in so large and complex a nation not everyone prized these attributes at all times. But most of them did so often enough that the school, the warrior band, the congregation, the farm village, the business enterprise—closely knit, manageably sized, and organized like families—became typical building blocks of Japanese society.

However durable, the social system of old Japan changed somewhat in outward design during the seventeenth and eighteenth centuries. A semicentralized polity under a powerful feudal ruler soon tied various regions more closely through networks of transport and communication. Education began to spread beyond the aristocracy, creating a basis for common discourse. Most importantly, a web of economic interaction began to draw the nation together through regional markets. By 1800 the country was slowly converting from a feudal class system inherited from the medieval world of 1185–1573 to a status hierarchy based on wealth, talent, and personal connections. The layered stratification imposed by the Tokugawa military government shortly after 1603 had gradually yielded to a more open condition of society, in which vertical aggregations of competing interests were ranged side by side like elevators.

As a transitional phase of social evolution, the era marked by a group status ladder presuming inequality but also mobility had reached its apex by World War One. Thereafter large enterprises gradually dominated the economy, especially during 1941–45 when the four largest of them gained control of nearly one-quarter of all corporate and partnership capital. The result was that Japan's hierarchy of status, in which elemental social groups still formed the nucleus, grew more flaccid without coming unstuck. Within the brief space of 150 years, society passed from a feudal order based on birth to a vertical arrangement of collective interests and then to the looser class system of contemporary industrial capitalism that has begun to characterize social relations in recent decades.

In 1800 only the military aristocracy still derived its position from inheritance. Otherwise the nominally horizontal classes of official social policy—priests, farmers, artisans, and merchants—were in fact vertically sorted into groups and clusters displayed in parallel ranks. Some trading enterprises, for example, enjoyed opulence and privilege at the top of commoner society and others existed in poverty and ignominy below. When the legal prerogatives of the warriors were finally erased in the 1870s, Japan's elite became one of landlords, traders, and (slightly later) industrial capitalists in name as well as in fact.

Now the doors to higher status were thrown open to all; the artificial distinction between feudal lord and commoner evaporated; and a blend of achievement by education, patronage through personal connections, and fortuitous circumstance created a highly competitive society of contending interests topped by a relatively accessible and remarkably stable elite of wealth, property, and power. This social system, despite the growth of industries, cities, and new labor-capital relations during World War One, was still largely intact when Japanese troops exchanged shots with the Chinese Twenty-ninth Army at Marco Polo Bridge.

Revisiting the War Era

"It is one of the perversities of human nature," former U.S. senator J. William Fulbright said in 1974, "that people have a far greater capacity for enduring disasters than for preventing them, even when the danger is plain and imminent." This is precisely what happened in Japan. Her people met calamity in 1945 because an incremental process of decisions four years earlier, unchecked by foresight or better judgment, took the country to war against Britain, the Netherlands, and the United States.

Why did ordinary citizens endure the disaster once the danger became apparent? They did so because of twin fears—of the unknown and the authorities—according to the diary of Yoshizawa Hisako, a home economist:

> Most people already believe that we won't win. They just think about how miserable it will be if we lose. From what country people say, they're being driven to their wit's end and no longer think it's worth it, that there's no reason for winning. Even though you hear ordinary people saying these things, still the public listens to the government and the army and meekly keeps on working. This is so that if we lose, it won't have been the people's fault. Only when the war situation is good are we told to leave everything to the military. When things are bad, we're told that it's a total war for all the people. [January 12, 1945]

Yoshizawa clearly believed that no one wanted to be blamed for quitting, so everyone carried on. No people can fully prepare for losing a war, but the shock of surrendering was enormously jarring to the Japanese because most were so unready for it.

A quarter-century later the impact of defeat was still very powerful. "People often say they wish they could return to their youth," Kitayama Mine said in 1970. "Those must be the words of someone who grew up when times were happy. No matter what I do, I can't erase the memory of that wretched war—I spent my youth during that abominable era." For most Japanese the years from 1937 to 1945 are a "dark valley," a memory until very recently too bitter to recall with detachment.

In Japan and elsewhere, Marxists and other determinists have dismissed the era as an inevitable consequence of capitalist greed; liberals have often written it off as a horrifying but temporary setback in the country's progress toward a modern, open society. Aided by the indulgence normally conferred on the aging, the memoirs of persons who lived through the war at home began to reach a receptive audience in the 1970s. Whether nostalgic for the past or worried lest it somehow recur, nearly all Japanese who remember wartime at all recall it as a critical period in their lives.

In revisiting the war era, the first task of this book is to find out what the experience meant for ordinary people who lived in Japan during 1937–45. The second is to discover how much World War Two transformed modern Japanese society. The narrative proceeds both chronologically and topically toward answers that are generally valid, even though they may be inadequate responses to the equally important matter of what the war meant to any particular person who lived through it.

Chronologically, the cascade of diplomatic and military events from Marco Polo Bridge to Hiroshima is bisected almost at midpoint by the December 7, 1941, attack on Pearl Harbor. Japanese usually refer to the period from July 1937 to December 1941 as the China incident or the Second Sino-Japanese War, depending on their point of view. Nearly all of them call the conflict between December 1941 and August 1945 the Pacific War. Although some persons may claim it for the European theater alone before December 1941, World War Two seems to be the most appropriate label for Japan's overseas military operations during the whole period from 1937 to the surrender. The domestic history of the era resolves itself into four main phases: (1) early mobilization, from July 1937 to September 1940; (2) consolidation and regimentation, from September 1940 to May 1942; (3) full-scale general participation, from mid-1942 to late 1944; and (4) destruction and defeat, from late 1944 to August 1945.

Helpful as this periodization may be, history is happily much more than facts and dates. It is thus also worthwhile exploring three sorts of topics connected with wartime life. The first is mobilization, society's muster for all-out war as directed by the state. Mobilization is most crucial in a total war, one which requires participation by all members of the national community. Mobilization involves ideologies, propaganda, finance, public organizations, and economic and political controls of many kinds. It also needs a willing populace. The second topical category consists of the social changes that occurred in the daily routine and the life cycle because of war. It includes people working, eating, playing, growing up: wages, prices, minority employment, and women's roles in field and factory; food, nutrition, and rations; entertainment, sports, the arts, and crime; the family, fertility, education, and health care. The third category encompasses the ravages of war: people moving to the countryside to flee enemy bombs, suffering from hunger and war weariness, and dying from mammoth air raids.

Mobilization conforms generally with phases one and two of home-front life, July 1937 to September 1940 and September 1940 to May 1942. Likewise stage three, from mid-1942 to late 1944, is when many of the changes in daily living happened, and most of the ravages were compressed into the final phase of the war (late 1944 to August 1945). But the matchup between periodization and topics is inexact. Chronology is indispensable because it matters very acutely at what point in the war a phenomenon occurred: people are more likely to accept a minority co-worker when they enthusiastically support mobilization than later on when they are fatigued and dispirited. A thematic tack is equally important because periodization alone is helpless to clarify social processes that both interconnect with one another horizontally and extend vertically across eras in time. Taken together, the two approaches offer guideposts toward a cogent understanding of wartime Japan.

The aim, in brief, is to provide an account of the Japanese people at war that both describes conditions in a country increasingly under siege and explains what was happening to society at large. The narrative recounts government policies only briefly; for the most part it tells a story of daily life among civilians and its significance for the society they comprised. It is mainly an urban history, since a majority of the people lived in cities for most of the war and much of the drama occurred there. The account deals primarily with women, children, and the aging, because so many adult males were conscripted for service far from home. In no sense is it a story unique to the Japanese, whatever the distinctive twists of their history. The narrative compares Japan to the other countries that fought World War Two whenever it seems prudent to do so. Based as it is on the subjective records and recollections of those who experienced wartime, the account may sometimes seem more partisan than dispassionate. At least it is a reassurance to remember that the first historian, Herodotus, knew that among the many snares of scholarship, biased testimony was the simplest for readers to detect.

2

"Extravagance Is the Enemy"

"By being cold, we were reminded of the soldiers who were fighting for our country in northern China," recalled someone who went coatless all winter to her elementary school once war broke out with China. "In this way," her teachers told the children, they were "to learn to discipline our bodies to withstand cold weather."

There have always been a few Japanese who wore no coats, sometimes for self-mastery through physical toughening, more often because they could not afford to own one. But never before 1937 had the state fought a war by requiring its people to undergo such austerities, because never before had Japan undertaken a war of total mobilization—economic, political, and social as well as military.

Spiritual Readiness
and Total War

The eloquent symbolism of shirt-sleeved schoolchildren emulating far-off soldiers, although obvious in retrospect, was obscure to the Japanese at first because most of them were only dimly conscious of the war and many were unfamiliar with wars at all. The conflicts with China in 1894–1895 and Russia ten years later had been Japan's first foreign battles fought by conscripted commoners, not aristocratic warriors. By 1937 the sketchy image of those engagements, among old-timers who remembered them at all, was that they were brief, victorious, and disrupted the home front very little. For the generation which led Japan into World War Two, these successful encounters were the events that shaped their awareness of war. But fighting was remote from the personal experience of most ordinary people, the more so because they had been preoccupied for two decades with political upheavals at home or simply with making a living during hard times. Warfare, on the whole, was only a minor factor in forming their consciousness of public affairs. It was the period 1937–1945 that turned war and peace into the dominant cultural motifs of modern Japanese society. The first way it did so, as the shivering schoolchildren found out, was when the state began stirring awareness of the crisis in China through the national spiritual mobilization of 1937–1940.

The government's planners realized very soon that the war on the continent was going to take a full-scale effort. An introduction to the first national general mobilization law of early 1938 noted that

> the special characteristic of modern wars is that they are wars of national strength. To achieve the objectives of the war, we must perfect the national general mobilization if we

are to expect the army and navy to struggle to the utmost. . . . We must mobilize our entire resources, both physical and spiritual; it is not enough merely to provide sufficient munitions. An essential requirement for achieving the goal of victory is for the country to do its utmost to make people's livelihoods secure and harmonize the various aspects of national life necessary for prosecuting the war.

The authorities started rallying people's support for the war even before passing this law, and with good reason. For one thing, in July 1937 the country was more ready militarily for war than psychologically. For another, the government was well aware that the tangible social groupings comprising the nation at large were not instantly tractable when orders came from above. The war at home began with ideological standardization because in the 1930s it was so notably absent within society as a whole.

There was little joy to the war in Japan, especially considering that most countries which are not themselves invaded at the outset usually feel a temporary burst of war fever. The mood was dour, not gay or even keyed up. There were few bright posters, hardly any platforms decorated with bunting, almost no marching bands—and when there were, the musicians played gloomy melodies unlikely to perk up a nation that found little exuberance in trudging off to fight the Chinese. Not only were people preoccupied with internal matters, but they also knew that there had been no real provocation and that Japan's more likely enemies were to be found elsewhere. The lack of exhilaration among the public helps explain why the government labored so hard at spiritual mobilization and why the movement, from start to finish, had such a humorless mien.

A glum-looking Premier Konoe Fumimaro, addressing delegates to the first national spiritual mobilization convention on September 10, 1937, stood in Tokyo's Hibiya hall beneath huge wall posters that proclaimed nothing so bold as "Down with the Bandit Chiang Kai-shek" or "Liberate Asia from Western Imperialism," but the much more modest epithets

"National Unity," "Loyalty and Patriotism," and "Un-tiring Perseverance." To these sober slogans were soon added the blandishments "Respect Imperial Rescripts," "Protect the Imperial Country," and "Work, Work for the Sake of the Country." With guidance from the cabinet information committee and the home and education minis-tries, a "people's movement" for spiritual uplift propagan-dized the public ceaselessly for the next three years. It held lectures, distributed publications, led pilgrimages to shrines and imperial tombs, saw men off to the front and welcomed the injured home, and encouraged people to practice judo and kendo. The movement used local subcommittees, often based on existing veterans' organizations, to focus attention on the war. Soon these groups were enforcing cooperation by labeling the reluctant as "unpatriotic" or "traitors." Columbia Records (Japan), Ltd., quickly sold a million copies of Se-toguchi Tōkichi's "Patriotic March," commissioned as the movement's theme by the central leaders.

"Despite the government's earnest efforts," according to one postwar appraisal, "the national spiritual mobilization ended up as nothing but inane, empty phrases the further the war dragged on." Its vague hectoring no doubt deflected the sympathies of many citizens. Curiously, however, the ab-stractness of the campaign was probably its real strength. It was easy for people to remain indifferent to the slogans but hard to oppose them. Few could sneer when the Russo-Japanese War song was revived: "Our soldiers, of all the world most brave/ . . . now leave the land that bore and bred them;/ never to return except as victors." However cloying they may have seemed, almost no one could object when the army put up posters with "Chinese children clinging trust-ingly to the hands of a Japanese officer [that] carried an im-plied message—welcome to a nation carving new empires." Like every effective ideology, the spiritual mobilization was flexible enough to excuse almost any exercise of public power, regardless of its doctrinal vacuity. Perhaps most im-portantly of all, the movement broke ground for organizing the people into community and neighborhood associations later in the war. The tension between ideology and organization was eventually settled in the latter's favor, but Konoe's campaign was especially useful in the early months of the fighting when it showed individuals how urgent the crisis was.

Although citizen self-discipline was the first keynote after July 1937, the state soon devised laws to centralize war production and labor resources. When the national general mobilization bill was proposed, the political parties resisted it so tartly that Lt. Col. Satō Kenryō, a war ministry spokesman, was provoked into shouting "shut up!" at his interpellator during testimony before the Seventy-third Diet. The act, which resembled ones that had been passed with little opposition in France and Britain, was the basic enabling legislation that allowed the government "to apply controls to our human and material resources in such a way that the country can most effectively attain the objectives of national defense in wartime." The controls themselves could now be imposed by imperial ordinance, without coming before the Diet, although each ordinance had to be sent for advice to a mobilization council representing various interests. The law, which was approved on March 24, 1938, hastened but did not assure the decline of political party influence, since few ordinances were issued before 1940.

Not all persons accepted this expansion of public power over their lives meekly. The critic Kiryū Yūyū, writing in February 1938, noted wryly that

> It is the season for national spiritual mobilization. The smaller producers, especially the farmers, have cast aside their parents, their wives, and their children to go off to war. Even though we keep on performing "extra labor service," or what might be called "superhuman service," on behalf of the imperial state, the upper classes—especially the capitalists—plunder our labor in the name of national spiritual mobilization and the wartime system. . . . their profits are increasing almost without limit. Despite all this, isn't it strange that they show no national spirit nor any trace of patriotic conduct?

But for most, patriotism soon became associated instead with the imperial throne and other symbols of nationalism flaunted by the spiritual mobilizers.

The War Goes Public

"As the war front expanded," recalled the essayist Takeuchi Yoshimi, "mobilization orders grew more intense. Young men with sashes made from Japanese flags were packed into troop trains and sent off by children's brass ensembles playing 'Protecting the Home Front.'" The focus of it all was the emperor, he wrote: "The war gradually became commonplace and started to affect people's lives externally and internally. Group pressures arose, such as the compulsion to remove their hats felt by passengers riding streetcars in front of the imperial palace and the Meiji shrine." Later in the war Tokyo streetcars stopped at the point nearest the palace on their routes so that passengers could rise and bow deeply in worship. Public meetings everywhere in Japan began with the same ceremony, and even though no law required people to bow, the "social pressure was too great to be ignored."

"Extravagance is the enemy," city residents were told early in 1938, the same spring that the first hot dog stand opened, with much brio, in the Ginza district of Tokyo. While the American fad was spreading to other cities, authorities in the capital warned people "don't be wasteful" and urged them to shirk luxuries. In the rooftop pool of the fashionable Ginza Matsuzakaya department store, shoppers were treated to a mock battle between electrically driven boats representing Japan, the U.S., and Britain, while a narrator explained the urgency of consumer restraint. In June the finance ministry kicked off a savings campaign, using the spiritual mobilization movement to disseminate such exhortations as "let the housewife save for her family" and "save for yourself and for the state."

Little Frugality in Occupied China: Japanese women and Chinese men, richly clad in their respective national styles, encounter each other on a Tientsin street lined with rickshaws in October 1938.

Frugality and savings, as the government official Aragaki Hideo made plain in mid-1938, "are purely precautionary measures." Japan "still has plenty of materials to spare, and the people have as yet felt no such actual stringency in their clothing, food and housing as was experienced by the European nations during the World War." Despite Aragaki's aplomb, gasoline was strictly rationed starting in March, charcoal-burning automobiles made their appearance in June, telephones—even for the military—could not be installed because copper was scarce, and whale, salmon, and shark skins were being substituted by deft craftsmen where leather had been used before. By day the summertime streets of Tokyo were crowded, Aragaki concluded, and "thousands of citizens go shopping or strolling as peacefully as ever while guns roar and their compatriots fall in battle on the Chinese continent." By night the drive for restraint had begun to darken the Ginza amusements a bit. The novelist Nagai Kafū gently noted that while the government was preparing to close the theaters it was also recruiting prostitutes to attend the troops abroad, but he added that "the prohibition against neon signs must be described as an enlightened act by our unenlightened military government."

Japan's first full summer at war included a few public ceremonies planned by the spiritual mobilizers, especially those held on July 7, 1938, to mark the anniversary of the Marco Polo Bridge affair. That morning the Tokyo *Asahi* newspapers sponsored a somber parade, with more than 10,000 marchers, from the Yasukuni shrine to the palace plaza, to "guard the home front." Throughout the empire, a minute of silent prayer was observed at noon. By the end of the next summer, such rituals were being held on the first of each month, now known as Public Service Day for Asia. Fortunetellers were told by the state to give only happy forecasts, and schoolchildren and office workers were exhorted to show self-denial by eating "rising-sun box lunches," a pickled red plum on a field of white rice in the pattern of the national flag—an economy that seemed luxurious later in the war when polished rice was scarcely available at all.

Citizens were expected to worship at shrines, donate their time to public service, and forgo amusements. Japan's enormously thriving entertainment industry closed for the day, with festive consequences unintended by the state. Public Service Day became a holiday for all the girls who worked in bars and coffeeshops, and many young couples spent their time window-shopping or walking together in parks and public gardens. In February 1942 the authorities switched the observance to the eighth of each month and renamed it Imperial Edict Day, to commemorate the declaration of war against the U.S. on December 8, 1941. The public formalities included an antic *coup de théâtre* in December 1942 that was reminiscent of the seventeenth-century Japanese Christians who were forced to renounce their faith by trampling a crucifix. In the wartime version, a woman recalled, "someone drew a large stars-and-stripes flag on the busiest street in downtown Tokyo—Ginza—and made pedestrians step on it. Most of my acquaintances dismissed the incident with the thought: How foolish can people get!"

However peculiar, ceremonies of all sorts helped Japan rally for war by regularly drawing large numbers of people into rituals held in the open. Sad though they may have been, the obligatory brass-band sendoffs both made the soldiers leaving for the front feel appreciated and let those staying behind feel involved. Even having to keep a stiff lip during the public rituals at the station when the remains of a loved one killed in battle arrived was psychically integrating for the survivors. The spiritual mobilization used ceremonies shrewdly to reduce the gap between public and private feelings by palliating the hostility and resentment that people might otherwise have allowed to burst forth.

Extravagance was the enemy, not just on formal occasions but in everyday life as well. The spiritual mobilization leaders ostracized showy dress starting in 1939, urging men instead to wear a national civilian uniform in order "to conserve material and promote increasing interest in national defense projects." Women were asked to bear the far harsher burden of setting aside their dresses and kimonos in favor of *monpe*, the drab peasants' pantaloons worn in the northeast. Men at least could evade the frugality campaign by having their civilian uniforms tailored from pure wool, but there was no way *monpe* could make even the most refined lady look chic. At first women wore them only at air raid drills and other public events, but deeper in the war they were seen more and more often because other clothes were so scarce.

Cosmetics and permanent waves were banned in 1939 as unnecessary luxuries, and the spiritual mobilization movement placed children on streetcorners to accost well-coiffed women with "let's cut out permanents!" Hairdressers were restricted to just three curls per customer, a restraint that must have taxed their artistry to the utmost. But despite the patriotic blandishments many women continued to have their hair done, even when charcoal replaced electric dryers late in the war, on the principle that "a happy woman is a more efficient woman, even in war-time."

Since 1937 the National Defense Women's Association had sent members clad in white aprons to see soldiers off at dockside or to ask passersby on downtown streets to sew one loop each in "thousand-stitch bands," to be given to departing servicemen as "a symbol of thousands of Japanese women's trust and faith." Soon the association had young girls send "letters

Girls with Curls Unwelcome: Woman with a severe hair style reads a community council poster: "People with permanents will please refrain from passing through here."

of encouragement" to soldiers at the front whom they had never met, even when they received coarse answers in reply. It also mustered vigilant matrons to stand on streetcorners with handbills to be distributed to stylishly dressed women, urging greater sobermindedness in light of the national emergency. By 1940, the bureau of municipal social education in Tokyo discovered, the year-long campaign against luxuries was having scant effect. In one hour the bureau scrutinized 1,172 women pedestrians at a downtown intersection. Twenty-seven had unseemly hairdos, 163 were dressed in extravagant foreign styles, 172 wore overly expensive kimonos, and 192 had elaborate accessories. Not only was the drive for self-restraint ineffectual; no amount of moralizing from the spiritual mobilization could conceal the huge textile shortages by 1940. The strictures of a tightening war economy, not stern pieties from streetside dowagers, eventually drove citizens into the approved styles. No law ever formally required men to put on civilian uniforms, or women to wear *monpe*, except the law of supply and demand.

Using the News and Banning Bad Books

The program to rally civic-mindedness soon spread to the mass media, which had always been susceptible to pressures from above. The quality of Japanese propaganda toward enemies and neutrals during 1937–1945 was indifferent, but it was generally quite effective at home. Like Britain in the First World War and Germany in the Second, Japan made good use of the media to dispense propaganda in the classic sense—truth or fiction deliberately spread to help a cause. The government also used time-honored techniques to stamp out unwelcome opinions and cow its opponents into silence. Both the myth and the cudgel turned out to be effective instruments for getting people to accept the war, through radio, the press, and movies, as well as the publishing industry.

Propaganda, like most other aspects of the mobilization, was rather poorly coordinated during the first three years of the war. The army, navy, foreign ministry, and imperial general headquarters each had a separate press service, and the cabinet created an information bureau of its own in September 1937. The army news office soon put out a set of pamphlets to show its cooperation with the national spiritual mobilization, one of which declared that

A firm belief in the ideals of the Empire and its mission must be implanted. . . . A spirit of self-sacrifice for the country must be fostered and internationalism, egoism, and individualism which lead to forgetfulness of the State, to evasion of control essential to the State and to conduct contrary to the interests of the country must be eradicated. . . . Japan's unique civilization must be promoted. . . . Education of a very intellectual type must be abandoned; stress must be laid upon moral training.

Most news management, in the sense of positive manipulations of information, took place through the single news agency that had been created by merging earlier wire services into one public corporation in January 1936. Known as Dōmei, it received all its political directives from the cabinet information bureau and was the only official source for out-of-town and international news. Aided by Dōmei, the daily newspapers cooperated actively with the spiritual mobilization (although they had little choice in the matter). But Japan's propaganda before Pearl Harbor was mainly directed at other Asians and its future adversaries in the west, and most of the state's dealings with the press early in the war employed the negative manacles of suppression.

Any government can find a legal basis for trimming the sails of the press, and the Japanese authorities soon uncovered acts dating back to 1893 that permitted wartime censorship. New press restrictions were voted in 1937, and additional rules were announced every year down to 1941 under the national general mobilization law. The army used its military police, the Kenpei, to enforce strict controls over military information and troop movements. Sensitive political and economic topics were generally checked by the home ministry's thought police, or Tokkō, which had been established in 1911 to suppress leftwing movements. Newspaper editors began submitting stories to the home ministry for advance approval during the war, rather than risk punishment after an unwelcome item appeared in print. Nevertheless, fines and imprisonment were often imposed, and most papers had "jail editors" to represent them behind bars when sentences were handed down.

Censorship, like most forms of psychological terror, is probably most effective when it is arbitrarily imposed. Its randomness and unpredictability are far more intimidating than a blue pencil or a blackout uniformly applied. Yet the authorities decided to take even more direct steps than mere news management in order to control what people read. On the pretext of conserving paper, the home ministry and local police forces drummed hundreds of newspapers out of existence between 1937 and 1939, consolidating local dailies in most prefectures into a single regional paper. Morning editions were cut back to four to six pages from the usual eight to fourteen, and evening papers now ran two to four pages instead of six to eight. The metropolitan police censors in Tokyo pruned the number of periodicals from 11,400 in 1936 to 7,700 in late 1939. The number of women's magazines by 1941 had dropped from eighty to seventeen; art magazines fell from thirty-nine to eight. The victims of these blunt shears had no support from the judiciary. Even if they could have afforded lawyers, the freedom to publish was not available at any price.

"Dangerous thoughts" are what most proscribed outlooks were branded, yet the erratic manner in which dissent was purged suggests that ideas were most dangerous when they seemed to threaten how power was organized. Pornography had been the bête noire of the home ministry's book censors in the 1920s, but dangerous thoughts became the leading pretext for bans in the next decade. Before 1937, the state usually harassed authors rather than editors or publishers, but once the war in China broke out the bureaucrats caused endless headaches for publishing houses when they insisted on inspecting proofs before publication. Most publishers were unhappy with this prior restraint, but some struggling firms welcomed it because a book, once approved, no longer risked being removed from sale in the stores. More than 20,000 books a year were appearing in the late 1930s, and normally the censors had just five days to disapprove of a title. Understandably enough, their favorite method of control continued to be hounding certain authors who were offensive to the government. Publishers were confronted with lists of writers whose works could not appear, which by 1941 included not only leftwingers but also the authors of antiwar stories, romances, and even comic books.

Personae non gratae on the campuses found it harder to publish their writings as well. The liberal economists Yanaihara Tadao and Kawai Eijirō were driven from their professorships at Tokyo Imperial University in 1938–1939 for speaking out when the institution cooperated with the war. Kawai was first acquitted, but when the prosecutors appealed the verdict he was found guilty of "desecrating the position of our sacred emperor, supporting communism, and trying to eliminate the private property system." A few days before the November 1940 ceremonies honoring the 2,600th anniversary of the Jinmu emperor's ascent, the mild-mannered Waseda historian Tsuda Sōkichi found four of his books prohibited because they questioned the divine origins of the imperial family. By 1941 the state had suppressed the works of such popular writers as Niwa Fumio, Tokuda Shūsei, Oda Sakunosuke, Hayashi Fumiko, and Nagata Michihiko. In the extreme case of Tsuda, none of his books had ever sold more than 6,400 copies—but the state apparently persecuted all these writers less for the doctrinal content of their volumes than for the challenge they seemed to present to the established order.

Radio was much easier to maneuver than the print media, and it soon became the main propaganda vehicle for the cabinet information bureau. Since 1934 all stations in Japan had been absorbed by the public broadcasting corporation, NHK. Once the war began, the state expanded radio audiences by waiving the monthly subscriber fee of one yen (about 30¢) for large families and those with men at the front. In 1938 Japan had only one-fourth as many radio receivers per capita as the United States, so the authorities gave away AM radios in poor villages—but banned shortwave sets, assuring a monopoly on what people could hear. Beginning in January 1938, the government broadcast ten minutes of war dispatches and news of the spiritual mobilization movement each evening at 7:30. Like Japan's newspapers during the war, NHK carried few reports of the European theater even after the fighting began in September 1939, and the Dōmei press agency remained its only official source of news throughout the period. Controversial political developments were never reported, and starting the day Japan bombed Pearl Harbor listeners could no longer even hear weather forecasts because they might aid the enemy.

Since movies, of all the media, are the most absorbing for the audience and the least subject to distractions, it is surprising how little heed the government paid them during the early mobilization. The censors had always scanned films from abroad for socialism as well as kissing, and no Russian productions could be shown. When the home ministry began to withdraw American and British films, there were still plenty of domestic movies to replace them. In 1937, a record year, Japanese studios poured out 580 features and nearly 2,000 newsreels and other short films. Yet there was still a market for foreign movies, especially ones from France while they were still available early in the war.

The state ordered producers in 1937–1938 to support the spiritual mobilization by depicting truly Japanese emotions and portraying respect for the family system, and in April 1939 the motion picture law imposed both negative controls on film distribution and positive guidelines for producing propaganda. Gradually such items as *Japan Stands Alone* appeared, showing her as the defender of Asia against the aggressive U.S. Navy. Still it was not until 1940 that the home ministry began to censor scripts in advance, and the state was usually content in the beginning of the war to assure what people could not see rather than manipulate what they could. Like most other aspects of the spiritual mobilization, media policy during the first three years of the war was more hortatory than Draconian, but the legal and organizational apparatus built during this period made it easy to apply much stricter controls after 1940.

Cultivating the Young

As a supposedly "people's movement," the national spiritual mobilization lasted just three years and mainly acted as a trumpet to rally sentiment for the war quickly. Most of its activities were hurry-up enterprises: parades, pamphlets, ceremonies, streetside admonitions to frugality, nightly broadcasts on NHK. But the campaign also had a bearing on long-range socialization for millions of Japanese schoolchildren through military drill, student labor service, educational broadcasts, and eventually a showy curricular and organizational reform in 1941. The education ministry was proud of its autonomy and often wary of the army, cabinet, and home ministry officials who led the spiritual mobilization; nevertheless, schooling for Japanese children soon fell in step with the movement's main aim of getting the nation ready for war.

Even before the Marco Polo Bridge episode, new ethics texts (*Shūshin,* appearing November 1936) and a volume called *Basic Principles of the National Essence (Kokutai no hongi,* published May 1937) had been introduced to play up Japan's cultural distinctiveness among elementary pupils. In January 1938 the education ministry brought out a pamphlet, "National Spiritual Mobilization and School Education," that showed teachers how to work the China crisis into each subject area. Already schoolchildren were forced to bow to the emperor's portrait and hear the imperial education rescript of 1890 recited at regular intervals; now they had to join in new activities to correct the earlier "overemphasis on intellectual training"—with their classroom hours shortened correspondingly.

For one thing, the students had to undergo more physical training, and their daily calisthenics (taisō) were eventually renamed body drill (tairen), carrying obvious military overtones. School sports after 1938 grew more martial, with baseball increasingly displaced by marching, judo, and kendo. For another, boys in the upper elementary grades and secondary schools were required to take frequent military training, an unpopular regimen that the army explicitly admitted was intended "to build up the morale of the nation, rather than to serve primarily as a measure of preparedness." Moreover, the obligation to perform school labor service cut still further into class time as a result of the spiritual campaign. At first the tasks meant occasional work on specific neighborhood or community projects, such as cleaning streets or parks. The labor service program intensified after Japan declared "a new order in East Asia" on November 3, 1938, the anniversary of the Meiji emperor's birthday. On the pretext of helping Japan strengthen herself to lead the lesser countries of Asia, students now had to give as much as ten days at a time for gathering charcoal, picking up leaves, and other jobs no longer routinely performed in a slowly tightening war economy. After Pearl Harbor, student workers proved even more important when labor grew truly scarce.

Radio broadcasts to the schools, first developed by NHK early in 1935, were systematized under the spiritual mobilization despite the education ministry's fears about losing control over their content. Beginning with a "teachers' hour" for elementary instructors in 1938, the broadcasts spread directly to pupils and in September 1941 were legally incorporated into the curriculum. Because their content could be changed

An Earnest Salute: Ill-clothed schoolboys greet a tattered reservist before military drill at Koga National School, Ibaraki prefecture. Most wear wooden clogs because rubber for sneakers was scarce.

instantly, unlike textbooks, the programs were handy devices when changes in instruction were imposed. Their themes grew more militaristic after Pearl Harbor, and soon pupils were listening to "Frontline Diary" and "Greater East Asia Co-Prosperity Sphere Lectures." Useful as they were in reaching millions of young citizens, the broadcasts were only peripheral ornaments to the basic curriculum, and doubtless for many students they were entertaining diversions rather than classroom material to be taken seriously.

Once they graduated from elementary school, most children kept on pursuing their spiritual training in a form of continuing education devised for young working people. Since only a minority of prewar Japanese boys and girls continued their education beyond the compulsory six years of grammar school, the government had set up youth schools for teenagers in 1935 so that they could get part-time vocational and military training. Based on local youth associations and training institutes, the schools met for three hours or so each day while the pupils also held jobs. In April 1939 the national education commission, under the authority of the education ministry, made it obligatory for boys to attend the youth schools for five years if they were not studying elsewhere. Evidently this requirement was not fully enforced because young people's labor was often too valuable, yet in 1941 three-quarters of the thirteen to fifteen age group was enrolled.

What happened in Japan's schools during the spiritual mobilization was a hint of much larger changes after 1940. The education commission, starting in 1938, recommended that primary schools be revamped to offer not only ordinary skills but also "basic training of the people in conformity with the moral principles of the Japanese empire." The reforms, which took effect in April 1941, required students to attend elementary schools (renamed national schools) for eight years and youth schools part-time for another five. Even more military training was wedged into the daily schedule, and secondary education was more tightly integrated. As the official history of the education system noted after the war, these

structural changes were never put into effect because of wartime conditions, but the shift in curricular content was
weighty. Although classwork in the national schools was nominally split into four teaching categories, the education ministry insisted that "there is to be no division of learning, nor
any separation of subjects of study, and the bulk of the instructional content will deal with training imperial countrymen." In a system that the state claimed would "complete
the holy war" to bring "eight corners of the world under one
roof," it is small wonder that flags flew in every classroom, rituals venerating the throne increased, and Christians were
asked "Which is greater, Christ or the emperor?"—by now a
rhetorical question in the eyes of the state.

"Training imperial countrymen," the education officials
concluded, meant revising the national texts of 1933 twice
during the war, once in 1940–1941 and again in 1943. Two
recent studies of these schoolbooks agree that the state emphasized the same virtues and goals in its texts throughout
the prewar and wartime periods. All six editions between
1903 and 1943 stressed the national essence, Japan's rise to
prominence, and pressures from abroad. But new versions
were needed to keep up with the empire's expansion and
world diplomatic events after 1937, and the manner of pre-
sentation grew more romantic and less formal by the sixth
text of 1943. Schoolchildren were now taught that the Shinto
sun goddess would protect her divine land through mystical
powers that drew man and nature together. In the same vein
was *The Way of Subjects* (*Shinmin no michi*), issued by the education ministry to all schools and community organizations in
August 1941 as a handbook for young persons. This remarkable document attacked "individualism, liberalism, utilitar-
ianism, and materialism" in one breath and offered an elaborate rationale for Japan's overseas activities. The state spent
most of its energy making younger pupils aware of the war,
but not even university students were free from the program
of spiritual elevation. Their curriculum was further national-
ized in 1940 when Tokyo and Kyoto Imperial Universities announced courses on "The History of Japanese Ideology" and

"The History of the Japanese Spirit." In August of the same year, instructors were forbidden to use the Bible as a text because it was "detrimental to the moral education of the Japanese."

Lyrical as the school texts may have been about Japan's destiny, their aura of fantasy did not stand in the way of badly needed technical education after 1937. The spiritual mobilization leaders, it is true, forced cuts in elementary school class hours. Rather like the Nazis, certain officials talked for a time about a "Japanese science" based on "the imperial way." But the government soon shifted more students into technical areas, and it converted most public commercial institutes into technical schools. The result was that there were three times as many science and engineering graduates in 1941–1945 as a decade earlier. To encourage basic research, the state formed a series of federations and societies in 1940, capped by a technology agency two years later to coordinate policy. Japan's scientific and technical shortcomings in wartime stemmed from inadequate financing, equipment, and leadership much more than from a preoccupation with ideology. Given the deficient resources available to them, for example, it is amazing that Admiral Tanegashima Tokiyasu and his research team developed jet aircraft to the experimental stage before the end of the war.

The government's language-instruction policies, on the other hand, were as short-sighted as its science policy was practical. Zealous officials in the spiritual mobilization branded English as the language of the enemy in 1937, and soon citizens found that Japanese terms derived from European languages had been replaced in official pronouncements by ersatz native equivalents. Perhaps it was understandable that a *sukāto* (skirt) might seem more respectable when it was called *hakama* (traditional Japanese skirt), but people were surprised to learn that *poketto* (pocket) was now *monoire* (put-things-in) and that *uesuto* (waist) had turned into *dōkakori* (torso encirclement). Although not unsympathetic to these efforts, the education ministry treated the question with discreet inaction. It issued no national ukase against teaching English, in deference to those who knew how vital it was for scientific research, but instead left the matter to the local school districts. Faced with demands for more military drill and student labor service, the local authorities usually took the ministry's silence as consent to eliminate English classes from the middle schools, and by 1943 the language had virtually disappeared from the curriculum below the university level. Even in cosmopolitan (although tightly policed) Tokyo, the well-known Tōyō Eiwa Women's College felt obliged to change its name from characters meaning "English-Japanese" to ones signifying "eternal harmony."

Elsewhere the state took up the campaign against English words with élan. Signs in roman letters came down from parks and stations; cigarettes sold by the government monopoly changed their names from Cherry and Golden Bat to Sakura and Kinshi. A woman's *parasōru* (parasol) became her *yōhigasa* (western-style sun umbrella) and, more uncomfortably, her *burajā* (brassiere) became a *chichiosae* (breast restraint). Imagine the confusion of the radio audience in 1940 when baseball announcers suddenly began to use utterly unfamiliar Japanese words in place of English-derived equivalents. *Sutoraiku* (strike) now became *honkyū, bōru* (ball) was *gaikyū*, and *hitto endo ran* (hit and run) turned into *kyōsōda*. Most ludicrous of all was the attempt to discourage children from calling their parents *mama* and *papa*, as though the authorities could root out many generations' usage in the most elemental social unit of all. However foolish the government's attitude toward teaching the language, the campaigns to stamp out words of English origin after 1937 suggest the limits on a state's ability to mobilize its people. Bureaucrats could remove the offending terms easily enough from the controlled press and radio, but they were quite helpless to dictate what words the nation, as a people, used for communicating within itself.

If extravagance and the English language were the true enemies, Japan had scarcely defeated them when the spiritual mobilization came to an end in September 1940. By then the movement had overstayed its welcome and become an irritation to many, but as a messenger to make the war crisis better known it had done a thorough job. How fully ordinary citizens applauded the war at this stage cannot easily be known; some did so enthusiastically, others reluctantly, and still others not at all—often at peril to their personal liberty. Thanks to the spiritual mobilization, the country fell into a routine of parades, ceremonies, slogans, and broadcasts that made it almost impossible to ignore the war. The press was under restraint, radio was completely controlled, and the schools had been gently but firmly bent to serve the state. It might still not be easy for a citizen to accept the war in conscience, but it was now much harder to oppose it in public. Japan's persistent spiritual campaign, for all its somber anomalies, had brought the war home to every doorstep and won the participation, if not yet the support, of most who lived within.

3

Getting Organized for War

"Honor home" was the inscription on little plaques outside every house in Japan with a man at war. Slowly but noticeably, daily living at the end of the 1930s grew tighter because of the battle in China. If they had somehow escaped the moralistic browbeatings of the spiritual mobilization, people now could not help knowing there was a war on when they went off to work, out to do the shopping, or over to the neighborhood bar. Starting in 1939, the wearisome fight in China gradually forced more and more preparedness at home. If fantasy had marked much of the spiritual campaign, now the events abroad and pressures in the marketplace began to bring the country to terms with reality. Whether honor homes or not, most families found it easier to cope with concrete actualities than with fanciful spiritual illusions as they confronted day-to-day living. During the second and third years of the war, these tangibles included economic disarray, tightening webs of neighborhood and labor organization, changing standards of public health, and a growing pinch on what people could buy and how they could spend their free time.

The Economy Heats Up

By 1939 anyone could see that Japan was involved in a real war. The unruly but stubborn Chinese Nationalist army had retreated the previous October deep into the interior, near the new capital at Chungking. There it dug in for a war of attrition, one that cost the Japanese army an astounding 185,000 lives even before Pearl Harbor. Prime Minister Konoe's "new order for East Asia," unveiled in November 1938, meant occupying strategic cities and communication routes all over China, often at great peril to the Japanese troops posted in distant regions. In May 1939 the army began an enormously draining engagement with Marshal Georgi Zhukov's Soviet divisions at Nomonhan, on the Mongolian-Manchurian border. The jolt of such far-flung operations on the continent inevitably made waves at home. So did the spectacular summer drama of 1939 in the west: the Nazi-Soviet nonaggression pact of August 21 and Hitler's invasion of Poland a fortnight later. Now Europe, like Asia, was burning.

With the Europeans self-occupied, the Chinese recalcitrant, and the Americans reproachful, Japan's leaders were more eager than ever to expand their new order. The government could see that the opportunities and the risks abroad demanded an even firmer industrial base at home. By 1940 the military expenditures in Japan were double their 1937 level (6.81 versus 3.27 billion yen), and the munitions procurements helped to drive up the output of durable goods 36 percent in the same period. Heavy industry, which had accounted for 58 percent of industrial production when the war with China began, climbed to 73 percent by the end of 1941. The new factory openings drew hundreds of thousands of workers from the farms, and by 1940 the proportion of civilians employed in agriculture had dropped to 42 percent from 48 percent a decade earlier. Not included were many people still listed as farmers who had taken jobs moonlighting in the war plants.

Despite the urgent situation abroad, heavy industry in Japan expanded as it had before—through inducements resulting from the political process, not by military fiat. The army and navy still had to have their budgets approved each year, and imperial ordinances under the March 1938 national general mobilization law had to be screened by a fifty-member council not notably partial to the military. As late as 1940–1941, in the words of the economist T. A. Bisson, "Japan's economy was financed and operated by private enterprise, which disposed of profits and dividends with relatively slight government interference. Control, in the sense of comprehensive state plans enforced on industry, was still in embryonic form." The role of the government, as in Japan's prewar economic development, was still mainly that of chief customer, although the products it purchased were a good deal more portentous than the railways and school buildings of earlier eras.

Ordinary people did not have to work in a defense plant to be affected by the swollen economy. Inflation was so bad during the first three years of mobilization that real consumption per capita fell 17 percent between 1937 and 1940, despite the seemingly good wages in the munitions factories. With the year 1936 as 100, the retail price index had risen by 1940 in the U.S. to 101, in Germany to 104, in the U.K. to 125—and in Japan to the shocking figure of 175. Clearly the state had ineffectual control over the wartime economy, but not for lack of concern. Within a month of the Marco Polo Bridge incident, it had announced an excess profits ordinance, and the next summer price ceilings were set for certain product lines. But it was easy to evade these rules, and the fired-up manufacturing sector kept on driving prices higher. When war broke out in Europe, the cabinet knew that inflation would probably become contagious, as it had during the First World War, so the government suddenly announced a price freeze on September 19, 1939, fixing rents, wages, and general consumer prices at their September 18 levels. The cabinet had grown impatient with selective controls and now gambled, unsuccessfully as it turned out, that a general freeze would attract voluntary compliance. But the only thing that stayed frozen that winter was the family hearth—from a sudden shortage of charcoal.

Organizing the Neighborhoods

The spiritual mobilization was a misfit in the tightly structured administrative world of wartime Japan. As a creature of the cabinet, it became something of a brass ring on the bureaucratic carousel, up for grabs by the home, finance, education, or service ministries. Most often it was claimed by the home ministry, when concrete organizational activities were at stake. Without stepping out of character as a morale-building enterprise, the spiritual campaign ornamented a favorite home ministry scheme: organizing civilians into neighborhood associations and community councils.

As time passed it was natural that the spiritual movement joined in this sort of venture. When the war dragged on into 1939, people's vim for ideological readiness sagged and more broadly based mobilization took hold instead. The spiritual campaign correspondingly turned more practical. Its central federation had been created when the war first started under Arima Ryōkitsu, a man who mixed his roles splendidly (he was an admiral turned Shinto priest and now a spiritual mobilizer). In March 1939 the federation was placed under a new spiritual mobilization committee headed by General Araki

Sadao, the education minister. The movement began to help gather scrap metal, show consumers how to economize, and solicit savings from schoolchildren and housewives. In August the home ministry goaded the central federation and the spiritual mobilization committee into announcing seven principles for daily living: rising early, gratitude and thanks, cooperation for Japan, public labor service, strict punctuality, thrift, and physical and spiritual discipline. If no paragon of practicality, the list was at least less abstract than Konoe's melancholy calls for loyalty and unity two years earlier. Still, it was in the drive to build neighborhood organizations that the spiritual campaign functioned most concretely.

Since 1930 the home ministry had been trying to solidify local administration, euphemistically known as self-rule, by forming community councils and neighborhood associations in every city, town, and village in Japan. A community council (*burakukai, chōkai,* or *chōnaikai*) normally included several hundred households or an entire village, and the neighborhood association (*tonarigumi*) was designed as a subunit of the council with ten to twenty families. Both were supposed to be informal citizens' organizations to plan community affairs beneath the ward, town, or village assembly, which was the lowest-level body legally recognized in the local government system that had been created in 1888–1890. Now, in the late 1930s, the spiritual movement helped form councils and neighborhood associations, but their most important activities were concentrated in the period after Pearl Harbor.

Starting in the seventh century, powerful Japanese rulers periodically made commoners form small residential groupings for mutual surveillance, often patterned after the medieval Chinese *pao-chia* system of collective responsibility. As feudal community organizations died out in the nineteenth century, they were gradually succeeded by two sorts of intermediate groups. One was the voluntary association, like those found in many countries, established locally for specific purposes such as street-sweeping, fire-watching, tending the local shrine, marketing grain, guarding against diseases, or planning recreational outings for schoolchildren. Apart from small-time merchants' associations, the voluntarist tradition was much weaker in the cities than in the countryside. The second category of intermediate organizations included all the civic groups created around the beginning of the twentieth century with direct aid from the government: reservists' and veterans' organizations, agricultural associations, thrift societies, women's guilds, and youth clubs. These nominally "half-bureaucratic, half-people's" groups were unquestionably weighted in favor of the state, but like the more voluntaristic associations they met residents' needs and could not have flourished without support from below.

Times of stress were a fillip for both types of groups. The depressions of the 1880s and 1920s, as well as the monstrous Kanto earthquake of 1923, were true disasters that forced people to cooperate spontaneously—often leading to permanent community organizations. The government, for its part, seized on the Russo-Japanese War and the depression after World War One to build local associations through its rural improvement campaign in 1905 and the village rehabilitation scheme of 1932–1935. What the home ministry tried to do in the 1930s was to subsume both the voluntary associations and the government-sponsored societies under the new rubric of community councils, without formally abolishing the older groups because of strong local feelings.

It is easy to guess why the bureaucrats were eager to bring these functional associations into their orbit. By the 1930s Japan was a much larger, infinitely more complex society than forty years earlier when the local government system began. Villages were no longer quite the stable, cohesive communities they had been before industrialization disrupted their self-sufficiency and skewed their social hierarchy. The cities had always been more depersonalized, more chaotic, and their ferocious growth since the start of World War One made them sometimes seem ungovernable. With a crisis in China atop it all, the home ministry pushed even harder to convert random bands of fire-fighters and street-sweepers into community councils that would help with local duties as well as drum up ideological support for the war. The councils soon took on more administrative than political functions. After Pearl Harbor, their tone became matter-of-fact, pragmatically focused on getting the job done in a time of siege.

In 1938 and especially 1939, the spiritual mobilization spread its exhortations through community councils wherever they existed and helped set them up wherever they didn't. The councils also engaged in savings subscriptions, keeping parks clean, drilling for air raids, and sometimes even collecting taxes. In 1938 the home ministry tried to parlay the council movement into a major reform of local government—one that would make community councils and neighborhood associations legally a part of the administrative apparatus and thus compulsory for all municipalities. The plan was denounced by the political parties, rival bureaucratic agencies, and many local bodies, each of which saw the scheme as a power play. The ministry cleverly set the proposal aside until 1942 but kept on using the spiritual mobilization to form more councils anyway.

Community Councils and Neighborhood Traditions

The first push to start community councils came in early 1938, when spiritual mobilization leaders and the home ministry began setting them up to mark the fiftieth anniversary of local rule, April 17, 1938. Osaka, Japan's second city, responded with formidable zeal. It distributed half a million handbills urging "let's form new community councils, desired by all city residents," and by the day of the ceremonies it claimed 2,699 councils, compared with just 344 of them two months earlier. Kobe and Yokohama quietly followed suit, using their public health cooperatives that had long existed for preventing dockside epidemics as cornerstones for the new organizations.

The councils in April 1938 were transparently nothing but paper entities, confined almost wholly to whatever long-standing activities they had carried out before being renamed community councils. Tokyo is a good example of how the organizational shell began to take on substance in 1938 and 1939. The city fathers decided to use the April 17 festivities to issue an "Outline of Provisions for Community Councils in Tokyo," a detailed list of instructions to the city's 3,061 councils that was emblematic of the movement as a whole. The outline announced a great deal of structural frippery and then identified the councils' purpose: "to cooperate in self-rule, contribute to expanding the public good, and plan for the advancement and fulfillment of people's livelihoods, in accord with the traditional good customs of neighborly mutual aid and joint responsibility."

The councils were asked to work with police and fire officials, arrange for festivals, help with public works, take care of sanitation and public health duties, guard against fires, tend the aged, keep order, and reform public morals—nearly all the services of local government, and at no pay. The neighborhood associations, the document concluded, "will serve to implement the detailed business of the community councils." In the early stages of wartime, when well-dressed women still shopped freely in Ginza and farmers enjoyed more prosperity than they had in two decades, this manifesto expressed only an ideal, not a literal set of expectations. But it was the first clear statement of a process of neighborhood involvement that eventually drew nearly every civilian into the day-to-day administration of the home front.

The city government soon discovered that Tokyo could not be organized by fiat or exhortation alone. Her six million residents usually had little in common with their neighbors, and no sense of crisis yet prevailed in 1938–1939 to drive them together. Community councils seemed to work best when they conformed to political or postal subdivisions, although this often trapped them to the flypaper of administrative routine. Sometimes it also turned them into support organizations for the reelection of a local politician. And certainly not all volunteer groups relished the standardization that was being thrust on them from the city and the home ministry, whether they agreed with the spiritual mobilization or not.

Despite such ruffles, the community councils and neighborhood associations are occasionally regarded as a blunt "system of organizing and mobilizing individual citizens for the purpose of controlling them from above," based on the ancient notion of "conveying the will of the authorities to those below." In the months after Pearl Harbor these organizations took on so many duties, and drew so many people into their activities, that so concise a description is a poor fit. Even as they were forming in the late 1930s, it is not clear how authoritarian the councils and associations were. The government naturally pretended that these groups were spontaneous outpourings of public sentiment, which they manifestly were not. But without some measure of local cooperation, it would have been impossible to thrust such organizations on the people from above. Tokyo, in particular, apparently shunned any pretense of uniformity and tried for most of 1938 to let local residents devise their own methods for establishing them.

For men supposedly creating local instruments of repression, the authorities were uncommonly sensitive to community feelings, especially in the countryside. Unlike the Nazi party blocs created *de novo* in contemporary Germany, the new bodies in Japan were as thoroughly rooted in society as the bureaucrats could make them, preferably based on producers' cooperatives or agricultural associations dating back to the nineteenth century. The authorities trumpeted village solidarity, as they had during the prewar economic improvement campaigns, "without questioning occupations"—a profound bow toward a conservative social order assuming the integrity of the village as a whole, even at the cost of a totally rational, efficient war mobilization that would corrode the rural structure by draining manpower.

Cultivating farm communalism was no mere romantic idyll for the state. Japanese villages had always retained a good deal of autonomy, even under the supposedly absolutist Meiji state in the late nineteenth century. Shortly before the Marco Polo Bridge incident, the anthropologist John F. Embree reported, village elders in Suye Mura were very reluctant to let Tokyo intervene to clear their debts, because they feared dependence on the government. The tradition of corporate independence forced the state to move very delicately when it entered the countryside to promote its community councils.

Signs of this official deference were extensive. The home ministry and the spiritual mobilization tried to work through the existing men of influence in the communities rather than impose new leaders—a classic pattern found ever since the Taika appointments of the seventh century. In Sengokuhara, Kanagawa prefecture, the community council leaders in 1938 included the village revenue officer, members of the village assembly, the local doctor, a school principal, the head of the reservists' association chapter, and the chief of the village agricultural society. The following year, according to the spiritual mobilization headquarters, the people who dominated community councils and spiritual campaign activities were mayors, public officials, school administrators, Buddhist clergymen, landlords, and farm organization leaders. By using local elites, the state undoubtedly hoped to ingratiate itself and also coopt the men of influence to support its community councils. No doubt, too, the neighborhood elders knew they were being used, yet as persons with responsibilities to fellow residents, they were a check on authoritarianism from above. In this sense the community councils helped to maintain the delicate balance between state and locality that had characterized Japanese administration for many decades.

The government paid careful heed to "traditional good customs" in its pronouncements, yet it sometimes treated them roughly in practice by forcing established recreation clubs or night-watch squads to turn into community councils and take on many of the duties announced in the April 17 outline. Friction was especially raw between the councils and the long-established shrine associations, which resisted the bureaucrats' efforts to merge their jurisdictions after 1937 just as stoutly as had their predecessors during the government's shrine consolidation operation in 1906–1912. In the most extreme cases, community councils tried to exercise the traditional local prerogative of ostracizing uncooperative families by cutting off their wartime food rations—an action that the state ironically had to suppress as "excessively authoritarian conduct," even though it was exercised from below in defiance of the home ministry.

When the bureaucrats appealed to neighborliness and mutual aid, they quite plainly intended to revive the past as a malleable ideal, not as an actuality appropriate to wartime living. This is how the spiritual mobilization lent its abstract ideology to the campaign for organizing citizens more tightly. Both movements used fantasies about a simpler, purer era to excuse wartime policies that were radically new. Nevertheless, as the attempts at ostracism showed, the old social customs extolled by the state set limits on how fully it could control people's lives, even in the midst of total war. By the time the two movements were absorbed into Konoe's "new structure" in September 1940, they had managed to establish 79,028 councils in cities and towns and another 118,430 of them in the countryside. Not all were yet active, but soon they would impinge more and more on the routine of daily life as the fighting wore on.

Patriotic Laborers: "The Plant as One Family"

By the third year of the war, people found themselves being drawn into new organizations in their workplaces as well as their neighborhoods. This was especially true in the biggest cities, where hundreds of thousands of new laborers worked long days and nights in the plants without striking deep roots in the community. Soon after the Marco Polo Bridge incident, the social affairs bureau of the home ministry ordered employers to stop overworking their laborers on the pretext of the war crisis. The bureau was well aware that employees were often being kept on the job for twelve to fifteen hours a day, and in some cases for thirty-six hours straight. These conditions, it noted, led to accidents, absenteeism, illness, and poor workmanship—and doubtless the bureau's officials feared that communism might flourish too. In October the ministry set twelve hours as the legal work limit and directed employers to give their workers rest breaks, two days off each month, and a shift system. In spite of the demand for their labor and the price controls imposed in September 1939, however, factory workers' wages rose less quickly than inflation between July 1937 and July 1940, slicing their real earnings by 8 percent. These were circumstances that would normally invite a torrent of union activities.

What happened instead was the evisceration of the Japanese labor movement, through an official campaign during 1938–1940 to establish patriotic industrial associations (sangyō hōkokukai) in every plant and enterprise in the country. Trade unions had a long but clouded history in prewar Japan, beset with chivvying from the authorities and paternalism from the industrialists. The prosperity of the mid-1930s drove their membership to 420,589 in 1936, a record before the end of World War Two, and good times also helped produce unprecedented numbers of strikes the following year, involving 123,730 laborers. Since 1926, private employers had been trying to set up patriotic labor societies, based on "the spirit of building the country," as a foil to the unions. Now that war was under way in China, the cabinet (and possibly the army, too) took note of the idea because good labor relations were urgent, and on July 30, 1938, it embarked on the patriotic industrial movement.

"Labor and capital are one," "industrial patriotism," "family harmony," "the plant as one family"—with slogans such as these, the patriotic industrial campaign glossed over the idea of class struggle and encouraged working people to accept the paternalism of their enterprises in lieu of unions. A single patriotic industrial association was created in each factory for everyone who worked there, from drivers and janitors to the president of the firm. The company bosses became the officers of the associations, snuffing out the very premises of unionism: worker leadership and representation in bargaining with management. Within a year 19,670 units, with 2,989,976 members, had been established; by December 1940, 4,815,478 workers (about two-thirds of the industrial labor force) belonged to 60,495 patriotic industrial associations. In the meantime, the labor unions had been pressured to dissolve, and by 1944 they ceased to exist at all.

Although most employers were delighted to see the labor movement wither away, they were unhappy to have the state intervene in management-employee relations. Tycoons who already complied with the labor laws were particularly annoyed to have the central leaders of the patriotic industrial movement meddle in their wage and benefit practices. In some cases, according to the history of the imperial rule assistance movement prepared after the war, both capital and labor "showed reluctance to form patriotic industrial societies, but the bureaucracy took a completely unbending attitude and finally used the power of the police to establish them semiforcibly." Yet it was much simpler to foist such bodies on wary businessmen than to assure that the managers would conform to labor policies developed in Tokyo. Given the state's rather headstrong approach to forming these associations, it is not surprising that big business proved to be so stubborn in the overall economic buildup for war.

When it set up the patriotic industrial groups, the government appealed directly to the enterprise paternalism that big business had developed early in the twentieth century as a response to the unions. In this sense the state used tradition, especially the image of the factories as families, to justify a form of labor organization that was utterly modern in intent—harmonious war production. How successful this effort was would not be clear until later in the war, but the framework for labor-management cooperation had been almost completely erected by 1940. Like the drive for community

councils and neighborhood associations, the patriotic industrial movement drew on the past to attract support for new
organizations serving wartime purposes. A crucial difference
is that the unions were a good deal weaker than the local voluntary associations, and thus could be absorbed with much
less fuss. Interestingly, the government also established patriotic farm associations in 1938, but they were mere shells for
most of the war because other strong village groups—above
all, the family—supplied labor effectively. As with the community councils, the main aims of the patriotic industrial societies were practical, not merely political. The government
set them up not to crush unionism, which it had long accepted
as inevitable, but to deal with an economic emergency
brought on by the haphazard gunfire one dark night near
Peking.

Battling the Germs, 1937–1940

As recently as a century ago, both soldiers and civilians still
faced the ancient wartime menace: death by epidemic, not
battle wound. Not until World War One did preventive medicine improve sufficiently to qualify the disease-to-wound
death ratio, and contagious illnesses became a truly minor
source of mortality only with the Second World War. Naturally, the Japanese government was concerned to protect its
people's health once mobilization began in mid-1937—
another sign of its practicality amid the bluster of spiritual
mobilization. Like many countries in World War Two, Japan
underwent a partial but significant improvement in health
care, especially during 1937–1940.

More social welfare legislation was passed in the heat of the
military emergency than in the preceding two decades. The
motive was explicitly instrumental, not humanitarian. Since

1875 the home ministry had supervised health matters, through its hygiene and social affairs bureaus. Desultory discussions about a new welfare ministry had taken place since the mid-1920s, but now the army's concern for the condition of its recruits provided the impetus. The new welfare ministry began operations on January 11, 1938, to protect the health of the country "with a view to strengthening the nation's military potential" by overseeing medical care, labor, unemployment, and other aspects of social welfare. However militaristic the intent, the results of founding the ministry were certainly favorable for ordinary Japanese.

The government quickly adopted laws revising the relief regulations, providing protection for mothers and children, creating old-age homes, orphanages, and day-care centers for the poor, limiting working hours for laborers, and extending workmen's compensation to shop clerks. More important were two actions affecting nearly everybody, the enactment of a national health insurance law and the inauguration of public health centers throughout the country.

The health insurance law made protection available to many persons, especially farmers, who until now had no assurance against illness. It went into effect on July 1, 1938, and provided for a national health insurance association in each community. Families could join at their option, with premiums supported partly by the state and partly by contributions from the insured, depending on their means. By the end of 1938, 578,757 persons belonged to 168 local associations; by 1942, bolstered by more laws that broadened the plan, it insured 15,901,199 persons through 4,446 associations. According to the welfare ministry, by 1945 41,409,450 citizens were covered through 10,432 local health insurance associations. Although it was criticized as inadequate, the program was a vast step forward from the uneven traditional system of private protection, and it anticipated the comprehensive health-care insurance scheme adopted soon after the war.

Public health centers were authorized under laws passed in April 1937. Guidance centers for infant care had existed since the turn of the century; now, pressed by military needs, the state planned 550 centers and 1,000 branch units during the next ten years to instruct residents in health care, sanitation, and nutrition, and to provide physical examinations. By April 1938 forty-nine centers had opened, and three years later at the height of the program there were 133 of them, at least one in every prefecture. To train public health workers, an institute was founded in 1938 with help from the Rockefellers, and three years later regulations were announced setting uniform guidelines for training public health nurses. These moves had particular effect in the countryside, where doctors were scarce and health care spotty. The prefectural center in Fukui, for example, was especially helpful in combatting malaria and tuberculosis from the moment it was opened in 1938.

For public health centers and medical care to work effectively, an adequate supply of well-trained physicians, dentists, nurses, and other practitioners was essential. By World War Two most physicians in Japan were graduates of the medical schools of universities, although some had been trained in technical institutes specializing in health care. At least 46,882 of Japan's 52,581 physicians in 1935 are thought to have been medical school alumni; by 1939, the total number of physicians had grown to 64,324. In that year there were also 23,311 dentists, 29,833 pharmacists, 121,059 nurses, and 62,307 midwives listed in the country, the last full wartime year for which figures are available. Thereafter most younger doctors were drafted for military service, so that by 1944 the city of Iida, in Nagano prefecture, had no doctors at all under age forty. Generally the supply of medical practitioners in Japan was adequate throughout the war, never exceeding the ratio of one physician per 2,000 citizens considered the minimum norm.

The government also took steps during 1937–1940 to regulate the price and quality of medicines, establish gymnasiums, playgrounds, and physical training programs for children, and provide for a new system of postal life annuities to accompany the existing postal life insurance plan, effective September 1939. The state promoted medical as well as other scientific research through the federations and councils established between 1940 and 1942, although the military authorities offered only lukewarm support because they distrusted many civilian researchers. Obviously the state could have done more, especially in funding the new programs. But it did enough by way of protecting its citizens' health to transform the government's policy permanently from one based on relief to one predicated on welfare.

"Waste Not, Want Not, Until We Win"

By the winter of 1939–1940 most people in Japan could tell that war was slowly driving them into a closer, more confining relationship with their state. Even if the superstructure of mobilization committees, community councils, patriotic industrial associations, and health centers was too hazy to be comprehended, there was no mistaking that wages and prices were supposed to be frozen, that rice was short, or that cotton goods were under strict government ration. Extravagance was still an enemy, but it was harder now to find tempting luxury items in the stores. Signs began to spring up instead: "waste not, want not, until we win."

Despite the price controls imposed in September 1939, the economic police began to look into complaints that shopkeepers were gouging their patrons as goods became harder to find. Even the government seemed immune to its own rules: the tobacco monopoly raised prices on November 16, to the particular annoyance of the army, its chief customer. More worrisome was the sudden scarcity of rice, the one requisite of every diet in the country (there are no oruzophobes in Japan). Until 1939 domestic production and colonial imports from Taiwan and Korea kept the nation well supplied, but suddenly bad harvests in Korea and greater military purchasing left the shelves bare in certain rice stores in November of that year. The problem turned out to be partly one of distribution, but it foreshadowed the true lacks that occurred the next year, which is when rice had to be put under ration. By 1940, one reporter noted, Zen monks were refusing rice offerings and taking vows to live on vegetables and fruit, but not on the twenty-second of each month—a fruitless day, by government decree. In an excruciating pun on the prime minister's name, one wag began calling the cabinet of the corpulent Admiral Yonai the "no-rice cabinet"—and the habit caught on.

It also turned out to be a no-luxury cabinet. On May 10, the state announced that stores could no longer carry nonessential merchandise. It gave retailers until October 7 to sell off their inventories, a day marked by price-slashing, bargain-hunting, and unemployment for the craftsmen of proscribed items. Citizens were ordered to sell their gold to the government, "but a great many of them hid their gold watches and rushed to jewelry stores to buy chrome ones instead." Under these circumstances, it was predictable that a black market in restricted goods soon flourished.

Matches and sugar were rationed starting in June 1940, the latter at half a kilogram per person per month, and charcoal joined the list in December. If it was available at all, coal was now usually mixed with slate and charred wood. Clothes made of staple fiber (bark and wood pulp woven with small amounts of wool and cotton) began to appear that year, and shoes—especially leather—were hardly available at any price. As in America and elsewhere during the war, shoe repairmen were swamped with trade: the forty cobblers in Arai, a town in the snowy north, were "delighted and worked day and night." Gasoline was limited to thirty liters a month for private cars, and taxis could no longer be found after midnight to take late revelers to their unheated homes.

In cabs or on foot, there were fewer places for people to go for amusement, since restaurants had been hit both by the food shortages and by limits on their prices and hours of operation. The government began to save rice by brewing sake from sweet potatoes, and drinking hours in the bars were confined to the period from 5 P.M. to midnight. One report has it that in late 1940 twenty million liters of "sake" were produced from acorns and consumed by the public.

Some golf courses were plowed under for farmland, and those who played the remaining ones were allowed to purchase just two new balls per season, to the delight of small boys who sold lost balls retrieved from ponds. Since citizens were discouraged from driving to places of amusement, Prime Minister Konoe set an example of sorts by having his chauffeur stop a few hundred meters short of the club entrance when he played in August 1940. Then, wrote someone

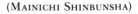

(MAINICHI SHINBUNSHA)

Last Tango in Tokyo: Men purchased a strip of ten tickets for one yen (about 30¢ at the time). Each ticket was good for one dance with a dance hall girl, lasting about three minutes. The dance halls were closed by government order on October 31, 1940.

who observed him, he walked "the remaining distance with his golf bag slung over his shoulder." Other citizens were quick to catch on. They parked a bit short of the theaters to avoid having their cars towed by the police, who frowned on private automobiles in the entertainment centers. Golfers were criticized as self-indulgent, and they had to make to do without caddies, an "unnecessary luxury." But skiing suddenly became popular, since the government ruled that it was good for people's health, and thus permissible.

The state was less charitable toward Japan's forty-seven Rotary clubs, which were deemed incompatible with the new order in East Asia and possibly the vehicles of a secret Jewish-communist movement as well. To the chagrin of most Rotarians, their groups were turned into "East Asia service clubs." The government also took a dim view of dance halls, whose records already suffered from the effects of bamboo phonograph needles now that steel ones had vanished. On Halloween night 1940, most dance halls hired live bands to play "Auld Lang Syne"—not so incongruously as the calendar suggested, because at midnight, by government edict, they closed their doors forever. Perhaps saddest of all, the post office announced as autumn came to an end that it could no longer deliver New Year's greeting cards, even to "honor homes"—a sign of the joyless year ahead.

4

Tightening the Drum

"Spies," the home ministry warned, "do not necessarily go about carrying reagents for developing code messages or worm into high society to entice general staff officers, as we see in the movies." Instead, they "gather information by legitimate means" and send it along to the enemy to be evaluated. With these stern words the Japanese government issued a defense security law in March 1941, darkening the clouded climate of public assembly and discussion still further. During July the state held the first of its annual midsummer antispy weeks. An antispy week consisted of warning people to be vigilant through films, pamphlets, notices, even matchboxes—which were otherwise in short supply—showing "an enormous finger against a giant mouth." To simplify things for the monitors, only Japanese, English, or German could be used for international phone calls. This caused particular consternation among the Italians in Japan, the more so now that the two countries were allies. These episodes are emblematic of the intense way the Japanese authorities got everyone even readier for total war in 1941–1942. By the time this consolidation was completed, society was organized as tight as a drum.

Prince Konoe had returned as prime minister in July 1940, a month after France fell. Both events seemed promising to the Japanese. Konoe "was greeted with overwhelming popularity," a recent writer has concluded, because his tantalizing "new structure" sounded a fresh note just when life at home, like the war in China, had turned flat. Diplomatically, too, there were favorable signs when the new administration resumed Japan's earlier talks with the Nazis, who now ruled western Europe. Soon the cabinet announced an alliance with Germany and Italy, signed in September 1940, that opened Southeast Asia for Japan to exploit.

The skittish optimism of late 1940 evaporated, however, as Japan entered the new year. Konoe's domestic reforms, at first so attractive as an escape from political listlessness, turned out to be more structured than new. Internationally, what had seemed so appealing the previous autumn—moving into Southeast Asia—was now dangerous and uncertain. By increments Japan and the United States were moving toward conflict.

Japanese soldiers marched into Indochina in July 1941, causing the Americans to cut off steel, petroleum, and other resources by freezing Japan's assets in the United States. In negotiations during the next four months, neither country gave way on the American demand that the Japanese pull back their troops in China. In the autumn a stymied Konoe yielded to General Tōjō Hideki, who replaced him as premier on October 18, 1941. War became inevitable at a crucial conference of Japanese leaders on November 26, for two reasons: the diplomats were making no progress and Japan's strength, above all her oil, was slowly draining away. As soon as the ships could be launched and the weather had cleared, the imperial navy attacked Pearl Harbor on December 7. What had been desirable before was mandatory now: getting totally organized for war.

The New Organizational Pivot

Japan was pinned down abroad and politically inert at home when Konoe started his new structure campaign in the summer of 1940. The hope was to give new direction to the war effort; the result was a standoff in which the political parties were the big losers and the recently created civic organizations were extended and reorganized. Because it was confined to political and social mobilization, the new structure movement made little difference to the economic buildup that continued under the cabinet planning agency until a unified munitions ministry was started in November 1943. As a pivot for organizing society, the new structure worked at two levels in September 1940, the same month that Japan was redefining its new order in East Asia much more grandly as the Greater East Asia Co-prosperity Sphere. On the upper level, the campaign merged the political parties into the new Imperial Rule Assistance Association, a massive federation of citizens' groups, through which Konoe apparently hoped to thwart the military services. At the same time the new structure smothered the media and the world of letters with much tighter controls. On a lower level, the movement stepped up the drive to begin neighborhood associations on every street in the country.

In a superficial way the Imperial Rule Assistance Association resembled the mass organizations of contemporary fascist states in Europe, but politically it turned out to be a thin reed and soon played into the army's hand. The parties found it hard to resist the reform wave, but not so the Diet: it cut the imperial rule association's budget from fifty to eight million yen in early 1941. Neither the home ministry nor the great corporations relished the threats this new organization seemed to present them. Big industry neutralized the new structure through Minister of State Hiranuma Kiichirō, a pro-business bureaucrat whom Konoe put in charge of the imperial rule assistance movement in December 1940 after it had failed to put down the army and navy. The result was a deadlock, with generals, financiers, and bureaucrats watching one another suspiciously across the void left by the dissolved parties. As a vehicle of political integration, the Imperial Rule Assistance Association broke down almost at once. Its vast efforts at social mobilization were most persistent but not much more effectual, because they amounted to little more than a reshuffling of the large-scale organizations already in existence when the diffident prime minister reclaimed power in July 1940.

Like many state-sponsored groups before it, the imperial rule association was labeled a "people's movement" from the moment the premier announced it on September 27, 1940. In fact it was consistently used by the Konoe and Tōjō cabinets to try to centralize the intermediate organizations in society at large and put them on a war footing. Its first chance to rally the public came on November 10, 1940, at stately ceremonies held all over the empire to mark the enthronement of the Jinmu emperor, whose dazzling reign supposedly began in 660 B.C. and lasted seventy-five years. Then the association started integrating the various labor groups that had been formed during the past few years, especially the patriotic industrial societies in the war plants.

On November 23, a date now celebrated as Labor Thanksgiving Day in Japan, the government founded the Greater Japan Patriotic Industrial Association to bring the factory units under Konoe's new structure. The number of workers in the local patriotic industrial groups continued to grow, reaching a peak of 5,514,320 members in June 1942. Under the new national association, each factory planned recreation for its laborers, offered them productions awards, and later in the war distributed extra rations of rice, barley, and sake.

Centralized patriotic groups were also set up in commerce, farming, and marine transport during November and December 1940, all for the purpose of "diffusing the patriotic spirit" in the various occupations.

Although each of the unified labor associations had identical structures, managements, and budget procedures, it is unclear how smoothly they coordinated the work of their local branches. Since the Imperial Rule Assistance Association itself never became politically dominant, it seems likely that its suborganizations, such as the Greater Japan Patriotic Industrial Association, drew their greatest strength from their well-established local branches in each company. Meanwhile a good deal of wildcat labor violence broke out in 1941 because of the wage freeze and long hours. By 1943 the number of strikes and stoppages had risen to 279, its highest level since 1937. Considering the huge numbers of persons who worked during the war and the pressures on them to produce, labor relations overall were certainly quite harmonious, perhaps more despite than because of the nominal centralization under the new structure. Whatever its shortcomings as a mass movement, the Greater Japan Patriotic Industrial Association poured amazing energy into its rallies, lectures, and panel discussions, and brought the war to Japan's workplaces much more systematically than had been true before Konoe began his latest movement.

The Imperial Rule Assistance Association followed the same scenario with other key social organizations that were now made part of the new structure. One of the largest was the Greater Japan Youth Association, officially established on January 16, 1941, by merging four youth-group councils dating back to the 1920s and 1930s. Age-group clubs for boys and girls arose in the rural areas of Japan late in the nineteenth century, designed for recreation and community service. Starting in 1915 the education and home ministries began to encourage them throughout the country, and the councils formed after World War One were intended to bring the local chapters under a degree of state leadership. Amalgamating these societies in early 1941 was the last step in a long government drive to control the young people's groups, which now numbered 36,299.

In the next year and a half, the Greater Japan Youth Association built its membership from 4,428,239 to 14,215,837, mainly by bringing in nearly all young people from age ten to twenty-five, especially those in cities. Most of the local clubs kept up the same voluntary activities as before the unification, but the state now used them to drum home the aims of the war and to marshal work teams to perform spot jobs in neighborhoods and on the farms. As with the labor associations, the individual youth clubs apparently were far sounder than the new national association, but there is no question that young people in the local groups were now involved with wartime activities far different from the traditional recreation and shrine festivals of earlier years.

Women, too, were soon brought together by the Imperial Rule Assistance Association under a huge national organization. In the years before the war, dozens of private women's groups had grown up to promote such goals as suffrage, consumer rights, socialism, birth control, temperance, and world peace. There were also three major federations of official women's organizations, sponsored respectively by the home ministry (later by the welfare ministry), the education ministry, and the army. One of the first actions of the new structure movement was to combine the three into the Greater Japan Women's Association, submerging all the private groups beneath it. Unification was first proposed in the Diet in early 1941, but the bureaucratic agencies fought one another so hard to control the new organization that a compromise could not be reached for nearly a year. When the association finally started, on February 2, 1942, all married women, and single women over age twenty as well, were expected to join "to fulfill all the responsibilities of women in wartime." More precisely, "the final objective of this organization is to fulfill service to the public as women in line with traditional ideas of womanhood." The press put it more succinctly: "its main purpose is to make good mothers." The full effects of these efforts would become apparent only later in the war.

Like the labor and youth groups that formed in 1940–1941, the Greater Japan Women's Association was nominally a "people's movement," and by one florid account it was established "because voices swelled up from the masses of women seeking a rational women's organization." Having paid this obeisance to spontaneity, the same report then noted that bureaucratic jostling hurt the association's efficiency, as did poor matchups between its central leaders and the officers who ran the local branches. The old three-way division lasted long after the merger, and the organizational confusion died down only near the end of the war.

These conclusions, from the authoritative but hardly disinterested history of the Imperial Rule Assistance Association, are corroborated by other records showing how uncertain a grip the unified women's organization had on the 19,310,000 persons who supposedly belonged to it. After the war, Kubota Ai, a housewife in Kuwano village, Nagano prefecture, recalled the contradictory instructions about who should join and what the dues should be in her local chapter after it was founded on April 16, 1942. At a national meeting of Imperial Rule Assistance Association leaders in September 1942, the well-known women's advocate Yamataka Shigeri denounced the lack of uniformity in the clothing styles being promoted by the Greater Japan Women's Association. And competition for the time of many younger women sometimes caused strains with the local Greater Japan Youth Association units, since those between ages twenty and twenty-five were expected to belong to both groups. By all accounts the women's associations served best throughout the war at their familiar tasks from before the merger, particularly comforting injured soldiers and bereaved families.

One of the ironies of the organizational tightening is that the most effectual group formed under the Imperial Rule Assistance Association was a namesake that came into being at least partly to undermine the parent association itself, which was still under business influence thanks to the efforts of Hiranuma. The new body, known as the Greater Japan Assistance Adult Association, began on January 16, 1942, with a good deal of help from the army. Starting with Fukui prefecture, it drew together various adult clubs, especially in the villages, into a support organization to plump for candidates favorable to the army in the forthcoming elections for the lower house of the Diet, held on April 30, 1942.

Through a separate political committee, the Tōjō government used the imperial rule assistance movement to recommend 466 candidates and mobilized the police and much bureaucratic pressure to help them win. All but eighty-five were successful. Among those elected were at least forty who were also supported by the Greater Japan Assistance Adult Association. Although the adult association did not really offset the bureaucrats or the financial community within the parent group, it gave the army quite a rich rural base, reaching 1,300,000 members by 1943. In the unruly climate of wartime politics, this reservoir of civilian strength was a menacing auxiliary weapon that gave the generals a bit more leverage over their governmental rivals.

With the April elections out of the way and a tractable lower house in office, the Tōjō cabinet decided to overhaul the Imperial Rule Assistance Association by legally bringing all civic organizations under its umbrella—although in practice most were there already. The purpose of the change, the government deadpanned, was "to strengthen their objectives and functions." The main difference is that the association now had budget access to the national treasury and uniform fiscal control over the labor, youth, women's, and other similar groups. In a classic administrative compromise, the new arrangement made the cabinet the general overseer of the newly integrated association but gave various ministries the job of supervising its activities. Now the reshuffle that began in the fall of 1940 was completed. Far from curbing the generals and admirals, the Imperial Rule Assistance Association had become a giant organizational sponge, wielded at the pleasure of the military-dominated state. Its cumbersome sogginess is doubtless the main reason why the association, having absorbed all the citizens' groups, became almost useless to the authorities after mid-1942.

The state reorganized the organizations during 1940–1942 out of its own political necessities as much as from a need for tighter social control. In most cases the elemental strength of the workers', young people's, and women's associations continued to be at the plant or community level, not at the central organizational pivot. Even in politics the standardization was incomplete. The Diet, hemmed in by the mobilization law of 1938, met infrequently during the war, but it did meet. The semicontrolled election of April 1942 had returned eighty-five candidates opposed by the Imperial Rule Assistance Association, including such critics of the state as Nakano Seigō and Ozaki Yukio. As late as March 1945, by-elections were still being held to fill vacancies in the Diet. Throughout the whole period, the Imperial Rule Assistance Association proved to be a vague and enigmatic apparatus, not a smooth instrument of social mobilization in the hands of the generals and admirals who dominated the cabinets. The military services had enormous influence in Japan after 1940, but more because the simple necessity of fighting a war had tightened the drum strings than because of any cleverness at integrating society under mass organizations.

Push and Squeeze: The Media at War

Clumsy as the large-scale associations were, still it is a fact that life was very systematized in Japan during the war—perhaps more so than in any other country except the U.S.S.R. (Paradoxically, Japan was also the least well mobilized of the major powers in relation to capacity for a full war effort.) During the organizational consolidating that went on in 1940–1942, people's habits and choices became more and more restricted in two main ways. One was the outright control of information, discussion, and worship by the government. The other was the growing effect of neighborhood organizations on daily living, stimulated partly by the authorities and partly by the pressures of an economy of scarcity. In both instances, war itself, not just a baleful state, drove civilians into a common quandary and hedged their personal freedoms very tightly.

The government treated the media to a mixture of propaganda and suppression, as it had in the early years of the China war, but news policy became much more smoothly coordinated after the cabinet information bureau was upgraded to an information board in December 1940. The board absorbed both the publicity and the censorship duties scattered among various agencies—except for the imperial general headquarters, whose outrageous untruths only complicated the board's work throughout the war. Although it suffered from the chronic bureaucratic disease of factionalism, the cabinet information board met the government's domestic needs quite systematically in its dealings with the press, the book trade, radio, and the film industry. The result was a sharply controlled current of news reaching households around the country.

Dōmei, the official wire service, was the board's chief means of spreading war news written to show Japan's position to her people in the best possible light. Stories from abroad were carefully trimmed to remove anything offensive to the military services or other ministries. Severe as it often was, the correspondent Otto D. Tolischus observed, at least the screening was "open, official censorship." Although its negative, repressive activities were usually more dramatic, the board stepped up its positive management of the news after Pearl Harbor and under a new president, Amau Eiji, became a rather suave propaganda unit starting in April 1943.

On the pretext of saving newsprint once again, the government created a Newspaper League in November 1941 to allocate paper under instructions from the information board. On the principle of one newspaper per prefecture, the league and its successor deliberately shrank the number of dailies from 454 to just 54 within two years. Those that remained were limited to a dividend of 7 percent, but their circulation grew to nearly thirteen million, a rate of one paper for each 6.18 persons or virtually one per household. The wartime state not only blanketed the country with a controlled press but also hurried the drift toward oligopoly that made the top three dailies into giants after the surrender.

The day after Pearl Harbor the cabinet information board called a rushed meeting of news executives to explain which types of stories they could report and which they could not. Both NHK and the papers were warned that news must now be prepared "as much as possible in cooperation with the government." By February 1942, the Newspaper League had been restructured as the Newspaper Council, which could revoke the membership of any reporter whose views it disliked and put him or her out of a job. What the council was for publishers and editors the Patriotic Publicists' Association soon became for journalists, technical writers, and public relations personnel. Established by the information board in December 1942, the publicists' association was expected "to take the lead in the empire's internal and external ideological warfare" through publicity planned in cooperation with the agencies of state. Before the publicists' group was officially inaugurated, its leaders traveled to the Ise shrine to report their plans to the gods, an action caustically described by the magazine *Bungei shunjū* as "an unprecedented affair in the history of the modern Japanese press."

By coloring the news to its taste, rationing stocks of paper, and badgering journalists to join various federations, the information board unquestionably weighted the flow of information in the state's favor from late 1940 onward. But there are hints that the controls were far from absolute. The cabinet needed journalists and printers if its messages were to reach the public, and few writers apparently lost their credentials. The political and military analysts still published their commentaries, carefully censored, in the major dailies. The political scientist Claude A. Buss, interned near Tokyo for much of 1943, observed that the Japanese papers contained huge amounts of war news while he was there. On the other hand, the navy crammed its Midway casualties into a single hospital in Yokosuka to obscure that defeat from public view, and the proceedings of the 1943–1944 Diet session were very heavily censored before they were transmitted to the press. Still, in the last year of the war the information board apparently used its cudgel less often, to build confidence in its reports at a time when the military general headquarters was issuing war reports based on fantasy rather than fact. What the activities of the cabinet information board seem to show is that the state realistically understood that a news management operation, to keep on working, has to maintain the hypocrisy gap between the ideal and the actual at a reasonable level. Even then, as became apparent in 1944–1945, it was impossible to hide a losing war from the public for very long.

Book publishers, organized as the Japan Publishers' Council, found their supplies of stock scarce at best and sometimes absent altogether if they ran afoul of the information board. The number of titles tumbled from 28,138 in 1941 to just 5,354 the next year and only 875 during 1945, among them such improbable volumes as translations of Hegel's *Theory of Dialectic Change,* Hesse's complete works, Bergson, and T. S. Eliot. With livelier amusements curbed by the state, wartime might be expected to produce a huge audience for new books—and in fact library circulation nearly doubled in one northeastern town, Sukagawa, between 1941 and 1943. But genuine shortages of workers and materials, as well as the information board's harassments, forced the industry to contract. So did the Japan Publishers' Association, after it was founded in March 1943 to replace the publishers' council under the terms of a new ordinance restricting the industry. By one reckoning, the association reduced the number of book publishers from 3,664 to 204 within a year, presumably by forcing all but the most powerful to suspend operations or enter into mergers with larger firms. The survivors were instructed by the publishers' association to become "fighters in the ideological war and producers of paper bullets."

Still the war was a poor time for quality manuscripts. Even if they were not conscripted for factory or military duty, authors had to make do under the controls on news and academic freedom. Often there was neither the leisure for reflection nor the prospect of finding a publisher when one's book was completed. Nearly all writers cooperated with the war out of civic duty, and most joined the Japan Patriotic Literary Association after it was started by the information board in May 1942. One of its members stated after the war that the association "always obeyed the wishes of the state. It took the lead in spreading knowledge of national policy and disseminating publicity." Soon the officers of the literary association sponsored such works as *The Tradition of Loyalist Thought (Sonnō shisō no dentō)* and *The History of the Japanese Spirit (Nihon seishinshi)* by the philosopher Watsuji Tetsurō, and *The History of Japanese Thought (Nihon shisōshi)* by the Shinto scholar Muraoka Tsunetsugu. At the same time, a well-known group of scholars in Kyoto labored to justify Japan's expansionism by calling for "a new world view and a new moral energy." By the very nature of the book trade, however, the Patriotic Literary Association was less directly propagandistic than the publicists' organization, and in some ways it may have helped protect the interests of writers against the state. Still it nurtured uniformity and a distinct policy viewpoint rather than the creativity and liberating environment that usually lead to good books.

The state saved its sharpest blade for the magazines, with their huge circulations that made them especially inviting to the censors and their leisurely deadlines that made them easy to control. "It is the special habit of the ignorant to believe things frivolously," wrote Hiraide Hiizu, the top justice ministry investigator, in a 1944 book on magazine censorship. In this patronizing vein the government took pains to curb the big weekly and monthly journals, whose publishers were obliged to join the Japan Publishers' Cultural Association after it was started by the information board in December 1940. This group's main weapon was its ironfisted hold on newsprint, which allowed it to be "the main staff of the ideological war," the information board said. The publishers' organization reduced the number of magazines from 1,970 in

1940 to only 965 in 1944—many of them tiny or irregular, special-interest journals. "Unfriendly critics" were forbidden to write for the mass-market magazines, and editors were expected to clear the names of contributors and résumés of the main articles with the publishers' association in advance—stiff medicine for Japan's secretive and highly competitive magazines.

The most spectacular repressions affected two of the largest monthlies, *Chūō kōron* and *Kaizō*, whose top editors were replaced with persons more acceptable to the government after the Yokohama and Tomari incidents of September 1942. The former involved the arrest of fifty-nine individuals associated with *Chūō kōron* and other publications. The Kanagawa prefectural thought police accused them of constructing a "fearsome secret plot" to revive the illegal Japan Communist party through their writings. The Tomari episode occurred during the same week, when *Kaizō* was forced to fire its senior staff for carrying a historical article deemed opprobrious by the police. The author, Hosokawa Karoku, was jailed for his supposed communist sympathies. By comparison with Germany and other countries in World War Two, however, the Japanese government treated its press critics rather mildly. Only one person, the spy Ozaki Hotsumi, was executed for treason. But it is also true that the September 1942 incidents left at least three persons dead as a result of the torture they received in prison, which helped to bully the magazines even further into complying with the information board's orders. Bloodied but unbowed, *Kaizō* and *Chūō kōron* struggled on until mid-1944, when they were suddenly closed down by the state because, said Radio Tokyo, "their policies were incompatible with the proper guidance of public thought." Prime Minister Tōjō's reaction to the uproar, like Hiraide's, was more peremptory: "The masses are foolish. If we tell them the facts, morale will collapse."

The facts nevertheless made very striking propaganda in Japan's movie theaters, as the information board discovered when it began sponsoring films to raise morale after 1940.

Unlike the early years of the war, when the government had been satisfied to prescribe what could not be seen, the new policy was that the film world had "a çultural rôle to perform in the total program of our new national consciousness." Now the studios turned out many newsreels of Japanese troops on the continent and a number of home-front travelogues, such as one showing patriotic fishermen rising in the dark and plodding through the Hokkaido snow to the docks, so that Japan's supplies of seafood could be maintained. Despite earlier bans, films from abroad continued to play alongside the publicity productions. As late as December 4, 1941, the government censors cleared ninety-six American movies for release that month—only to rescind the permission a week later because war had been declared.

The next March the state gave producers explicit rules for movies that would promote national policy and strengthen people's feelings against the enemy. By now the ten major studios had been forced to consolidate into three firms, Shōchiku, Tōhō, and Daiei, and each of them was now allowed to make just two features a month (before the merger the monthly total had been about two dozen). Film stocks were rationed as carefully to the movie studios as newsprint was to publishers. The kind of movie the information board wanted was remarkably realistic: instructional films on factory training, neighborhood drill, even how to build a bomb shelter. Historical films enjoyed a boom too, especially when they showed Japan's brightest eras, such as Meiji. The three conglomerates found straight war films hugely profitable, with the theaters usually crowded. To one postwar critic the consequence of the government-industry collaboration was that "when the fighting ended there was hardly anyone in the Japanese movie world who had a clear conscience."

To bring its wartime messages home the information board naturally concentrated on the radio, the print media, and films. But it also urged composers to produce patriotic works in keeping with classical Japanese musical motifs and directed NHK to broadcast marches and war songs constantly on the air. Painters were exhorted to do war pictures, which they did in great numbers despite a lack of materials. The tropics, ocean scenes, and heroic murals were common. But the political restraints were mild. Fujita Tsuguji's *Gallant Death of Attu,* done in 1944, is considered an important innovation in style treating a theme unlikely to appear in film or print. A cluster of avant-garde artists who had encountered Picasso, Fernand Léger, and Le Corbusier in Paris founded the Free Artists' Association in 1937 and promoted surrealism and theories of abstract art with impunity throughout the war.

Thorniest by far was the matter of thought control. It was relatively easy to regulate the news and intimidate authors, artists, and film producers. By 1942 Japan had certainly regimented people's access to information as severely as any country involved in the war. It was much harder to dictate citizens' thoughts and beliefs, however, no matter how much the state confined the opportunities to express them. The government dealt with the major religions, for example, less by challenging their doctrines than by restructuring them under centralized rule. The religious organizations law, enforced in April 1940, placed all denominations and faiths under the home ministry, which administered them after November 1940 through its new bureau of religious ceremonies (Jingiin, reminiscent of the Jingikan started in the seventh century and briefly revived in the nineteenth). Nearly all temples, sect shrines, and churches cooperated with the authorities so that they could continue their worship unimpeded, although the members of such groups as the Jehovah's Witnesses and the Salvation Army were willing to undergo great persecutions for refusing to do so.

By 1941, the many splinter sects of Shinto were reduced to thirteen groups, Buddhist denominations were merged into twenty-eight branches, and the Christian communions were reduced to two, one of them a merger of thirty-three Protestant churches. Naturally it was particularly hard to be a Christian in wartime Japan, although believing in an enemy religion did not normally lead to jail unless one insisted on declaring in public that Christ was superior to the Shinto deities. The newer domestic religions seemed particularly suspicious to the home ministry's thought police because of their potential for disorder among the less well educated, who formed most of the membership. Their threat to order, not their theology itself, explains why Tenrikyō and certain Nichiren sects were pressed to show allegiance by modifying teachings that appeared to conflict with the state's doctrines of imperial supremacy.

But most religious groups supported the war actively. The state shrines were mobbed with pilgrims, especially during the New Year's season soon after Pearl Harbor, when attendance at the Ise grand shrine rose 25 percent over the year before. The mood then was buoyant, with prayers for the further success of Japan's forces, but great numbers also regularly turned out at the Yasukuni shrine, garbed in black, to pray for the spirits of the war dead. The enormous Nishi Honganji temple put its priests into the war plants, created recreation centers in its buildings, and even collected funds to pay for aircraft that were sent into battle christened with the temple's name. For the first time in its 1,100-year history, the Kongōbuji temple on Mount Kōya ordained fifty-five women in 1944 to replace priests who had joined the services or volunteered to work in the war plants. In this way Japan fell into a familiar wartime pattern: with or without state controls, organized religions—whatever the universality of their doctrinal messages—tend to cooperate with the war policies of the secular state.

Since neither the religious bodies, the publishing world, nor institutionalized education proved to be sources of threatening ideas, the question of thought control ended up as a matter between the individual's conscience and the terrifying police power of the government. Fear was probably an even more awesome means of standardization than the elaborate organizational restrictions imposed on workers, neighborhoods, and the media. If a dissenter could not turn to a group for support because the groups were all structured by the state, he or she was unlikely to speak out alone in the face of naked police power. Those who did were well aware that they might be jailed, and they usually were.

In 1943, for example, the prosecutors picked up 866 persons for allegedly violating the peace preservation act, which was the legal club for suppressing most dangerous thoughts since its adoption in 1925. Of these, 215 were indicted, and the rest presumably were either repentant or obviously innocent. The 1944 figures are incomplete, but they suggest that about the same number of indictments were handed up from among the 700 or so who were detained. The police bureau of the home ministry reported in August 1945 that incidents showing public unrest had risen from 308 in the year ending March 1943 to 406 the next year and 607 in the year ending March 1945. Outright antiwar and antimilitary acts grew from 51 in 1942 to 56 a year later, and 224 in 1944. Likewise the military police tabulated a great rise in antimilitary rumors between December 1943 and May 1945.

These were remarkably small figures for a country of seventy million persons. War-weariness, especially in a losing effort, easily accounted for the larger number of incidents late in the war. But the noisiest critics had already been jailed, converted to supporting the government, or cowed into staying quiet. In a culture with strong emotional pulls to the land, the family, and the throne, it was hard for even the most committed ideologue to resist an appeal to patriotism. Those who stayed on in prison rather than renounce their dangerous ideas, according to Patricia G. Steinhoff, survived more through force of personality than intellectual commitment. Silence was the refuge for most, such as the novelist Nagai Kafū, who could not support the war but understandably did not wish to risk jail by saying so. Yet for writers accustomed to speaking their minds, silence became its own prison, and among persons of conscience the moral burden of remaining quiet was a very heavy one.

After a regime sets limits on expressing ideas, as Bruno Bettelheim and many others have observed, they have to be enforced totalistically to retain their effect. The home ministry's thought police—far from being taken in by the state's own propaganda—evaluated the public mood very realistically in a January 1943 report on what might cause discontent. The list included battle reverses, air raids, consumer shortages (if things do not improve, it warned, "people will grow more and more dissatisfied, provoking class antagonisms"), war-weariness, and social strife among Korean and Chinese laborers who were forced to work in Japan. The way to deal with these problems, the ministry soon decided, was to demand total obedience. In "Basic Policies for Preserving Order," it concluded that any sign of discontent, if not suppressed, could lead to more outbursts. The director of the thought control bureau, Furui Yoshimi, echoed this argument when he told the Diet in September 1944 that "the government is prepared to place strict control over speech which is harmful to unity within the country." This is why the state harassed citizens even in the last year of the war, as Hatano Isoko wrote to her young son in a January 1945 letter describing how the thought police pestered his father because of his liberal views. Once the chain was in place, it could not be loosened—only snapped.

The historian Ienaga Saburō has ransacked the war era for scattered examples of civilians who opposed the government's military policies, but he concluded that the Japanese were powerless to establish an organized resistance. The reasons for this are deceptively simple. One is that the state had a monopoly on the instruments of violence. There was no way for citizens to resist the power of the police and the army. The other is that until very late in the war the government had enough organizational control, through labor associations, youth and women's groups, civic associations, neighborhood units, and the media, to blunt any sort of collective action against its policies. As a result, whether hunting out spies with matchboxes or muzzling the magazines with frameups, organizational coherence was far more decisive than ideological unity—although both were less than perfect in Japan during the war. The intensifying battle abroad and a powerful military leadership at home had tightened the organizational drum, but it was the war itself that eventually made the drum go slack by eroding the standardization and consolidation of 1940–1942.

5

Bringing the War Home

The top best-seller of the 1940–1941 season in Japan was a thick book with an arid title, *A Reader for Neighborhood Associations*. Part of the appeal was its blunt language:

Up to now, the main purpose of neighborhood associations has been social, and there is nothing wrong with that. But as neighborhood associations are steadily solidified, they will be obliged to cooperate more for daily living and have some connection with distributing commodities. . . . The associations that will be hardest to set up will be the ones in exclusive residential areas. The main reason for this is the great difference in the standard of living, both materially and psychologically, among their members. . . . Because they find that interaction is difficult, they don't want to associate with poor people. Thus if we can only eliminate this cause, we can set up meetings and expect to solidify the neighborhood associations.

No longer was the idea just friendly chit-chat or mere spiritual uplift. The war was coming closer, and it had to be confronted head-on—at the same time flattening the social pyramid. That winter the *Reader* sold 100,000 copies in its first five weeks, a time when each neighborhood in the country was becoming an organizational cell for sustaining the war.

Building Neighborhoods Out of Blocks

On the surface, Japan's rural communities in 1940 hardly resembled the villages of even a half-century earlier, let alone those of premodern times. As recently as 1890, the residential clusters in the countryside still seemed closer to their medieval counterparts than to the villages of World War Two, especially at night. After sunset they were dark, quiet, and often cold. It was vivid and unforgettable when the evening calm was interrupted by a gong calling illiterate villagers to the candlelit temple or by a flute inviting them to dance under paper lanterns near a local shrine. For poor cultivators who rarely traveled more than a few kilometers from their birthplace, this age-old style of life was accepted without question. So too was the natural village cohesiveness, regardless of income or status, that had endured since earliest times.

Coal, electricity, and the web printing press had changed nearly all of this by World War Two. Most farmers could now read, thanks to compulsory schooling, and electrification let them spend their evenings scanning big-city newspapers with reports of grain prices abroad which directly affected their incomes. The same high-speed railways that delivered the daily papers let farm people visit places their parents had never seen, and perhaps never imagined. The chance to make big money in the cities had lured away many of the richest land-lords. Their exodus shook the village order at least as hard as the advent of the industrial economy, with its damage to local self-sufficiency. But beneath the changes was a residual social integrity left from premodern times, a point not lost on the spiritual mobilizers when they began setting up village com-munity councils in the late 1930s.

Most of the reorganizing that happened after Konoe called for a new structure in September 1940 was tangential, if not irrelevant, to village society. For consistency's sake, neverthe-less, the state was determined to construct community coun-cils, at least pro forma, throughout the countryside. In Febru-ary 1941 the authorities told each village's council to become "one in practice" with the established agricultural associations and producers' cooperatives, as well as youth, women's, and veterans' groups, in the interests of wartime solidarity. Stable villages were important, the government believed, for feed-ing the nation and preventing unrest. But in fact even with the drain of young men to the cities and the services, the rural communities were so steady that the new councils and neigh-borhood associations beneath them worked much less well than the existing organizations they were meant to subsume. As in the late 1930s, giving the state more leverage over the villages was the real goal, one the government continued to seek very tactfully out of deference to local leaders whose co-operation was needed more than ever. This is why the big drive to organize neighborhoods under the new structure took place in the urban residential blocks of Japan.

The Japanese city is sometimes called a network of villages, but that image no longer really suited most urban areas at the time of World War Two. By then the city was actually a patch-work of individual houses, clustered around shopping streets and connected by rail lines to large enterprises in downtown centers. Often the only things that people living near one another shared were the same commuter station, the same grocery store, or the same school for their children—bonds that were far from meaningless, but a great deal less than the strong community pride still found in the countryside. Being neighbors in the city meant little more than living side by side.

When the home ministry issued Order No. 17, "Essentials of Providing for Community Councils," on September 11, 1940, the government began a gigantic piece of social engineering to prepare everybody for a concentrated war buildup. Its main targets were the relatively unstructured residential districts of the largest cities. The edict restated why active community councils were needed, and it also set out the framework for building neighborhood associations beneath them. The councils were expected to

1. Organize and unify people who live in cities, towns, and villages based on the spirit of neighborhood solidarity. . . .

2. Organize the basis for planning people's moral training and spiritual unity.

3. Cause all national policies to prevail among the people and help national policies be put smoothly into effect in every respect.

4. As regional units of control for people's economic life, to demonstrate their essential function in enforcing a controlled economy and stabilizing people's livelihoods.

The order and auxiliary regulations issued the same day directed that "the community councils organize every household within each district" so that "universal participation" could take place all over the nation.

Before September 1940 the program of starting community councils had relied so much on the persons of local prominence that it had reached the bounds of its effectiveness, especially in the cities where well-established neighborhood leaders were harder to ferret out. Without forgetting its ties to local elders, the government now reached beyond them to draw in every citizen by the strongest sort of urging short of legal compulsion. As in the spiritual mobilization of the late 1930s, the state invoked a romanticized past when it appealed to "the spirit of neighborhood solidarity," precisely because so little of that sentiment existed in the cities. The authorities deferred to the group nature of Japanese society by deliberately trying to mobilize people in units of ten or fifteen households, not as individuals or isolated families. Once again tradition was being dressed up to dance to a modern tune.

Without a doubt the scheme of community and neighborhood organizations was highly structured, yet the group conventions on which they were built suggested something different from sheer authoritarianism. Instead the many thousands of elemental residential associations brought to mind Japan's nineteenth-century hierarchy of status in which cohesive interest groups, arranged side by side like elevators, competed with one another for advantage in a society that was at once stable and fluid. What was more, the simple fact of getting everyone involved in neighborhood units had implications for leveling as well as for heaping up. Participating was not the same as having an equal voice, but it meant belonging to a tangible organization of neighbors who needed to get along with one another too much to tolerate heavy-handed authority. In a country that has always preferred interminable discussions and consensual decisions, it was *de rigueur* to accommodate everyone's views at least occasionally. When war forced the wealthy to rub elbows with the poor, as the *Reader for Neighborhood Associations* noted, the social pyramid probably grew a little less steep as a result. No one could safely claim that the Japanese neighborhood associations were instruments of democracy, but as time passed they took on more and more practical duties imposed by war itself and often had to improvise on their own authority, beyond the discretion of the embattled state.

"Neighborhood association," remarked Komori Ryūki-chi, who belonged to one. "It's fair to call this a term that makes memories of the war well up among us Japanese." Understandably so, for although the community council may have been left to local persons who enjoyed administrative matters, hardly anyone could avoid the neighborhood groups once they were systematized in the wake of Order No. 17. Reliable nationwide figures are scarce, but the Imperial Rule Assistance Association calculated that in July 1942 there were 1,323,473 neighborhood associations in Japan and additional ones in Taiwan and Korea as well. In the six largest cities, where the government's greatest efforts were spent, there were 282,175 associations by April of that year, with an average of eleven families in each.

Right after the September 1940 order, the Tokyo authorities named eight duties for neighborhood associations in the capital: liaison with the community councils, acting as a neighborhood social group, air and fire defense, counterespionage, crime prevention, encouraging savings deposits, reforming daily living, and distributing commodities. With certain variations, like sanitation, labor service, and honoring soldiers and their families, these remained the chief activities down to the surrender, both in Tokyo and elsewhere. In all these enterprises, the emphasis was on doing things together as neighbors. *A Guidebook for Neighborhood Association Meetings,* for example, published by the city of Tokyo in 1940, called for full discussions of policies in the neighborhood meetings, putting the public interest uppermost and reaching a consensus of the group. Individual competition, the booklet warned, should be subordinated to collective harmony.

With so many units doing so many things, the new structure had helped bring the war home to every street in the country. The state was boldly trying to build neighborhoods out of residential blocks—scarcely child's play in a country under siege. By hounding city-dwellers into working together, the authorities hoped to manufacture enough community sentiment to get Japan through the crisis. As one of their most lyrical apologists explained to foreigners in 1944, life in the neighborhood associations made "living collectively much more comfortable than living alone . . . life can be very pleasant even during the stringent period of war! The hostile, icy atmosphere of the immediate past has given way to friendliness and helpfulness." If the ice had melted, it was doubtless because people anywhere unite in a crisis, not just because the state had nourished a hothouse "spirit of neighborhood solidarity."

Guiding the
Local Organizations

Soon after it announced the campaign to build neighborhood associations, the home ministry was briefly nervous that the Imperial Rule Assistance Association, proclaimed a fortnight later, might take them over within the new structure. When the bureaucrats saw how thin a shell the assistance association was, they discreetly began to cultivate more local leaders to manage the neighborhood units. This was a delicate errand, since the state neither wanted to offend the low-level public servants (whose duties the associations would partly assume) nor wished to tie its hands by depending entirely on local persons of established influence. Disregarding objections from the home ministry, the cabinet eventually decided to put the neighborhood associations under the Imperial Rule Assistance Association after all. In "Policies Regarding the Organization of the People," announced on May 15, 1942, the government made it clear that the existing officers of community councils and neighborhood associations were to be confirmed in their posts by the assistance association.

The parent group had the right to place aides in any community or neighborhood unit it wished, although in practice it decorously deferred to the local leaders in almost all cases, "to avoid duplication of efforts." Exactly as with the large-scale labor, women's, and youth groups that were nominally absorbed at the same time, the Imperial Rule Assistance Association became the titular organizational hinge on which the neighborhood groups revolved. When the neighborhood and community associations were actually integrated into the imperial rule association on August 14, 1942, the move drew fire from below. One critic was Ichikawa Fusae, the tough-minded women's leader, who told the *Asahi* newspapers that "there will be problems with our operations henceforth. . . .

although they call it strengthening, all they have done is make the structure more complicated and increased the number of officials." The absorption revived an ancient administrative riddle: the investiture of existing leaders in new roles by a powerful state meant they might be seduced into supporting its centralizing aims, but it was equally likely that a private usurpation of public power might occur. Since the Imperial Rule Assistance Association was abashed about using its right to appoint new leaders, it seems very likely that the community and neighborhood groups went on settling most matters, as in the past, among themselves.

One of the touchiest of these was financing the local units, a problem that the state never fully resolved before the surrender. In 1940 a general tax reform increased central revenues at the cost of regional fiscal autonomy, just when wartime chores for local bureaucrats were piling up. The city of Kagoshima, for example, actually took in fewer taxes in 1940 than 1939 because of the reform (3.0 versus 3.2 million yen), despite a growing economy, and the percentage of its local aid payments from the national treasury did not surpass the 1939 level (4.4 percent) until five years later. In the meantime, expenses grew enormously for all Japanese cities during the war—especially municipal office costs, whose proportion of the swollen 1945 urban budgets was 59 percent higher than in 1939.

At the same time, the neighborhood and community organizations were also carrying a big administrative load, without pay for their officers or much help with their expenses apart from the dues paid by each household (usually fifty sen or one yen per month). To encourage the neighborhood and community groups, on January 11, 1941, the home ministry ordered each local government unit to bear some of their expenses—an impossible demand, given the tighter incomes and larger duties of local bureaucrats. A 1942 survey showed that community councils in Tokyo still got four-fifths of their revenues from individual householders, who in effect were being taxed to support a new layer of local administration. Not until 1943 was funding regularized, but even then the neighborhood associations and community councils could not stay afloat without the spirit of voluntarism.

The event that transformed these groups most of all came on October 29, 1942, when the government officially made them responsible for distributing the food and clothing rations—an action propelled by the course of the war, not the leadership or financing policies of the state. Defeats in the Coral Sea in May and at Midway in June ended the growth of Japan's empire and implied even greater consumer economies at home. Certain products had been rationed since the war with China began, and formal allocations started in the cities, under municipal jurisdiction, in April 1941. But only in the fall of 1942 was the consumer prospect bleak enough to draw each neighborhood into the rationing network. Every community council was told to form a distribution department, headed by someone other than a shopkeeper, to watch over allocations to the neighborhood associations. Although this step presumably reduced hoarding and assured that rich and poor alike had equal chances to buy what they needed, it also interrupted the customary relationship between merchant and customer, giving Japanese consumers an unprecedented leverage in purchasing. In an economy of growing want, the state probably had no alternative to giving these powers to local residents, but the consequences for seller and purchaser could hardly have been imagined in more peaceful times. Until now, for most citizens the neighborhood association had involved air defense drills and other occasional wartime obligations. From this point on, it meant an intimate daily relationship to each household's purchasing habits for the rest of the war.

These new duties were a tremendous drain on the community councils and their neighborhood associations, and they often led to disputes over spheres of authority as well. Partly to resolve such tensions and partly to reassert its grip over regional administration, the home ministry in 1942 revived its old plan to incorporate the councils and neighborhood units legally into the local government system. When laws no. 80 and 81 made the changes official on March 20, 1943, the net result was that mayors, as the creatures of the home ministry, got much more discretion over the neighborhood groups and community councils, offsetting whatever influence the Imperial Rule Assistance Association still retained. One sardonic critic later wrote in the Ōsaka mainichi that "the brilliance of mayors as commanding officers in raising the output of food, timber, and fuel, increasing savings, collecting metals, and distributing commodities is ever more sparkling."

How much difference the latest innovations meant in practice is hard to judge. Mayors were apparently no more willing than the Imperial Rule Assistance Association to meddle with the local units, and in the meantime the assistance association was posturing to show its nominal control once again. Clearly the neighborhood and community groups were a political prize worth seeking, especially now that they were active on a daily basis. But it was equally obvious, as a top Imperial Rule Assistance Association official admitted on October 13, 1943, that "there has been a lack of attention to leadership and it is still incomplete." In other words, the community groups were ignoring the orders from above. The reasons for this probably relate mostly to the local leaders themselves.

What sorts of persons took charge of community councils and neighborhood associations? In the villages the answer is already clear: the old leadership class of local officeholders, teachers, landlords, and veterans' association officers dominated rural community councils from the start. Wealthy landlords, if any remained in the village, often served as council chairmen, a ticklish job that required them to represent the state and the village to each other. Finding natural leaders for the urban councils and neighborhood associations was much more complex, as the city of Tokyo frankly admitted in a 1941 reader for women in the neighborhood groups. Right to the end of the war, the government was never fully satisfied with the quality of local leadership and constantly issued edicts to encourage good persons to step forward, a further sign of how imperfectly the community and neighborhood groups were fitted to the apparatus of state.

Through painstaking investigations the sociologist Akimoto Ritsuo has produced a fairly complete profile of the persons who led the local organizations in Japan's biggest cities, based on data from the home ministry and the Imperial Rule Assistance Association. It is safe to assume, although most records are silent on the matter, that the leaders were overwhelmingly male and that a majority of ordinary members were women. In the community councils of Tokyo, Osaka, and Kobe, the top officials mostly represented the more well-established city occupations, such as merchant, manufacturer, and owner of urban rental properties. Altogether these persons accounted for 2,065 of 4,052 identifiable leaders. Company employees, lawyers, doctors, accountants, and clergymen were disproportionately under-represented, comprising 670 persons in the group. From figures developed in a December 1942 survey in five large cities, it is clear that families who had lived in their neighborhoods for a relatively long time formed the pool from which leaders were chosen: 87 percent of the chairmen and vice-chairmen of community councils had resided in their districts for more than five years. Most were recruited from men over forty years of age, and only a minority had received schooling beyond the elementary grades. In short, they were the urban counterparts of the local men of influence in the villages.

Being a city neighborhood association captain or council chairman was rarely a popular job and often became a nuisance, as Sutō Ryōsaku, a captain in Tokyo's Egota Yon-chōme area, noted in his diary for 1945. Although council chairmen and neighborhood captains were supposed to serve at least a year's term, a lot of them refused to stick it out and had to be replaced by someone confirmed by the local mayor or ward chairman. The assistant captains of the neighborhood groups usually rotated each month, since the post included bothersome chores like sending around notices, standing in line for distributed items, and supervising clean-ups. In Ōmori ward, Tokyo, the authorities were so bereft of leaders in November 1942 that they had to make a twenty-year-old girl a neighborhood captain, and in Wakkanai, a city in Hokkaido, an eighty-one-year-old man served as chairman of a community council starting in March 1943. Because the council leaders were taking on more and more duties, the home ministry began to make them grants in the six largest cities after November 1943 to help with expenses, but neighborhood captains were apparently pure volunteers. As in wartime New York State and elsewhere, serving in a council or a neighborhood association was an emotional outlet for the older, less well-educated man from a long-established family who had time on his hands but was ineligible for service at the front. It is just this sort of man who is patriotic in the abstract but unyielding in practice to arbitrary guidance from above.

The Local Groups in Action

The National Song "Neighborhood Association"

> *A sharp tap-tap-tap*
> *From the neighborhood association!*
> *When I opened the lattice gate,*
> *There was the familiar face saying,*
> *"Please pass along this notice board*
> *After you've read it,*
> *So others can be informed."*

> —words by Okamoto Ippei, music by Tokuyama Teru and children's chorus, issued by Victor records in July 1940

The notice clipboard, passed from door to door with space for each family to stamp its red-ink seal by way of acknowledgement, was the voice of the neighborhood association in wartime. It blanketed the residential districts as effectively as any of the mass media, linking the households between the monthly meetings of the group and the regularly scheduled activities like air-raid drills. Even today, in the uncensored and intensely high-technology information society of contemporary Japan, the neighborhood notice board is one of the ways the urban community keeps informed—although now about more prosaic matters like power outages, trash collections, or curbing the neighborhood dogs.

On the first of each month (later changed to the eighth to mark the declaration of war against the U.S.) NHK broadcast a half-hour program for the regular meetings of the neighborhood units, held at a member's home with at least one delegate from every household in the association. By the end of the war, the groups met whenever they could, usually as soon after the regular community council meeting in that district as possible. Members read such documents as *Way of the Subject* and discussed the nation's war aims, and they also worked out schedules for neighborhood duties such as night patrols, cleaning gutters, selling savings bonds, and the myriad other responsibilities they assumed as the fighting dragged on. Most difficult of all for the monthly meetings were chores such as settling unfair food distributions, when there wasn't enough for everybody. Members were irritated when they had to decide such things as how to divide nine eggs among ten families. The most common solution was by lot, but the unlucky were not always graceful losers.

The community councils operated somewhat more formally, but they dealt with the same sorts of problems connected with daily living. Each month they met between the twentieth and twenty-fifth, ideally with someone present from every household. In fact the authorities felt satisfied if each neighborhood association was represented. The agenda included worship of the imperial palace, silent prayers for the war dead, and remarks about Japan's war goals before turning to specific business. The minutes of a village community council meeting in Sengokuhara, Kanagawa prefecture, held on January 20, 1942, show that after these formalities the session was devoted entirely to notices from the village office. They concerned ceremonies to mark the declaration of war, air defense, national savings bonds, consumer commodities, preparing comfort kits for soldiers, collecting metal goods for the war, special prayers to mark the founding of the country on February 11, and the distribution of bean paste and soy sauce. If such occasions were expected to promote neighborliness through discussion and consensus, there was no hint of it in these proceedings.

The state quite evidently hoped to use such regular public events, as it had during the spiritual mobilization, to break down private reservations about the war effort and encourage people to join, if not enthusiastically support, home-front activities. This is why the government began awarding prizes to superior community councils in March 1942, an incentive scheme comparable to those used in the war plants in other countries. If not internally competitive, the neighborhood units certainly vied with one another to meet savings stamps and war bond quotas. "Going to the Sea" was made the national song in December 1942, to be sung in unison at all community council and neighborhood association meetings. Everyone was doing things together in groups, something most city people had not done very often since they moved in from the countryside.

Not everybody was happy with such forced togetherness. Early in the war, women complained about having to pass the notice board late at night or having to open their homes to their neighbors' prying eyes when the air defense captain inspected each house for fire safety. Later, when American B–29s bombed most cities to ruins, these same housewives were no doubt glad for any help they could get in fighting the flames. Others resented supporting group functions they would rather do themselves, such as the doctor who refused to pay his assessment for inoculations and insecticide to the community council. Homeowners with good fire insurance or supposedly fireproof houses were sometimes reluctant to pay the council for night fire-watch patrols. The war drove state and citizen into the classic stymie of public versus private rights, a dichotomy that had not fully developed in Japan before the rise of occupational specialization, big cities, and relatively autonomous households in the twentieth century.

The most sensitive nerve touched by all the neighborhood togetherness was the family tradition. The modern city household led a relatively independent, self-reliant life separate from those around it. Urban housewives, spared the need to work full time to help support the family, poured even greater care into the rearing and education of their children. Although it no longer necessarily meant a large number of relatives from several generations under one roof, the family was still the fundamental social unit—one that had to be mobilized, the state was well aware, if the home front was going to pull its weight.

The home ministry endlessly reminded people to be thoughtful toward those living "in the three houses opposite and one on either side," not just their own household. Given the logistics of modern living, it was inevitable that people would do this anyway when the war worsened. With relatives scattered all over the country, the city family was forced in an emergency to rely on neighbors, as Mishima Sumie noted: "The traditional Japanese family sentiment for turning to relatives in case of need was superseded by a democratic way of not feeling ashamed to disclose one's plight to non-relatives, and to ask them for help." Even though families at first may have resented the neighborhood group's intrusions, the great bombings at the end of the war left them no choice but to cooperate. Yet the family was also an anchor in the potentially chaotic flight from the cities once the B–29s began their fearsome raids.

When households were asked to send a representative to some neighborhood event, it was usually one of the women who went. At first, Takahashi Aiko observed in her diary for March 27, 1943, people who could afford maids normally sent them rather than a family member to the bucket relays and air defense drills. Later, anyone who was free was sent, usually the wife or mother once a large majority of eligible men had been drafted for military or labor service. In May 1944, as wartime duties piled up in the neighborhoods, the *Asahi* reported on women who helped to run the associations:

Bucket Relay: Women practicing air defense in the Meiji Gaien stadium, Tokyo, November 1943. Most are wearing peasants' pantaloons (monpe) and hooded air raid shrouds.

Recently everything from the distribution of cotton thread, socks, and toilet paper to repairing shoes, umbrellas, and pots and pans is being carried out by the neighborhood associations. Especially with manpower growing insufficient these days, everything from buying national bonds, collecting money for postal savings and insurance, and tax payments to delivering the mail has been left to the neighborhood associations. Thus the responsibilities of the neighborhood association captain have piled up and expanded. . . .

Since the captains have many occupations and places of work, there are many cases in which women do their duties for them. There are days when the wives of captains are entirely absorbed by work "on behalf of the neighborhood association." It is said that a certain captain's wife had only sixty days out of the entire year for her own life.

Despite this account, there is every indication that more men than women ran the neighborhood associations and no question at all that males dominated the community councils. Nevertheless, since most of the routine duties were being handled by women, it meant that more of them were participating in events outside the house than in peacetime—an experience that was very likely to change their long-range outlook on themselves and their families.

Most citizens apparently felt more satified with their neighborhood associations than with the community councils, from a survey of 450 Tokyo families taken by a Tokyo Imperial University research team on November 30, 1945. At the time the neighborhood units were still distributing food but not carrying on their more disagreeable wartime duties, something that may have affected the findings. Of those who were questioned, 65 percent felt satisfied and 17.5 percent dissatisfied with their neighborhood associations, whereas 37 percent were satisfied and 43 percent dissatisfied with the community councils. People apparently thought of the councils as unresponsive administrative units, whereas the neighborhood groups were rationing units dealing directly with families' daily needs. Nevertheless, 38.2 percent expressed the belief that the neighborhood associations did not place enough emphasis on local cooperation or self-help.

Whether contented or resentful, hardly anyone was unaware that the councils and neighborhood groups were bringing the war to Japan's residential districts. In 1947 the prime minister's office surveyed 3,000 citizens, and only 14 percent of the men and 6 percent of the women had not heard of the local organizations. More than 77 percent had been active in neighborhood work, about a third of them voluntarily and the other two-thirds because they had to. Most of the reluctant remembered that they simply "didn't feel like it," although a few called such service "disagreeable work." The survey, unfortunately taken after the fact but fortunately conducted when people could speak freely, came up with nearly identical results in cities, towns, and villages. The young and the well-educated participated least often and least willingly, and nearly half of the 3,000 recalled the neighborhood experience with some negative feelings, although doubtless these were mixed with more general attitudes about the war era itself.

Between them, the state and the fighting brought war home by driving people into busy neighborhood activities, particularly after rationing became a local responsibility in late 1942. Tocqueville is probably right that wars menace a society less through direct military intervention than by swelling the power of the government, but wartime Japan happily escaped the nightmare of a rootless mass society enslaved by huge centralized institutions. Instead the Japanese authorities mobilized their citizens by deferring to the corporate tradition, using the family to form larger groups rather than smashing it, and cooperating with old-time local leaders as opposed to the type of social reconstruction attempted in the Soviet Union. The Japanese tried to fight a thoroughly modern war by conserving a social tradition. The changes that occurred were brought on mostly by the hardships of war. The national crisis forced the humble and the lofty to stand in the same rice lines, sing the same war songs, and battle the same bomb fires. It brought people out of their homes and into new relationships that affected their attitudes, and no doubt their behavior too, long after the fighting ended.

6
Working

When we farmers occasionally went to Tokyo, people would be gathered in a huge crowd in front of the kabuki theater trying to buy tickets. We could not bear the idea of sweating so hard to produce rice to be sent to city people who amused themselves like this.

—A farmer, early 1943

Today some older men came as labor volunteers from the Tōhō Electric Company. They were intellectuals without experience in farming. . . . They pulled on brand-new cotton army gloves and helped us very earnestly with the farm work that was so unfamiliar to them. . . . This made us happy.

—Tanaka Ningo, a Kyushu farmer, June 1945

One of the most tantalizing indiscernibles of modern history is why people work and how they feel about their jobs. Before occupations became specialized and big industries developed, nearly all Japanese worked like peasants everywhere—to subsist and pay their taxes. In more recent times, the urban money economy began offering people cash incentives to get them to take jobs so they could buy goods and services unimagined (and uncraved) by their village forebears. Total war artificially tangled the work/reward ratio in Japan by restraining wages, changing factory rules, and trimming the choice of jobs. As these two farmers knew, it also intensified the complex feelings workers had about themselves, their occupations, and the people who consumed their products in an industrial economy that was just two generations old.

Pearl Harbor was the decisive event for the country's overall economic mobilization, even though the cabinet did not expect a dragged-out war. When China was the main enemy, the industrial preparations for full-scale fighting had been more leisurely than they soon became when America joined the war. Conversion had begun in earnest in the spring of 1941, when many of the textile mills were turned into munitions plants, at a time when big business, the military services, and the civil bureaucracy could not otherwise agree about how to plan the buildup. By the end of 1941, control boards had been set up in a dozen major industries, and early the next year the state announced eight plans for raising industrial output by mobilizing labor, capital, energy, transport, and the like. These programs foundered less because they were tardy than because they were not fully integrated and needed more natural resources than were available, particularly under a blockade late in the war. Although the Americans overrated Japan's economic potential, the wonder is that production held up as long and as well as it did.

Work's Small Rewards

Much of the reason why Japan could keep up the fight is that more citizens took jobs and worked longer hours than ever before. Labor statistics for the war years are unusually diaphanous, but it is clear that civilian employment grew from just over thirty-one million in 1937, a boom year, to nearly thirty-three million in 1942. After that the heavy military draft cut the adult work force slightly, but 1.8 million students who were mobilized for full-time war work raised the total number who were employed in February 1944 to roughly 33.5 million—averaging eleven hours a day in the factories and, at busy seasons, even longer in the fields.

This growth in the work force resulted from natural population increases in the 1930s, not from a mass flight from the countryside. After the Marco Polo Bridge incident, the number of agricultural workers held nearly steady at just under fourteen million, although they were often not the same individuals. By 1944 many of those listed as farmers were women replacing men drafted for factory or military service. Not only did new workers join the labor force, but millions of persons shifted jobs as well. The number of people in commerce dropped from 4.9 million in 1937 to 2.5 million in 1944, whereas manufacturing gained 2.3 million workers and mining an additional 290,000—most of them Koreans and Chinese usually imported under duress.

Like all the main countries involved in World War Two, Japan met its labor needs through a combination of inducement and coercion, but its main program for mobilizing workers fell between the two. On the one hand, incentive pay was offered in certain industries where labor was especially tight, and all workers were bombarded with appeals to their patriotism in light of the national emergency. Early in the war the government also promised each factory and mine employee an extra three liters of sake per month "to alleviate fatigue and provide sufficient energy for the next day." On the other hand, although outright conscription for factory work accounted for only 8 percent of male civilian employees at its peak, the threat of being drafted presumably forced a lot of reluctant men into the war plants.

Labor enrollment began in November 1941, when men aged sixteen to forty and unmarried women between sixteen and twenty-five had to register for possible service. Only the men were actually drafted for war work, by the familiar white summons that was nearly as dreaded as the red notice for military induction. Altogether perhaps 1.5 million men were conscripted for factory duty, many of them from family enterprises. The drift toward oligopoly speeded up as a result, with 11,000 small shops forced to close in Tokyo alone by mid-1943. Each spring the government worked out a labor mobilization plan, and it used the patriotic industrial groups, neighborhood associations, and the local police to help persuade workers to take war jobs before actually drafting them. Late in 1943 the twelve-hour limit on the workday was set aside, together with other protective laws, but these changes apparently had little practical effect on productivity or the average hours worked. In February 1944 the national labor registry was expanded to cover men aged twelve to fifty-nine and unmarried women from twelve to thirty-nine, but once again only the men were called for service. In late 1944 a wide-scale job freeze kept 4.5 million workers from leaving their jobs in critical industries. Unmarried women and students were mobilized in various volunteer corps during the last year of the war, but the Japanese were never fully coercive in dealing with their labor needs. Perhaps more compulsion would have been beside the point, since the production downturn in late 1944 mostly resulted from deficiencies in raw materials, not labor.

Whether driven into the war plants by white summonses or simple economic necessity, most workers earned progressively less as the war went along because their total income rose much more slowly than the cost of living. Factory employees continued to be paid by seniority, education, and sex, and the war did little to unravel the intricate scheme of worker allowances, semiannual bonuses, and fringe benefits that had developed in the years before 1937. The wage-and-price freeze of September 1939 had little effect after Pearl Harbor, yet despite the great need for them Japan's war workers actually earned a third less in 1944 than in 1939, because of huge inflation. The real wages of German workers that year, by contrast, had fallen only 2 percent since 1939, and in Britain and the U.S. they had risen by 21 and 39 percent, respectively. It certainly paid to be on the winning side. At the surrender in August 1945, the Japanese factory employee was receiving only two-fifths as much as in 1934–1936—and working longer hours to earn it.

With those slender wages the worker had to carry a tax load that was 250 percent heavier in 1944 than just four years before. Because it expected a brief war, the state first resorted to bond issues to finance the fighting, an action that speeded up inflation. Then it continually raised both direct and indirect levies, imposing a withholding plan and taxing the few remaining luxuries and entertainments almost out of reach. Another drain was the national savings program, enforced by the patriotic industrial units and the neighborhood associations through persuasion that was really a tax—the more so when postwar inflation sliced the value of the worker's deposits almost to nil. The savings program, which was probably as important as taxation for financing the war, meant that families were putting 21.5 percent of their incomes into savings by 1944, up from 11.6 percent in 1936. The periodic donations of metal goods carried out by the neighborhood associations added one more burden to the household economy, and farmers were often expected to contribute part of their crops as well. For those with cash to spare or the hope of winning some, the finance ministry announced a lottery in January 1945 to raise funds for the national treasury, with a top prize of 100,000 yen—payable in savings bonds that soon became almost worthless.

The main reason inflation was more severe in Japan than any other wartime country except China was that national spending rose nearly twenty-fold between 1937 and 1944, most of it financed by Bank of Japan bonds. For consumers this meant an average rise in their real living costs of more than 20 percent every year between 1939 and 1945. Inevitably an economy of dearth produced a black market. By mid-1943 half of the 2,000 city families surveyed by a price-policing group admitted that they bought black market vegetables and seafood, even though only 20 percent of them were well enough off to be able to afford it comfortably. In March 1944 black market rice cost fourteen times the legal price, and by November that year it was up to forty-four times its official level—only to soar another seven-fold, in the case of Gunma, by July 1945. As other consumer items grew scarcer during the summer of 1944, most black market prices swelled to approximately ten times the legal charges. The government had quite evidently lost control over costs in the porous economy, and the overtaxed, underpaid consumer suffered for it.

Unlike the Nazis, the Japanese made hardly any effort to keep consumer goods in the stores during their buildup for war. In this Japan resembled America, where consumer production fell 30 percent in the first six months of the war. The difference is that in Japan it kept on dropping to the end. The index of consumer output fell from 136.5 in 1937 to 102.7 in August 1940, close to the 1930–1934 average of 100. In 1941 consumer goods accounted for approximately 40 percent of national income, a figure that plunged to just 17 percent by March 1945. Another sign of how ordinary people were being squeezed was that until very late in the war the military had first claim on what merchant fleet remained, at a time when the public badly needed rice from Korea. When civilians finally got priority, an authoritative study noted, "this decision represented a tacit recognition that the war had been lost."

Working obviously paid fewer rewards as things got worse for Japan: prices rose faster than wages, taxes climbed steadily, many employees were frozen in their jobs, forced savings shrank their incomes, the black market gouged them (although without it many of them would have gone hungry), and the economy pared down its output for their consumption. No wonder some workers complained or that the government was afraid many more of them would do so. The number of strikes and work stoppages in 1943 reached 279, its highest level since the Marco Polo Bridge incident. That was the same year the home ministry, in "Basic Principles for Preserving Order," decided to suppress all protests harshly. Already its thought police had prepared a sampler of laborers' complaints, in a report on "Trends Among Conscripted Workers":

Meals are extremely coarse fare. What's more, since there are few side dishes, you can't stay healthy. This is why people are deserting. . . . Wages are terribly bad. From our miniscule incomes, food and clothing expenses are deducted; we get no pay as soldiers do for sickness or death. . . . Since the only ones left at home are my mother and baby brother, life is agonizing. It's all they can do to live on their modest income. . . . There are such punishments as the guardhouse and wage cuts. It really makes you feel as though you're in jail.

Food, clothing, health, work rules, wages—all the classic grievances of working people, magnified by the unnatural context of compulsory war work.

Despite its resolve to put down such grumbling, the government knew that sabotage was a constant threat. The thought police, in December 1943, listed a number of obstructive incidents among plant workers and noted that "there is a tendency for them to happen frequently." Most, their report acknowledged, were predictable outbursts over work conditions or the frustrations of trying to make a living. "Although it would still be difficult to conclude that such actions were planned by ideological elements," the police warned, "we need strict vigilance against the tendency for this dissatisfaction and discontent to run wild and turn to direct action." The home ministry logged a steady list of sabotage incidents throughout the war, but verifiable statistics are not available. As in the case of strikes, the problem of sabotage seems to have been modest rather than serious.

Nevertheless absenteeism, moonlighting, and shoddy work were chronic, if not widespread. *Diamond,* a Japanese industrial journal, reported a 10-percent absentee rate in the war plants in 1943 and estimated a 15-percent figure for 761 leading factories in mid-1944. Dr. Tsukada Isaku, a physician, said on NHK that one-third of the workers claiming to be ill from pneumonia or beriberi were not sick at all and that absenteeism ran as high as 40 percent in some plants. General Mori Masamitsu told the *Asahi* newspapers in July 1944 that 10 percent of the aircraft manufactured in Japan were rejected by the air corps as defective. In the last year of the war, a number of employees apparently slacked off on their official work to take well-paying second jobs, such as temporary day labor to clear fire breaks.

Still it is a fact that more persons worked during wartime

than ever before, and nearly all of them put up with its diminishing rewards rather than resort to strikes, sabotage, or malingering. They did so because they had no real choice. If not fit for military duty, adult males still faced the labor draft—enforced by the police—if they did not voluntarily pick a war job. And nearly every family needed wage-earners to pay the steep taxes and high prices for daily necessities. The state organized its civilian labor supply adequately, if incompletely, to meet most of its production needs, but it was the market pressures of a worsening war economy that kept most of its workers on the job to the end.

Growing Much, Delivering More, Eating Less

Farming paid somewhat better than factory labor during 1937–1945, but the cultivators hardly benefited more from working than did city people. The number of farm workers remained just below fourteen million through early 1944, and then rose more than a million at the end of the war because of people fleeing urban bombings. The rural labor supply held steady because women and some older persons replaced the 2.8 million men and 650,000 young women who are thought to have left farming for the services or the factories. By 1940 women formed a majority of the rural work force, 52.2 percent, a figure that rose to 57.6 percent by 1944—when only three out of every ten farmers were males between ages sixteen and sixty. Those men who were still left in the fields were frozen in their jobs effective March 1944, to choke off the stream of male labor heading for the cities and keep farm production high. Nakawada village, in Kanagawa prefecture, had just sixty men left in its farm labor force of 143 by 1943, thirty-two of them over age forty-six. In Tamura county, Fukushima prefecture, the male/female ratio dropped from 92.9 males per 100 females in 1940 to 81.3 in 1944. Wartime was the springboard to Japan's recent *san-chan* farm system, operated by grandmother, grandfather, and mother while father works in a factory.

Considering the turnover of personnel, food output stayed surprisingly high before 1945, when production suddenly fell. Through 1943 the overall farm output stayed very close to its 1933–1935 averages, and rice crops just about matched the prewar level through 1944. A somewhat larger population, the greater military demand for food, and a drop in imports helped cause the consumer shortages of 1943 and thereafter. But domestic agriculture bore up amazingly well—the more so because the lure of off-hour factory employment cut the proportion of full-time farm families to just 34.4 percent in 1943. When the crops finally dropped off, inadequate fertilizer, worn-out equipment, smaller areas under cultivation, and disastrously cold weather were more to blame for the dismal harvests than a lack of pluck on the part of fieldhands. By the surrender, shortages of gasoline and chemicals had practically driven farmers back to the technology of the feudal era.

Although the individual grower was scarcely aware of it, wartime did a great deal to improve ordinary farmers' livelihoods by weakening the big landowners. To insure rural harmony and high output, the state took actions that incidentally (but not deliberately) made it less profitable to be a landlord. In 1937 the government came up with new regulations to lift a million families out of tenancy by helping them buy their own farms. Another law the next year extended the rights of those who remained tenants. All farmers benefited from the agricultural insurance law of 1938, although the new plan removed from landlords their traditional function of tiding tenants over after a bad harvest. To reduce inflation, land rents were controlled starting in December 1939, an action that helped tenants and hurt property owners. Similar controls on the prices of farmland weakened landlords who might want to sell.

But it was the food control law of 1942, an act made urgent

by the war, that helped tenants and self-cultivators the most. Since late 1940 a system of delivering quotas to the state had let tenants pay their landlords in money, not in crops that grew in value before the landowners sold them. Now, in 1942, the state controlled the production and marketing of basic food crops at set prices, dealing directly with the producers. Under this cash system, the landlord who personally cultivated none of his or her holdings had to buy rationed rice like the ordinary city resident. The law allowed the government to pay rice incentive bonuses to the actual producers, making them even richer in relation to large landlords. In exchange the state steadily increased the proportion of the crop it took under the delivery program, from 54.4 percent in 1941 to 64.5 percent in 1945, a sure sign that the quota system was working. Kubota Ai, a farmer in Iida, observed that it was also a system that was very demanding when crop yields fell at the end of the war. Still the land, rent, and marketing schemes imposed by the state to keep output high strengthened tenants and self-cultivators in relation to landlords, a hint at least of the much greater reforms that came after the surrender.

The irony of wartime agriculture is that so few village families profited tangibly from these long-range improvements, at least while the fighting was still going on. "How many times have they told us," asked an elderly farmer, Watanabe Kiyoshi, in 1942, "that we occupied this or that country and that we're keeping on winning, yet we haven't added a single one of the rice fields we've been waiting for." The home ministry thought police, although preoccupied with stamping out rowdyism in the war plants, reported in March 1943 that villagers were furious at the production quotas enforced through the community councils:

> They tell us "deliver, deliver," so then they come and take away at a song the rice we sweated so hard to produce, to the point where it's hard for us to eat. I can't stand it. Are they telling us to work without eating? Is it good if farmers die? Instead of being forced like this to go to the trouble of

growing rice, it'd be better if we just grew our own food and used the time left over from farming to earn money elsewhere.

They were also angry, the police noted, at their niggardly fertilizer rations and the flinty officials who extracted their output. In 1944 the number of tenancy disputes was down by two-thirds from before the war, but there were still 2,000 incidents that year. Harried by tight land, high rents, and greater inflation, many tenants by 1944 doubtless sympathized with the farmer who said wistfully, "If a man has tried his best and failed, he is still just as good a citizen as the man who meets his quota without even trying."

The delivery system certainly worked well enough to confound anyone who assumed that farmers in wartime would always hold back a constant amount for themselves. Rural families ate 11.5 percent less rice in 1944 than 1941, even though the total supply was slightly larger. Then in 1945 their intake fell another 7.4 percent, as millions of city people crowded into the villages to flee air raids. But thanks to the bonus plan, at least farmers were well compensated toward the end of the war for the rice they marketed. The basic price paid by the government for 180 kilograms went up from forty-three yen in 1940 to forty-seven yen in 1944, but by then the actual grower received a subsidy of 15.5 yen—which rocketed to 245 yen under the strange market conditions of 1945. With rents nominally stable but actually lower because they were no longer paid in kind, tenants were unquestionably better off under the incentive program than before. Their numbers increased a bit late in the war, when city families were willing to enter tenancy rather than stay on under the threat of urban bombings. Agriculture somewhat belatedly paid good cash rewards for both tenants and self-cultivators, mainly because of the rice bonuses, and the index of real farm profit jumped from 100 in 1942 to 170 in 1944 thanks to a 21 percent increase in wholesale farm prices.

Yet the anxiety of cultivators is easy to appreciate. Like city workers, their labor was controlled and their output requisitioned to meet war needs. They consumed less for all their effort, and they usually paid the same high prices as city people for the goods they bought—apart from black market farm products. Although their long-range legal rights had been strengthened by the new ordinances, farmers lost most of their wartime profits to taxes and the forced savings campaigns run by their neighborhood associations. Then inflation cut the value of their savings after the surrender by 90 percent, leaving growers little to show for their extraordinary efforts to feed the nation well.

Toil and Trouble

By Pearl Harbor Japan already had a full-employment economy. Practically everybody who wanted a position already had one. This was a politician's dream but a mobilizer's nightmare, because it meant inducing the reluctant to switch jobs or to seek them in the first place, not just staffing the war industries from a ready pool. When the labor pinch began to hurt in 1943 and especially 1944, the government turned to students, the elderly, Koreans, Chinese, convicts, prisoners of war, and finally additional women to boost the basic civilian work force of approximately 18.5 million adult males and 12.7 million adult females. These persons formed a crazy-quilt pattern of employment near the end of the war, one that was complicated in 1944 by exempting farmers from conscription on the one hand but drafting hundreds of thousands of the most highly skilled laborers out of the factories for military duty on the other. Work for all these employees became more troublesome late in the war, and if they were Koreans or Chinese they sometimes paid for it with their lives.

Long before the B-29s leveled the big cities, a stubborn problem for factory workers was the basic one of how to get to their jobs each day. The mass transit system developed in Japan after World War One was a victim of fuel and equipment shortages by 1941, the year the government began testing gasoline made from shale and sardines. In Hokkaido, by one account, steel rails were replaced with wooden track. The military authorities in Hiroshima banned civilians from streetcars and buses in 1942, forcing them to walk or ride bicycles to work. Long-distance passenger trains were cut back early in 1943 to give priority to military and industrial needs, and later that spring the Tokyo streetcars began to pull trailers converted from old buses that could hold fifty additional passengers. Starting in April 1944, trips beyond 100 kilometers required a good reason—and special permits from the police. Even the dead no longer traveled in style: wood was so scarce that coffins had to be used over and over again. Train tickets often took a long wait in line, and to claim seats passengers climbed aboard through the windows, which stayed wide open even in winter. Although American bombardiers did not destroy most of the urban commuter lines, passenger service was cut even more sharply when the heaviest raids came in the spring of 1945.

Once they got to work, many employees found themselves staying longer hours and being asked to take fewer days off when the manpower vise tightened. The government primly told its own 2.5 million civilian clerical workers in January 1943 that they "have too many holidays. There is no way we can condone this in light of the brave men at the front and the industrial workers behind the lines." So public offices were to be closed only on the tenth, twentieth, and last of each month, and banks and corporations were expected to do the same. Other workers were forced into the munitions plants when their employers were put out of business by the state. Dressmaking, typing, and art schools were closed down, as were most of the prep schools that tutored students for entrance examinations. Small enterprises that managed to stay open had to spare an employee twice a week for labor service, according to a Tokyo furniture store owner whose clerks helped deliver mail in the neighborhood. Finally, in September 1943 the authorities banned men from working in seventeen occupations, including sales clerks, railway ticket-punchers and conductors, and barbers. Conscription placed a de facto limit on males working as delivery boys or dry cleaners, and in Okayama the local officials forbade gardeners, tree surgeons, and tombstone cutters from practicing their trades for one year starting in June 1944. Even NHK had to get along without its regular technicians to jam the Voice of America broadcasts from Saipan each evening at six.

The military draft was heaviest by far during the last year and a half of the war, and the tightest civilian labor squeeze took place between April 1944 and the next October, when war production began to level out. By then nearly two million students above age ten had been put to work in volunteer units. In February 1945 the figure reached three million, which was more than two-thirds of the age group and nearly a tenth of the entire civilian labor force. Since at least 1938, public schoolchildren had done labor service from time to time, especially on the farms, and many apparently enjoyed it for the time off from school it afforded for a few hours or as much as ten days. Once they were conscripted for full-time duty after the spring of 1944, however, they found it hard and exhausting work. And the students still had to go to school, although most of them got just six hours of classwork per week, usually when teachers visited the factories. They were paid, like all Japanese workers, by age and sex, but money was deducted from their wages for school fees and compulsory savings. Urabe Takeyo, a housemother in a girls' factory dorm in Tokyo, recalled that the students never had time to do their laundry or change their bedding, which was filled with lice. The young workers lost weight because of their meager cafeteria meals, and "only the lice grew fat." But to Tanaka Ningo, the three students who helped him complete his planting on schedule in early July 1945 were worth their weight in gold.

When workers grew scarcer in 1944, the munitions and welfare ministries found that the elderly were staying on in their jobs or returning to the labor market in surprising numbers. More than two-thirds of the men and nearly a third of the women aged sixty or older were working in February 1944, the majority of them in the fields, despite the firm custom that the elderly should enjoy a leisurely retirement. Like workers of all ages, people over sixty had to take jobs to make ends meet—as sharp a prod as any government labor plan.

As the war buildup moved along, the cabinet had few qualms about putting more than half the nation's 50,000 prisoners to work in heavy industry. They were joined by most of the prisoners of war, who exceeded 30,000 by the surrender. A much greater help were the nearly 1.3 million Koreans who came to Japan during 1937–1945, most of them to work in mining and heavy construction. They were supplemented by more than 38,000 contract Chinese laborers, of whom 564 are said to have perished on shipboard before ever reaching Japan. These foreign workers enriched the labor supply by about 4 percent, compared with the 20 percent of Germany's wartime work force that came from occupied areas.

Since inflation rose faster than wages for all industrial employees in Japan, these minority groups did not prosper from their new jobs. They normally worked in segregated units under police guard. The government did little to improve housing, education, welfare, or the long-standing cultural tensions between Japanese and Koreans, other than to force the newcomers into the Concordia Society—primarily a control mechanism. It is axiomatic that wars are often fought for freedom but rarely for equality. In the case of Japan's minorities, World War Two brought them neither. Unlike black Americans during the same period, who overcame some barriers by participating quite fully in industry and the services, Korean residents of Japan and the Burakumin outcastes hardly improved their status at all. Only the Burakumin served to any important degree in the Japanese forces, almost always in the enlisted ranks.

Repression was the rule of thumb for both the Chinese and the Korean laborers. The state ordered employers to watch their Chinese workers carefully, on and off the job, on the theory that "the more kindly you are toward them, the more

Education in the Nation's Service: Women university student volunteers performing wartime factory labor duties.

presumptuous they'll grow. Thus there is no need to be kind or friendly." It is said that high-voltage lines were set up outside their barracks to keep the Chinese from fleeing and that their meals sometimes consisted of a single *man-t'ou* dumpling. Several thousand Koreans were forced to construct an underground supreme command headquarters in Matsushiro, Nagano prefecture, late in the war. Their whereabouts has never been established, and some people believe they were massacred to hush up the project. Chinese laborers rebelled against their supervisors in Hanaoka, Akita prefecture, in June 1945, and a majority of the 418 workers who died as a result of the episode are said to have been flogged to death. The foreign ministry has calculated that 6,830 of the more than 38,000 Chinese laborers died in Japanese hands. There are no official statistics for Koreans who died while working in Japan, but a reliable estimate puts the figure above 60,000. Their labor was indispensable to the mining industry and very helpful in dockwork and construction, yet the Koreans and Chinese received little but trouble for their enormous toil.

Japan's Underused Asset

Before the war Japanese women usually went to work after finishing their schooling but quit by age twenty-five, when they were expected to marry. About three-quarters of the married women who went on working did so in agriculture, but work was never supposed to interfere with their duties as wives and mothers. Even though three decades of industrialization had absorbed millions of female laborers, the demographer Irene B. Taeuber noted that as of 1940 "the major contribution of women remained the unpaid toil of the married women who assisted their husbands in field, shop, or house. Economic activity and social role were products of marital status rather than determinants of it." More bluntly put was the conclusion of the historian Inoue Kiyoshi: most women of working age "pursued household labor as wife-slaves."

By 1944 more women held jobs in Japan than ever before, yet they were less systematically mustered by the wartime government than any other social group. At its peak the number of working women exceeded fourteen million, which was 42 percent of the civilian labor supply in 1944. But in spite of the heavy military draft, the female share of the work force in that year was only 3 percent greater than in 1940 and just 7 percent higher than in the depression year of 1930.

Between 1940 and 1944, the nonmilitary labor supply lost 300,000 men and gained only 1.4 million women (including students), a modest 10-percent increase in the number of female workers. In America, by contrast, the number of working women jumped 50 percent during the war. In the Soviet Union, the proportion of women in the civilian labor force climbed from 38 percent in 1940 to 53 percent just two years later, mainly because of Operation Barbarossa. Fully 2.2 million of Britain's 2.8 million new war workers were females, and even in Germany, despite Hitler's legendary preference for keeping women in the home, their proportion in the civilian labor force rose from 37.4 percent in 1939 to 52.5 percent in 1944. These figures cannot mask the fact that female workers in Japan were a vital labor resource. Their contributions to the war economy were crucial. Without their labor, Japan could not possibly have fought a war; with more of it, the country could probably have fought a more efficient one. Why the state did not more methodically put women to work illustrates how slowly old social attitudes come unstuck, even in the midst of a total war.

It is tempting, but much too simple, to blame patriarchal officials for not mobilizing women more promptly and thoroughly. In fact the state was reluctant to conscript workers of either sex, and it never resorted to an outright labor draft of women at any point. The result was that relatively modest numbers of women took jobs outside the occupations traditionally open to them, despite the lure of higher wages and the whip of income lost because working-age men were absent from the family in the services. The government enlisted unmarried women for factory duty in two stages, through random exhortation until early 1944 and by systematic inducement thereafter. Although young women had to register for possible work after November 1941, they were never called since the state's labor needs were easily met during the first year after Pearl Harbor. But those who did look for agreeable work in 1942, such as Ōya Akiko, were turned away with "You'd better go to a munitions factory. These days, wanting to work in a corporation is unpatriotic." Crestfallen, Ōya later recalled, she returned home. "It was easy to brace myself with thoughts like 'making bullets helps the war,' but instinctively I knew I wanted to avoid that kind of thing."

The cabinet's attitude was revealed in February 1942 by the minister of welfare, Koizumi Chikahiko: "In order to secure its labor force, the enemy is drafting women, but in Japan, out of consideration for the family system, we will not draft them." Prime Minister Tōjō spoke somewhat more poetically on the subject: "That warm fountainhead which protects the household, assumes responsibility for rearing children, and causes women, children, brothers, and sisters to act as support for the front lines is based on the family system. This is the natural mission of the women in our empire and must be preserved far into the future." As in its campaigns to build neighborhood associations, the state was very cautious about upsetting the family groups that were the foundations of society.

Although these traditional attitudes toward working women predominated, public thinking was not unanimous. In late September 1942 the chairman of a prefectural assembly, Sakaguchi Takenosuke, told the Imperial Rule Assistance Association to use more women as agricultural technicians because the war meant that "the leaders and technicians in production, landscape gardening, animal husbandry, and every other specialty are insufficient and we are really in a fix. . . . I honestly believe we have no alternative but to encourage this activity by women." The next March a top cabinet planner, Minoguchi Tokijirō, duly noted the "extensive limits on a woman's strength in a physiological sense as well as special characteristics in an anatomical sense." But he cautiously advocated putting women to work anyway:

> Just as it is clear that we would not accomplish our war objective if we won the war but failed to establish greater East Asia, it is also very true that we cannot build greater East Asia if we do not first win the war. Therefore, in a full scale, all-out war economy, the problem is not to deny mobilizing Japan's women for production. Rather the problem is how to accomplish this mobilization of Japanese women while simultaneously giving rise to their special qualities associated with the household.

Although the state never found a happy solution, its planners were at least aware now that they faced a serious problem.

It was high time they did, since by early 1943 the war had bogged down, the economy was showing signs of strain, and there was a labor shortage. Nevertheless, the mobilization plan issued by the cabinet that spring still merely "urged" women to work in industry, a sign that the government remained ambivalent about the place of female labor. By late 1943 women who were not working were being criticized as "women of leisure" or as "unpatriotic," but Tōjō's idyll of Japanese womanhood by the hearth seemingly still underlay the state's policy of "using and discarding" the labor of women. The prime minister told the Diet in October that "there is no need for our nation to labor-draft women just because America and Britain are doing so." He argued that "the weakening of the family system would be the weakening of the nation," and he reminded the legislators that "we are able to do our duties here in the Diet only because we have wives and mothers at home." Rather than improving conditions for those who wanted to go on working, the government and big industry regarded the woman as temporary help, someone who should return home as soon as she was married. This was no change from prewar days.

The second phase of enlisting women workers, starting January 23, 1944, finally made something of a break with the past. On that date Tōjō told the Diet that women's volunteer labor corps (Joshi Rōdō Teishintai) were being created for aircraft manufacturing and other essential industries. A new registration of unmarried women aged twelve to thirty-nine was conducted in February, and neighborhood association leaders heckled eligible women into joining the corps. Those who did so had to serve a full year, later extended to two. It was hard for single women to refuse, but the new plan fell short of being a compulsory labor system. The national mobilization program for the spring of 1944 provided for these corps but cautioned that "due consideration shall be given to the limitations of women." In practice women who were badly needed at home were often excused, and at all times single women were urged to marry, matrimony immediately releasing them from further service. In spite of such prevailing attitudes, the state labor enrollment program functioned rather efficiently, considering that it was confined by statute to the unmarried minority of adult females. By March 1945, according to the labor ministry, 472,000 women had gone to work through the volunteer corps, although the welfare ministry estimated that half had been working elsewhere before.

Even before these figures had been assembled the perils of underutilizing women workers were explained in an inventory of human resources issued by the top war leadership in August 1944. This document, entitled *Current Condition of the Empire's Strength,* pointed out that male labor reserves were slim but that there was still a huge supply of potential female workers. In October the nearly four million women who were working in the war industries were frozen in their jobs by state decree. This action was the last major step taken to mobilize women. The labor pinch had already eased at the end of the summer, and materiel shortages were slowing industrial production more and more. After large-scale bombing raids began in November 1944 and people started to flee the cities en masse, the state quite simply lost control over the movement of workers in its war plants.

From accounts written by women in the volunteer corps, life in the war industries was grim indeed. Nakamoto Hiroko, whose school in Hiroshima ceased to function in the fall of 1943, was put to work in an airplane factory under conditions common to most women who worked in the war plants. The night shift had to sleep in the factory, which was plunged into cold by the complete lack of heating fuel. By 1944 she and her fellow workers received for lunch only a bowl of broth with a few noodles. Nakamoto lacked much involvement with her job since she was never told exactly what the steel she checked with micrometers was to be used for. Her incentive dropped even further, she recalled, when equipment and parts grew scarce and she was forced to stand idly for many hours without being permitted to read.

For those who lived in company dormitories, fatigue and filth were especially demoralizing. Urabe Takeyo's factory lodge near the Keio University campus in Tokyo held twenty-five girls who were exhausted by the nightly American raids. Living close to a noisy plant made sleep fitful at best, and the bombings meant that rest was nearly impossible. Smoke from the coarse fuel used by the factory coated the surroundings: "The entire neighborhood seemed black from oil." Urabe, in charge of having the girls' work uniforms laundered, found that the staple fiber from which they were made soon tore. Worst of all, they were a drab khaki color that depressed the volunteers' spirits, noted Iwase Tatsuko of Okazaki.

War affected the physiques as well as the emotions of working women in unfavorable ways. When Urabe inexplicably began to miss her menstrual period after moving into her company dormitory in April 1943, she was given a hormone injection at the factory dispensary and the opaque explanation: "Wartime loss of menstruation, shall we call it? It is a mental thing that has to do with nutrition." This phenomenon was reportedly also quite common among young women in the patriotic labor associations and women's volunteer corps. In a more general sense, the strain of factory work depressed many women employees. There was a good deal of emotional fatigue among young women volunteers after they had spent several months at the Toyokawa naval arsenal in Aichi prefecture. Although a few were returned home after treatment at the arsenal hospital, most were simply sent back to work with admonitions such as "carry on for the sake of the country" or 'there can be no apology to soldiers who have died honorably." Tomita Kimiko, a volunteer in Osaka, reflected the ennui of many when she wrote, "What pleasures were there those days? Lovemaking was impossible, there was no time for reading, and foreign music was prohibited." Long after the war she recalled her delight at surreptitiously changing from the standard *monpe* pantaloons to a dress in a train station ladies' room and going to hear the Asahi orchestra play Schubert's *Unfinished* Symphony.

Japan's labor needs during World War Two were satisfied primarily by redeploying male workers from nonessential industries, supplemented by three million students, a million older men, more than a million Koreans and Chinese, and fewer than a million new female workers who were not students. Nor were many of the women who were already employed when war broke out shifted into important positions of executive or production-line responsibility. Instead, most of them worked as before in the field, the marketplace, the kitchen, the stock room—wherever low-paid, light labor was needed. Women had actually outnumbered men in the factories before 1930, thanks to spinning mill jobs, but now they represented less than a quarter of the industrial work force. Another sign that women were less than fully mobilized for war work was the continuing presence of domestic servants, nearly all of whom were females. There were still enough well-to-do families in February 1944 to provide employment for 600,000 domestics.

It was not just the state that was skittish about putting women to work. It seems almost certain that public opinion—male and female alike—was no more favorable than the wartime leaders toward compulsory women's labor. It is true that women often lacked technical ability for industrial occupations, but the crux of the matter was that "traditional ideas of appropriate activity for women remained economic deterrents throughout the war years."

Time-honored values within the culture undoubtedly constrained the state's capacity to put women to work on behalf of the war. Yet in the absence of so many men, economic necessity forced more women to work than ever before, mocking the government's policy of keeping them at home. Despite the state's unwillingness to meddle too extensively with existing male-female economic relationships, the war made wage-earners of many women for the first time and as a result caused changes in their roles within the family that would have been difficult to imagine a decade earlier. For them, as for everyone who held a civilian job in wartime, working's main reward was its most basic of all: making ends meet in an economy of shrinkage that finally made white-collar executives pull on cotton gloves to help farmers plant enough rice to keep the nation alive.

7

Eating

Nukapan. Let me introduce our teatime specialty, rice bran fried in a pan. Mix wheat flour and rice bran, add a little water, and fry in a pan. Add no eggs or sugar. Fry for two minutes. It looks just like good custard. But it tastes bitter, smells like horse dung, and makes you cry when you eat it.

Since early times the Japanese have looked on the farmlands and broad seas around them as the fertile provenance of a varied and tasty diet. Hard work and a good climate have usually led to abundant harvests, in spite of a rugged topography that is only one-seventh arable. The people have nearly always lived in harmony with nature and worshiped its Shinto deities, a faith that has vitalized so much of the enormous human energy found everywhere in the Japanese economy.

Beginning in the 1880s, the marriage of traditional farming arts and modern agricultural science so greatly increased the prosperity of nature that even during a deep rural depression, from 1920 to 1935, the nation was better fed than in its long feudal period. It is small wonder that persons accustomed to such plenty in the marketplace found recipes like *nukapan* unappetizing—or that before the war was over some of them had bartered away their clothes and their possessions for a few liters of rice.

"The Rations Are In"

Except for prison or physical terror, feeling hungry probably demoralizes people faster than any other temporary privation, especially if they see a privileged few still eating well. There was no starvation in Japan during World War Two, although famine was a minor threat in the early months of the American occupation after the surrender. But there were plenty of individuals who were poorly fed, especially in the last phase of the war when there was just not enough food to go around. To head off these related problems—dispiritedness and undernourishment—the government in early 1941 began rationing basic foods, clothing, and other essentials to every home in the country. The official distribution program, although addled by endless snags, did its tough job rather well for most of the war. When it finally floundered and a black market grew rampant, the reason was less a lack of will or equity on the part of the state than a simple shortage of things to eat.

"The rations are in," a runner from the neighborhood association would shout up and down the block. Residents knew it was time to report to the captain's home or the local distribution center to pick up foodstuffs or other restricted items like fuel and clothing. Sometimes the assistant captain, a nettlesome office passed from family to family each month, would make the rounds to distribute goods to each home in person. Either way, once the neighborhood units were officially assigned their rationing duties in October 1942, the captain would ask for a consensus and instruct the local grocer which vegetables the group wanted. The grocer would give out the proper quantity, depending on the supply that day and the number of persons in the association. Citizens had at least this much control over what they ate—so long as there was still a variety to choose from.

On Christmas Day 1940, the first rice controls were imposed, with particularly inauspicious irony, on the festive rice cakes for the New Year's season. Formal rations began the next April in the six largest cities, and by Pearl Harbor the network of distribution centers covered the whole country. The aim was fairness; the means was a dual allocation system, to neighborhoods and companies, that helped keep laborers placated while assuring everyone a basic ration of 330 grams of rice a day. Adjustments were made for age, sex, fertility, veterans' status, and occupation. Although other grains and potatoes were occasionally substituted for rice, the state somehow managed to meet this basic ration through thick and thin until the last months of the war.

Suzuki Yoshiko, a distribution clerk, recalled that the rice stations calculated the amounts due each family per day and the number of days the standard 14-kilogram sack should last. Two or three times a month, depending on the size of the ration, someone would bring the family passbook, have it inscribed, and lug home the bulky sack—usually made of dusty rice straw because burlap was scarce. Women who ran short a few days before the next distribution sometimes implored, "Can't you please help me somehow?" The manager of Suzuki's center would often respond, "Your stomach looks big, so you must be pregnant," and give out the supplemental ration of 70 grams for expectant mothers. But elsewhere women who were not pregnant frequently got caught putting cushions under their kimonos to extract more allocations. For everyone, it was a case of catch as catch can.

It was also a case of hurry up and wait, sometimes for hand-outs that were unfair. "When word comes that there is to be a distribution," Takahaski Aiko told her diary on September 2, 1943, "we must leave our rice while it is cooking or our boiling laundry water made from precious fuel and run out. Even so, when we get to the distribution center, we have to stand in long lines and wait angrily while the clerks stare at the lines and merely smoke their cigarettes." Shopkeepers, for their part, complained about the intricate ticket system used to ration salt, clothes, soap, and other items. By June 1942 the distribution system had become a bureaucratic hydra, with thirty-five separate ticket books, taxing the patience and the wits of store owners everywhere. Because they were relatively nonperishable, rice, soy sauce, and bean paste could be precisely rationed. Most other foodstuffs were distributed to neighborhood associations without formal per capita rations, and unavoidably some people got more than others. Many an elderly aunt, never seen by anyone on the block, mysteriously appeared on families' ration lists. The justice ministry constantly threatened to fine or jail neighborhood captains and community council chairmen who tolerated these "ghost populations" in their districts, yet as late as March 1945 the council notice board in Saginomiya Nichōme, Tokyo, showed that the state had still not solved the cheating.

At first most consumers expected the shortages to end as soon as shipping tangles were combed out. Right after Pearl Harbor the head of the agricultural cooperatives boasted that "the longer the war lasts, the better will be food prospects." Three weeks later the government dampened such hopes with a stiff warning about overoptimism from the businessman-politician Fujihara Genjirō, and soon the neighborhood associations began to distribute seeds for vegetable gardens. When housewives grew annoyed at the long lines and skimpy allocations, the authorities responded with high-minded appeals to "patriotism for all" and "sacrifice yourself to the public good." Tokyo tried to shame the city's ration chislers with several "kindness and gratitude" campaigns in 1942, posting notices on storefronts:

1. We are all soldiers on the home front.
2. Sellers and buyers are comrades in arms.
3. Let's all help one another with smiling faces.

But it was hard to be altruistic, as the economist Kawakami Hajime noted in January 1943, when people were "thinking from morning to night only of food." Even if they didn't claim false rations or argue with their shopkeepers, surely everyone felt a little sad when the languid bugle of the neighborhood bean curd peddler vanished halfway through the war.

"Live by Making Do"

The material austerities grew much worse in early 1943. Taxes were raised in January, and cigarette prices went up by half. The government told people to get along by "making do" with substitutes, which often meant doing without. Whale meat and seal sausages never caught on, but nobody could avoid the new tin coins, twice as heavy as their predecessors, that were circulated "to economize on the consumption of aluminum which is an important war material."

Tokyo began to take on a shabby look. The iron rails from park benches were long gone, and the state began to collect statues, gongs, and the great hanging bells in temples for scrap. The French journalist Robert Guillain, noting that things like bicycles and pay phones often no longer worked, wrote that in 1943 "Tokyo, never a pretty town, has now become an ugly town. The capital wakes up a little dirtier each morning, as though tainted by the sinister night in which it has just been bathed." The authorities kept telling families to "deliver, deliver," not just valuables like diamonds needed for radio production but also artifacts such as pots and pans, glass, and dishes. As late as July 31, 1945, a Tokyo neigh-

Warm Hearts, Cold Hands: Schoolboys turn in their classroom stove for the national scrap metal collection, Tomigaya National School, Tokyo, May 1942. By then fuel was so scarce that stoves could not be heated anyway.

borhood unit in Egota Yonchōme could still scrape together twenty pieces of china and twenty-eight beer bottles for donation, although it is a wonder anyone wanted them by then. Even Mikimoto Kōkichi, the pearl king, responded by contributing his firm's silver "Bell of Peace," weighing 6.78 kilograms, created in 1924 for the New York World's Fair as a stand for displaying 10,024 pearls.

Much harder to cope with were the clothing shortages that forced the government to start rations through a point system on January 20, 1942. By that time men quite often wore the national civilian uniform and women were usually seen in *monpe,* saving whatever more stylish clothes they still owned for special occasions. To make new purchases, each city resident had a ticket allowance worth 100 points, but rural people were presumed to be less needy or more inventive, and so had to settle for merely eighty. A three-piece men's suit took fifty points but a civilian uniform only thirty-two. Shirts were twelve points, underpants four, socks just one—but overcoats fifty. In the first year of the new system, 29 percent of the points reportedly went unused, giving the state an excuse to cut the rations in half when textiles grew scarcer in 1944. Fortunately at least a touch of romance remained: brides, the authorities concluded, could be given special point allowances for their trousseaus.

To conserve leather and rubber, the government urged people to wear clogs rather than shoes or sneakers. The day the point system was adopted, Dr. Takagi Kenji of the Tokyo Imperial University medical faculty praised wearing clogs as "good exercise" that "enormously strengthens the little muscles at the tips of the toes." Shark skin and "sea leather" substitutes for cowhide quickly faded from use, but construction workers who could not get their customary work shoes repaired sometimes wore discarded ski boots. Finally even clogs had to be allocated through the neighborhood associations, by lot whenever there were not enough pairs for each family.

Like the food distribution program, the point system helped spread the scanty clothing supplies more fairly than by the open market, but as usual the rich were inconvenienced less by the restrictions. In September 1942 women were complaining to Ueda Kōichirō, a community council chairman, about the utter lack of cloth for diapers or for wrapping the stomachs of the pregnant. Meanwhile, he reported, "when you go to restaurants and hotels, there seems to be quite a sufficient supply of towels. The people are at their wits' end with desire for things such as this whose distribution was [supposedly] banned and would like to receive some. They never say they want things that are lacking, but they would really like to have the surpluses that are available of the things they most need." Yet even the hotels ran short by 1943, when there sometimes weren't enough fabrics to fill the rations. In June the cabinet announced an "Outline for

Implementing Simplified Wartime Clothing Habits," which regulated styles still further, with short sleeves now the norm even for winter, and restricted made-to-order clothing. But to help people feel better about the shortages, the government began giving out sunflowers free of charge.

A year later not even bouquets could hide the huge dearth of clothing. In June 1944 the neighborhood associations were made responsible for apportioning the most essential items, a silent confession that the ticket method no longer worked because very few new clothes could still be had. The November 1944 winter clothing distribution in Tokyo provided only one pair of socks for every fourth person and just one towel for each fifteen. Understandably the government preferred to let neighbors decide among themselves how to divide them up. Almost everywhere it was settled by raffle, leaving to fate what neither a free market nor the state system could accomplish: how to distribute too few commodities to too many customers. With much of what they wore now made of staple fiber, people by 1944 looked unnaturally dirty because they could not afford to wash a fabric that disintegrated after two or three washings. Finally the astringent scarcities of city living drove residents back to the primitive technique of bartering when Isetan, the elegant Tokyo department store, held a consumer's exchange at its main outlet in Shinjuku on February 3, 1945—a happening as bizarre as a garage sale in Lord & Taylor's.

Making do became watchwords for housing and utilities too after early 1943. The number of dwelling units remained just under fifteen million until the last months before the surrender, when American bombing raids accounted for most of the 24 percent of Japanese housing that was destroyed by war. But long before the B–29s began their attacks, the great industrial centers were overcrowded with workers who needed a place to stay. As early as 1940, the city authorities in Osaka discovered, more than four-fifths of all heavy industrial employees had fewer than seven square meters to live in. Construction of new housing throughout the country held up fairly well until 1943, when it is thought to have dropped to

80,000 units, down from 258,000 the year before. That same year rural families in the remotest districts found illuminating oil so scarce that they read by the light of animal fat, pine pitch, or even phosphorescent sea creatures, according to one report from Okinawa.

Coal and charcoal were already so scarce by 1941 that the posh Imperial Hotel in Tokyo had to regulate hot water for its guests. During the winter of 1941–1942 it was common for citizens to save fuel by using their home bathtubs only once every three days or so, a hardship that by 1944 seemed a luxury when the charcoal rations weren't often available at all. Wood was so lacking in 1943 that furniture dealers had to fudge the certificates of origin for their remaining wares, now likely as not to be made from black market materials. In mid-summer 1944, officials in Okayama tried to conserve fuel by telling families to unscrew one light bulb, use their lamps sparingly when supper was finished, and after ten o'clock not at all. The next winter some city people began burning their libraries for fuel, figuring that the books might soon be destroyed in an air raid anyway, and early in 1945 neighborhood associations began felling trees in the gardens of great mansions for firewood. Such green logs were no wetter than the driftwood Dr. Itō Ryōichi dragged home for cooking in Katase, once the city cut off his gas, all gasoline and propane had disappeared, and charcoal was no longer to be had. Tokyo's first fuel distribution of the 1944–1945 winter season took place on May 21, 1945, long after most residents had learned to cook with the charred ruins of a city now half-destroyed by bombs.

Sugar and soap were both rarely available after 1943, although the government showed a soft spot for little children by keeping up its regular allocations of rock candy as late as the day of the Potsdam Declaration, July 26, 1945, when the conditions for Japan's surrender were set. Takai Shigeko got around the lack of soap through the old farm trick of bathing with water in which cotton bran sacks had been soaked. She washed the family laundry in a mixture of lye and honey-

122 : VALLEY OF DARKNESS

locust pods and whitened the hot water with nightingale droppings. Smokers proved to be equally ingenious at finding substitutes. When the daily cigarette ration was cut from six to three in early 1945, people tried eggplant or persimmon leaves, knotweed, and cornsilk. But the most edifying solution, by one account, was to roll shredded black market tobacco in pages torn from pocket dictionaries.

As the war ground on and people's spirits fell lower, the state found alcohol an even better tonic for morale than candy or cigarettes. Clever bartenders earlier in the fighting had managed to evade the restrictions on selling sake before nightfall by decanting it into fresh bottles and selling it as cider. The fear of grain shortages led the government to close most of the bars by 1943, but small amounts of beer, sake, and wine were apportioned regularly through the neighborhood associations. The state induced wineries to triple their output between 1942 and 1944, for distributions along with beer that continued right up to the surrender. The public was presumably pleased to learn in February 1945 that sweet potatoes would no longer be used for artificial sake, since they were now needed for synthetic fuel. Instead the agriculture and forestry ministry set aside approximately 225 million liters of rice for sake production, still only one-quarter the prewar amount but a welcome gesture of business as usual to people with a thirst.

Small pleasures like these helped citizens endure an adversity that stood a half-century of better living on its head. The tawdry aspect of life in early 1945, even before the monstrous air raids, would have seemed rude enough when Japan began its modern economic growth in the late nineteenth century— and scarcely conceivable even as recently as 1943. By now people had donated their belongings and denuded their forests, given up the comforts of clean clothes and regular bathing, struggled through cold, dark winters with little fuel, and surrendered their buying power to a distribution scheme that often turned on simple chance. Somehow they had learned to live by making do, partly because they had no real alternative but partly, too, because the impoverished economy managed to eke out just enough of the most essential commodity of all—food.

The Family "Shopping," The Business "Lunch"

When Japan's prospects abroad and way of life at home turned gloomy in 1943, her people were realistic enough to see that shopping on the black market was the only way to get enough to eat. So many housewives bought the illicit produce, as Kiyosawa Kiyoshi wrote in April 1944, that "the crime soon became no crime" at all. Even before Pearl Harbor, the home ministry admitted, there had been a great deal of profiteering in controlled goods, but like everything else it grew much worse midway through the fighting against America. Nakajima Kenzō was amazed to come home early in 1943 from the service in Singapore to find the living standard more frugal than overseas. Otherwise, he observed, "life was surprisingly the same as before. Prices were higher, and the black market had become outrageous." One Sunday at the end of that summer 10,000 people are said to have gone out of Tokyo to Funabashi to buy sweet potatoes, and by the following spring thousands went even on weekdays to Chiba or Saitama prefectures to buy tons of groceries at several times the official prices. The time-consuming and troublesome task of getting food in the city, Hatano Isoko wrote her son on June 26, 1944, was a main reason why she was happier in Suwa, Nagano prefecture: "Here you can get as much as you want of that rice which has become such a problem in Tokyo."

The cabinet agreed that it was a problem, not just in Tokyo but in all the cities. The planning board was anxious enough to send its secretary to Okayama in September 1943 to inquire about the arms plants and people's daily livelihoods. He quickly found that food was the number one problem—its insufficiency, adulteration, clumsy distribution, and high price on the black market. After cataloging a great list of complaints and recommendations, he lamely concluded, "I do not believe in general that people are discontented with living conditions." The justice ministry was obviously afraid that they were, especially after black market prices shot up the next spring. In April 1944 it spelled out new rules about how each neighborhood unit should receive its allocations and how the fish and vegetable stores were to account for their sales. These steps helped erase black marketing by individual merchants, but they had no effect on farmers who sold directly to hungry families. The state found it couldn't really stamp out the illegal food sales, Akimoto Ritsuo recalled, because "it is plain to anyone that without them, it would have been impossible to go on living."

How literally true this assessment is cannot be known, because statistics on black marketing are almost as haphazard as those for gambling or other social vices. The black market peaked in mid-1944, when fewer goods became available through any channel. But munitions plants kept on sending trucks to the farms to bring back crops for their workers, and housewives in the last months of the war began to trade soap, cigarettes, cosmetics, or even their clothes to farmers, who arrogantly but understandably refused cash because of its relative worthlessness. Even the very correct neighborhood captain in Egota Yonchōme, Sutō Ryōsaku, regularly noted in his logbook that his wife took the Seibu Shinjuku train to Kodaira, a nearby farm area, to do what he discreetly called the family "shopping."

One private research group estimated that Tokyo workers' families used the black market in September and October 1944 for 9 percent of their rice, 38 percent of their fish, and 69 percent of their vegetables. In Osaka, according to another survey, the proportion of food that people bought on the black market rose from 18 percent in April 1942 to 24 percent two years later—then fell back again to 18 percent in March 1945 because black marketeers found it harder to supply their customers. By June, as war-end disorganization spread, the average daily amounts obtained from nonofficial sources ranged from 15.7 percent in Kyoto and 20.1 percent in Tokyo to as much as 35.9 percent in the prefectural capital of Yamaguchi. Yet the most interesting finding was that in Osaka the total amount of food eaten each day in March 1945 averaged 1,920 calories, down only one calorie from three years earlier. If the quantity of food held up, its quality and variety doubtless suffered by 1945. Still, between them the regular distribution and the black market managed to keep people reasonably well fed until air raids and mass flight from the cities skewed the allocation system in the last few months of the fighting.

For the millions of city office workers who regularly ate out at least once each day, there was no black market to replace the restaurants that had closed by 1943 for lack of food or help. Finally the government itself stepped in to create "hodgepodge dining halls," equivalent to the wartime "British restaurants" or the community kitchens of Germany. Here workers could register to eat "lunches" that usually consisted of a thin porridge garnished with potato fragments, a radish leaf, a bit of snail, or a few grains of rice. However grim the fare, people now lined up in front of the well-known Naka-muraya restaurant in Shinjuku as early as 9 A.M. for the noon meal. As of April 1944, 335 of these dining halls had been opened in Tokyo, and by the start of the new year there were sixty of them operating in the medium-sized city of Okayama, usually in the closed-down cafeterias of department stores and movie theaters. No one pretended that the dining halls served elegant meals, but the government was edgy enough about its food policies in mid-1944 to suppress its longtime critic, the progressive monthly *Kaizō*, for calling the hodge-podge soup "not nutrition but fat." Whatever their defects, both the black market and the dining halls were indispensable, and it is hardly surprising that the state was sensitive about feeding not just its soldiers and war workers but also its embattled population as a whole.

Weeds and Acorns

The winter of 1944–1945 was the toughest of the war for Japanese civilians. Housing was tight, in poor repair, and menaced by bombings after November. Clothing was scarce and food even scarcer. Luckily the mandarin orange crop along the Pacific coast was the best in years. But in Kyushu the special distribution to celebrate the New Year's holiday was even more austere than four years earlier, when only the rice cakes had been restricted:

.9 liter of sake
2 slices of salted salmon
a small quantity of herring roe
450 grams of sugar
50 dried persimmons
20 mandarin oranges

There was little nourishment and even less festivity here for the farm family of seven that received it, although the sugar must have seemed a godsend to people who were starving for sweets.

Domestic food production was still holding up pretty well, especially rice, but the amounts reaching consumers were pared down by several factors. One was a 90-percent drop in rice imports by 1945 compared with the prewar period, a result of shipping losses. Another was the tumid expansion of the armed forces. Although the proportion of rice distributed to the army and navy rose only modestly, from 2 percent in 1942 to 6.5 percent in 1945, the number of troops posted in Japan proper grew from one million at the start of the war to 3.5 million in 1945. The basic military ration was cut from 900 to 600 grams of rice in 1944, then to 400 grams in 1945 when civilians had to make do with just 300.

Not only was the overall supply smaller and the number of soldiers larger, but the bomb damage from the American

B–29s also threw food deliveries into confusion. By spring-time 130,000 tons of staples had been destroyed in raids on warehouses, and with the evacuation of the cities it was hard to make sure everyone was receiving a fair share. Ishii Tominosuke, a librarian in Odawara, observed that there was hardly any vegetable distribution at all in April and May because transport was in chaos. His neighbors began to eat wild grass, but Ishii considered himself fortunate because he could pick dandelions for soup from the top of his stone wall.

Despite all the hunger, the air raids, and the migrations of millions to the countryside, the community councils and neighborhood associations kept on functioning remarkably well. The Saginomiya Nichōme council in Tokyo sent around notice boards about food, air defense, draft examinations, and evacuation procedures right to the surrender. Sutō Ryōsaku's Tokyo neighborhood group in Egota Yonchōme continued to operate even under American occupation, with regular censuses of the district, monthly meetings, and welfare activities for its members. Unavoidably, there were disruptions. The author Yoshizawa Hisako wrote in her diary for April 8, 1945, about the shrinking dues being collected by her community council in Suginami as people fled to the mountains. She remarked that residents were growing more and more "dissatisfied with vacillation and fruitless discussions" at the council meetings. On June 27, Sutō wrote with asperity about his newly acquired duty of delivering newspapers and accepting payments for them. "From now on," he concluded, "we will stop settling how to distribute things at our regular meetings . . . newspapers will be handled separately." Henceforth, as captain, Sutō had to collect monthly subscription fees on behalf of the papers. He apparently resented this job, not just for the time it consumed but also because it interposed the association between families and publishers—with communal implications he thought inappropriate.

The local organizations kept on working in the face of a true emergency because people needed them, not just because the state continued to rely on the neighborhood groups as administrative units. When Tokyo announced plans in late March 1945 to hand out pumpkin seeds and fertilizer so that neighborhood associations could cultivate burned-out lots, the authorities found that resourceful citizens had planted many of the areas already. To help office workers whose hodgepodge dining halls may have been bombed, the government distributed bags of dried biscuits as lunch substitutes, starting in mid-April. More vegetable seeds came to the neighborhoods in May, followed by twenty million seedlings in June as part of an official plan to grow sweet potatoes for food and also for airplane fuel. The fermentation of potatoes grown by 5.5 million families, the munitions ministry claimed, would make enough alcohol to keep 400 bombers flying for a year. By that point it hardly seemed likely that people would have delivered a single potato to their state, however strong its coaxing, until they had held back enough for themselves. Most were no doubt relieved that surrender mooted the issue.

By the last weeks of the war eating had become a necessity, not a satisfaction. The basic ration of staples was cut 10 percent, people were urged to eat plantain, mugwort, chickweed, and thistle, and plans were devised to produce tons of pulverized food from potato stems, mulberry leaves, wild plants, and the residue of soy beans, peanuts, apples, and grapes. Pumpkin became a mainstay of most persons' diets. Families had long since turned loose their pet dogs because they could not afford to feed them. A year earlier the city streets had been full of prowling dogs, but by now they had mostly starved to death or been slaughtered for food. Finally the government announced a program to collect five billion liters of acorns for flour, because they "have just as much nutritive value as whole rice." But not even in the gloom of a lost war could Sutō Ryōsaku's family find them palatable:

This flour was difficult to cook with, since it was dried sweet potato vine, leaves, and acorns that had been turned to powder. At our home my mother used it to make dumplings. The children wouldn't eat them. Even when we told them to shut their eyes and eat, it was no good. If there had been some sugar or something to put on top, maybe they'd have gulped them down.

A Slimming Diet

Eating, like dress and shelter, was clearly a matter of making do for most people after early 1943. Mealtime was certainly less pleasurable, but it is uncertain how much nutrition was lost from the ordinary diet during the last two years of the war. Fish catches were cut in half by the lack of gasoline for the fleets, although the reduction hurt the fertilizer industry more than the family dinnertable. Livestock and dairy production, minor sources of food for most Japanese, dropped even further. The Bank of Japan calculated in April 1944 that the official distribution in Tokyo came to 1,405 calories and forty grams of protein per person each day, including 330 grams of rice, 200 grams of vegetables, 25 grams of fish, and 47 grams of soy products. The black market and other auxiliary supplies raised the total average daily intake in that year to 1,927 calories and 61.2 grams of protein. How adequate this was to sustain a long war is questionable.

By 1944 Japan had suffered a 17-percent drop in the average daily calories per civilian since the start of the war, compared with a 2-percent loss in Britain and gains of 1 and 4 percent in Germany and the U.S. In the 1930s, Japanese citizens had consumed an average of 2,265 calories each day. Now, in the midst of the war, two official agencies set the daily calorie and protein requirements for light and average male laborers at 2,200 and 2,400 calories, and 75 and 80 grams of protein, respectively. According to the Labor Science Research Institute, the actual amounts from all sources stayed between 1,925 and 1,975 calories and 60 to 62 grams of protein during 1942, 1943, and 1944. Then, in the year Japan surrendered, people took in just 1,793 calories a day—

although they ate slightly more protein, 65.3 grams. Calorie consumption was certainly constricted, especially at the very end of the war, yet even then the amount of protein people were eating held up reasonably well.

The food outlook by the summer of 1944 was dark enough to worry the new cabinet of General Koiso Kuniaki, who replaced Tōjō as prime minister on July 2. A staff report prepared for the top war leadership a month later, titled *Current Conditions of the Empire's Strength,* warned realistically that

> if we look at the national standard of living in 1944 from the viewpoint of foodstuffs, it should be possible to maintain the same level of distributon as the year before for staples only, although the rate of adulteration [of rice] with miscellaneous grains will rise. The supply of all other foodstuffs—vegetables, fish, and other foods with protein, fats and oils, and every sort of seasoning and relish—will unavoidably decline compared with last year. There is an obvious trend toward insufficient supplies of fuel, clothing, and other basic necessities of daily living. Thus in general the national standard of living in 1944 will become a good deal more stringent compared with last year.

Although this forecast turned out to be too glum, no one could deny that people were eating insufficient and poorly balanced meals at the end of the war.

The final months were the worst, as Ishii, Sutō, and millions of other civilians knew. Through 1944 the state's rice purchasing and distribution system worked well enough, and crops stayed fertile enough, to keep the national rate of substitutes in the basic ration below 15 percent. Even as late as May 1945, only 13 percent of the Tokyo ration was filled by potatoes or grains other than rice. Then in June, July, and August, the substitutes suddenly formed half of the total allocation. Yet apart from such unedifying offerings as weeds, pumpkins, and acorns, the distributions and the nonofficial sources bore up well at least through March, judging from the experience of Osaka. There the official allocations and total intake were almost precisely at their April 1942 levels, but by July the average daily consumption had fallen to 1,824 calories, down nearly 100 calories from March but still higher than the national average of 1,793 for the year.

Elsewhere the food situation by summertime was very stingy. Of five cities surveyed by the welfare ministry in June, only Yamaguchi reported that its residents were consuming more calories than the 1944 national daily level of 1,927. Worst off was Kyoto, where people were averaging just 1,677 calories a day. It is no coincidence that the U.S. Strategic Bombing Survey found after the surrender that nearly two-thirds of the adult population of the old capital had lost nine kilograms or more from inadequate diets.

All who endured the hardships of wartime in Japan concur that food grew scarce, particularly delicious food, but all agree too that the malnutrition found in Kyoto and elsewhere did not amount to mass starvation. In some respects the winter after the surrender was even more difficult for food supplies. Bitter memories of hunger and suffering may tempt some persons who lived through the era to accept historian Inoue Kiyoshi's impassioned claims that individuals unconnected with the military or bureaucracy just didn't have enough to eat. But the question was not one of feast or famine. To the very end people managed to find food, however sparse or untasty. Still it is a fact that eating simply was no longer enjoyable—perhaps the truest hardship of all in a land of abundance whose inhabitants have always taken their pleasures very seriously.

8

Adjusting

Dress Code, Hamada Girls' High School, Shimane Prefecture, 1944

Hair. No pins could be used. Hair was to be gathered and fixed with a rubber band in the back. Colored rubber bands were forbidden.

Blouse. Sailor blouse without ribbons.

Trousers. Peasants' pantaloons were the basic garment, sewed according to specifications. A colored ribbon indicating the year in school was attached to the upper part. . . . the size and position of pockets had to conform to instructions. In them we put four things: paper, handkerchief, hand towel, and foot towel. The foot towel was needed because, apart from coming and going to school, we went barefoot, indoors and out, even in cold weather.

—*Kasai Yukiko, born 1930*

Even a people so animated and purposeful as the Japanese did not spend all their time between 1941 and 1945 at work, in the strict sense of gainful employment. But almost everyone was very busily occupied, within the firm limits of a national emergency. As the fighting progressed, persons who were not formally on the job—mothers and infants, schoolchildren, the sick, workers during the after-hours—found that they had to adjust their routines more and more. Marrying, bearing children, going to school, being ill, and using leisure time all took on new colorations during the war, with effects on those who lived through it possibly beyond measure. Although the state involved itself in each of these phases of daily life, it was the war that ended up having a greater influence on people's habits—as Kasai's bare feet show.

"Having Babies Is Fun"

Marriage and fertility have been as regular as any patterns of modern Japanese behavior, signs of how durable the family is as a structural unit. From 1900 to the Marco Polo Bridge incident, the marriage rate held steady at about 8.3 per thousand, then fell a little in 1938 and 1939 for reasons that may have to do with economic readjustments. The long-term divorce trend since 1900 was slightly downward, from 1.4 per thousand to 0.7 in the 1930s, dropping a bit further to 0.62 at the end of the decade. Birth rates, which are partly guesswork before the first full national census in 1920, fell steadily from 36.1 per thousand in that year to 30.8 in 1937, a normal decline for an industrializing country. Then, like marriages and divorces, births dropped a little more at the end of the

1930s, to 26.8 per thousand in 1938–1939. Not even the absence of 1.1 million men abroad on military duty by 1940 had much effect on these trends, since most of them were in their early twenties and not yet marriageable.

Although the armed forces eventually swelled to 8.2 million and three million persons lost their lives, the Japanese case confirms that modern warfare has unexpectedly minor effects on a nation's population in the long run. But this principle was beside the point even if it was apparent to Prime Minister Tōjō and the military authorities, who endorsed the idea of family solidarity and urged women to stick to their customary social norms. Even before Tōjō formed his first cabinet, the women's youth groups had begun to operate marriage counseling centers in the spring of 1941 that were supposed "to cause women to move from an individualistic view of marriage to a national one and to make young women recognize motherhood as the national destiny." The marriage improvement movement that resulted was linked with Tōjō's new fertility campaign. For many years Japan had told the world she needed more territory for her crowded population. Once the war to secure that living space broke out, the government suddenly decided the country was shorthanded and passed a national eugenics law to promote childbearing by outlawing birth control.

The state hoped to raise birth rates by nearly one-half. If all women cooperated, the target of three million births each year could easily be reached. From her comfortable Tokyo home in exclusive Daizawa, Tōjō Katsuko, the wife of the prime minister and the mother of seven, announced cheerfully that "having babies is fun," and she told her fellow countrywomen to shirk all luxuries so that they could afford to raise large families. The state promoted early marriages, set up matchmaking agencies, and asked companies to pay baby bonuses to their workers. The government lent couples wedding clothes if they were too poor to afford a ceremony. Families with ten children or more were promised free higher education.

In fashionable Suginami, the Montclair or Darien of

Tokyo, the authorities opened a school in June 1942 to train brides for Japanese men in Southeast Asia. The welfare minister celebrated the autumn harvest with commendations to 2,145 large families and extra education grants for the children of 246 especially prolific homes. On May Day 1943, citizens read an interview with Kimura Sada, a nurse in Kamanohata, Yamanashi prefecture, who said that "in this village a small-sized woman bears from seven to eight children, while the more strongly built have from 11 to 12 children. The babies are all extremely healthy. The mothers do not show the slightest signs of exhaustion and their cheeks are as rosy as in their girlhood days." Even the neighborhood associations followed Mrs. Tōjō's bid. Starting in the spring of 1943, neighborhood units in the Tsukishima district of Tokyo prodded unmarried men and women to register at the local public health center, which hoped to sponsor 700 marriages that year. The center promised to help provide homes for the newlyweds, maternity hospitals, and nurseries for the babies it expected would result.

Despite all the incentives, there was little change in the wartime birth rate. Between 1941 and 1943, when the state promoted its natalist policies most strongly, the marriage rate rose to about ten per thousand, up from 8.1 during 1935–1939. This increase partly reflected the cash and benefit inducements offered to soldiers for having legal wives, so that informal marriages, which customarily were not recorded until pregnancy or some other exigency occurred, were promptly registered. More importantly, the fertility campaign took place in a time of economic expansion, when young men could afford to marry somewhat earlier.

Births themselves merely held steady at the 1940–1941 figure of about 2.2 million per annum through the year ending September 30, 1944. The live-birth rate briefly regained its 1937 level of 30.8 per thousand but soon flattened out at 30.2. Then births plunged more than 10 percent during 1944–1945 and another 15 percent the following year. This downturn, a response to tougher times from mid-1943 onward, was tied to larger draft calls of potential fathers, internal migration to flee the bombings, economic deterioration, and lower levels of public health and nutrition that made it harder to carry babies to full term. Even sadder was the fact that those infants who were born in 1942 were skinnier than children born just two years before. Presumably because of poor diets during gestation, boys in 1942 averaged 1.8 centimeters shorter and 209.4 grams lighter than in 1940. For girls the figures were 2.3 centimeters shorter and 235.3 grams lighter. These children's prospects for making up the loss were dimmed by the strict rations on milk products for infants that had been implemented on November 1, 1940.

Under the best of circumstances a state has only limited leverage over so private a matter as the reproductive propensities of its people, and it is small wonder that Japanese women failed to respond more enthusiastically to the government's invitations to produce more children. Despite endless discomforts and three million war deaths, the long-term fertility of Japan's population remained quite unaffected. Even though the birth rate wobbled a bit midway through the decade, the 1940s as a whole continued the gently downward pattern of fertility found ever since World War One. Unlike the Soviet Union, whose nine million war dead were outnumbered by eleven million babies not conceived because of the conflict, Japan had a population in 1950 very close to the level expected if war had never occurred because postsurrender births soon offset the decline in 1944–1946.

Millions of families were separated because of military or factory service, but there was no increase in marriage breakups. The divorce rate remained steady between 0.6 and 0.7 per thousand through 1943, the last wartime year with statistics, and it rose along with the marriage rate after 1945. The postwar jump in divorces probably resulted mostly from the legal changes in favor of women under the American occupation, not from wartime strains on Japanese families—whereas Britain's divorce rate had tripled as a result of World War One and America's doubled during 1940–1944.

If there was no permanent damage to marriage or childbearing in the abstract, three million individuals nevertheless died sooner because of the war than without it. Age structures and male/female ratios were disarrayed; schools, labor forces, and old-age homes would be alternately crowded and undersupplied for decades into the future. Still it is remarkable that neither Tōjō's natalist efforts in the early 1940s nor the ravages of bombing, malnutrition, and death in the later months of the war were enough to upset the reproductive habits of the people as a whole.

Learning by Doing

The official history of Ōmuta, a Kyushu city of slightly more than 100,000 during the war, includes among the endless statistics typical of its genre a passing note on primary education. Through the 1943 school year, the last with records, well over 99 percent of the age group was enrolled in the city's elementary schools. Attendance at every one of them was also above 99 percent. Even with allowances for generous roll-keeping by overenthusiastic or timorous instructors, the education system was obviously still open and functioning deep in the war. What turned it to tatters by 1945 was a combination of factory labor needs, flight from the large cities, and finally a huge dearth of supplies and equipment.

Growing up in wartime, for everyone from age seven until marriage or the draft, involved schooling and labor service. Although the period of compulsory education was theoretically increased in April 1941 from six to eight years, in fact most pupils were lucky if they received the old minimum. To release students sooner for war work, the education ministry cut back most secondary curricula in April 1943 by a full year. Once schooling was out of the way, everyone was expected to go to work, and after April 1944 all students over ten were soon mobilized for labor in the fields or war plants, practically on a full-time basis.

Because family ties stayed pretty much intact and young people were busy learning or working, the rise in juvenile crime was much slower in Japan than in most other countries that joined in the fighting. Arrests increased 40 percent between 1941 and 1944, then fell back precisely to their 1941 level the next year. But records were poorly kept at the end of the war, and it is hard to weigh arrest figures against the knowledge that the police harassed many young people, especially university students, when the state controls were tightest. Crime in general seems to have diminished in Japan's tightly organized wartime society, although most statistics are untrustworthy because of poor reporting and undermanned local police. The Hokkaido authorities offered a pithy explanation for the 35-percent dropoff in violations in their prefecture: "the spiritual unity of the Japanese people" under siege.

Education was a serious enterprise for the country's eighteen million students, one that more and more forced them to adapt to the national emergency. Their grade schools had been renamed national schools in April 1941 and their studies revamped because of the war. Even the cafeterias showed how education could do its part. Primary students returning from the summer vacation in 1942 were fed roasted sparrows for lunch, part of a government campaign to protect the rice crop from the birds. College men and women soon grew used to seeing pyramid markers on top of empty desks, honoring their classmates who had gone off to war. During alerts the pupils wore air-raid bonnets, covering the head and shoulders like the upper half of a hooded jogging sweatshirt, to ward off sparks and debris—symbolically if not in fact.

Labor service became a much larger requirement for students above the third grade after June 1943. Their vacations and holidays were given over to war work, and the school year was shortened by as much as a third in some areas to keep children on the job longer. Andō Masako, a junior high school teacher in Nagoya, remembered taking her class two hours into the mountains to cultivate new fields in the fall of 1943: "All 600 pupils or so from the school cut down thick weeds and pulled out rocks and tree stumps. This severe work went on for thirteen days. . . . I was so tired that my hoe dropped, and I forgot whether all this had any effect in the war zone." No doubt the effect was even greater at home, since without Andō's students and millions of other replacements, food supplies could not possibly have held up so well and so long as they did.

That same autumn was when student deferments finally ended for most young men over nineteen in the universities and higher level schools. Only students in engineering or the sciences were excused from the callup. Altogether 130,000 men were inducted en masse, removing about a quarter of the total enrollment in higher education at a stroke. To mark the occasion, the cabinet sponsored a supremely somber parade in the Meiji stadium in Tokyo. "Thousands and tens of thousands gathered in a drizzle," Takahashi Aiko wrote in

(DŌIN GAKUTO ENGOKAI AND ASAHI SHINBUNSHA)

Underground Classroom: Elementary schoolchildren in a city air raid shelter. The boys sit in the front seats with crew cuts, the girls in the back with soup-crock haircuts.

her diary for October 21, 1943, "to see off the uniformed students with rifles on their shoulders." Each school group, led by a flag bearer, chanted "naturally we don't expect to return alive." The mood was taut, emotions were shrouded, and the scene was unforgettable to anyone who was there. This ceremony was perhaps the most elaborate public exercise of the war era, in a country that has always emphasized education in the nation's service—but also usually respected the campus as a sanctuary immune from current crises.

By the next spring, most students at other levels found their schoolwork more and more disrupted as well. All of them who were older than ten had to join "volunteer labor corps," beginning in April, for nearly full-time war work. Dejima Motoko, a fourth-year student at a girls' high school who had been mobilized for labor duty that year, recalled that "sometimes we still went to class, but it was in name only. There were only fragments of instruction." The only education that Yokoyama Jōji, a student at Tokyo's second normal college, got after June 1944 was on the job. He and 120 other students dragged great boxes filled with dirt all summer to build a 1,500-meter-long runway in Shimoshizu. But the strip was never used by a single plane, because aircraft production was cut by a shortage of materials. Learning by doing turned out to be a particularly bitter lesson for an eleven-year-old school volunteer in a large chocolate factory. He was caught helping himself to a piece of candy and forced to stand in front of Kawasaki station with a big sign saying "I am a thief."

The last year of the war affected teachers as greatly as their students. If they were not on active duty in the services or the munitions plants, instructors were often asked to supervise the student volunteer corps or accompany school groups who evacuated to the mountains from big cities after August 1944. That autumn Hoshi Imae, a grade school student in Iida, noted that because so many male teachers were being drafted, "women instructors, who before now had charge only of the lower grades, are taking over the older classes." Late in the year a mobilized male teacher from rural Iwate prefecture, Aibara Kiyoyasu, tried to visit his former pupils during their impromptu graduation ceremony in the Nakajima aircraft shops in Kawasaki, where they were now labor volunteers. The students were "lined up between the huge machines, and no one recognized their faces or what schools they were from." Then the motors started up again, Aibara wrote, and there was "no feeling of auld lang syne, no vision of your alma mater, no sense of spring, and no hopes were born."

Fighting Young Citizens, a fifteen-minute documentary released in September 1944, showed that the mood of schoolwork was just as grave for teachers and their pupils in the lower grades that autumn. Boys with crew cuts and girls with ponytails sat in a chaste classroom listening to the education rescript of 1890 and reciting rote phrases instantly when the teacher called on them. Textbooks at all levels were so scarce that old ones had to be copied over by hand. Nagai Kenji recalled filling in as a substitute teacher at Takahashi Higashi national school in April 1945, even though he was only seventeen. By then there were no writing tablets, no sheets of paper for art classes, and students "used old newspapers for practicing characters until they turned completely black." That same month classes at the public secondary schools were suspended, since 70 percent of the students were away as labor volunteers, but the primary schools and universities struggled on, despite air raids and evacuation, right to the brief summer vacation in August. In or out of school, Japan's young people got an education in hard work and perseverance that would have been scarcely imaginable in calmer times—a lesson many of them still seemed eager to teach their own children a generation after the fighting stopped.

Staying Well

Citizens were probably better off being sick during the early years of the conflict with China than before, thanks to the government's health reforms in 1937–1940, but after Pearl

Harbor a lack of doctors, facilities, and especially medicines made decent care a good deal harder to come by. During the last two years of the war, plain good luck helped the country avoid any big epidemics, since by then nutrition levels and drug supplies were probably too inadequate to counteract a really serious outbreak. Despite the appalling wastage of a losing conflict, people came through the era in a relatively healthy condition, little touched by medical disaster.

The government depended very much on local cooperation to keep its citizens well. After the fighting with America began, community councils all over the country were told to set up public health divisions to encourage good "physical and spiritual" standards in their districts. The home and welfare ministries ordered them to conduct simple physical tests, improve people's awareness of nutrition, assure adequate sanitation, and also promote marriages. One council in Kyōbashiku, Tokyo, responded by attracting 42,000 residents to the nearby public health center in April 1943 for basic physical examinations, diphtheria immunizations, and tuberculin skin tests or X-rays.

Once the threat of air raids turned tangible in 1944, neighborhood groups helped the health officials do what they could to prepare the public for disaster. In March of that year Takahashi Aiko wrote that "neighborhood association people are checking the blood types of the people they know in the vicinity, and everyone in each household is being tested too. This sort of thing is being done because it is urgently necessary, but in my opinion it is somehow inexpressibly sad that the time when this is necessary has now come." Circulars such as those distributed in Tokyo by the community council for Saginomiya Nichōme told citizens to have their health checked, get their blood typed, and receive shots to protect them against disease. Without the councils and neighborhood associations, the government's scattered public health centers could hardly have carried out these preventive projects on their own.

The parched consumer economy late in the war made it even harder to stay well. People's health was unmistakably jeopardized when food grew scarce after 1943, but slimmer diets apparently did not bring on waves of epidemic diseases. Deaths from tuberculosis rose from 203 per 100,000 in 1937 to 225 in 1943, the last war year with figures. Although the army was naturally worried about TB among its draft pool, the disease actually killed fewer persons under twenty each year between 1940 and 1943, and throughout the 1937–1943 period the majority of its young victims were girls. As a fatal illness, TB was increasingly rampant in the upper age groups during the war.

Among the main countries involved in World War Two for which statistics exist, only Japan had a higher tuberculosis death rate in 1940 than at the beginning of the century. The disease was an unavoidable problem common to all industrializing countries, not one peculiar to the war years, but the government could do little to solve it in the midst of battle. One estimate put the number of sanitorium beds in 1938 at only 10,000, with perhaps 1.5 million TB victims that year, and there was little chance that the state could expand its capital facilities so long as the war continued. Crowded city living after 1937 created conditions that spread the disease faster than the health officials could contain it, and reduced nourishment alone was probably less responsible for the rise in TB rates than poor housing, long work hours in dank factories, and bad sanitation.

Judging from the welfare ministry's rather unrefined statistics, there was no pattern of communicable illness during the war that could be linked directly to bad eating. A minor dietary irony, in fact, is that beriberi fell off because higher millage rates left more husk, hence more thiamin, in consumers' rice. Malaria was a nuisance mainly in Fukui prefecture, where quinine proved to be less deft at controlling the disease than draining swamps for new croplands, which killed the mosquitoes. Typhus was a threat near the end of the war because lice were so common. Morikawa Tamae, who fled with her schoolmates to a mountain spa in 1944, later recalled that despite daily baths and twice-weekly shampoos, "even when I was asleep, I itched from the black-headed lice. When

I got up and combed my hair, they fell out in clumps, and I could crush them with a snap. It was easy to find the crabs, but I hated the skin-lice, which were white and hard to hunt down." Lice may have been a curse, yet typhus cases fell by two-fifths between 1944 and 1945.

Dysentery, paratyphoid, and diphtheria cases rose substantially between 1941 and 1945, but cholera, smallpox, and typhus all grew much worse in 1946, presumably because more than 6.6 million Japanese were repatriated after the surrender. Scarlet fever cases, by contrast, dropped steadily from 1941 to 1945 and remained uncommon after the war. Penicillin became available in late 1944, helping the fight against germs, and there were great regional variations in illnesses throughout the war period. Some older residents of rural districts unfortunately did not seek medical care because they believed rumors that persons over sixty could not obtain it. Elements such as these make the disease statistics for 1941–1945 hard to interpret, but wartime living conditions in general, not food shortages alone, had a great deal to do with whether people got sick.

No group suffered more measurably from poor diets during the war than young people, who with few exceptions were shorter and lighter in 1946 than their counterparts in 1937. Both boys and girls averaged three centimeters shorter and one to four kilograms lighter, depending on their ages. The lack of nourishment made children especially vulnerable to myopia, trachoma, and rickets—the latter a result of inadequate calcium because milk was scarce. The government began testing schoolboys in 1940 for physical strength, and those who seemed weak in grenade throwing, chinning exercises, or the 2,000-meter endurance run had to take special training at one of 1,300 sports centers around the country. The reduced height and weight, the various diseases, and the diminished athletic skills of young people were all symptoms of how bad their diets and their wartime environments had become, with nearly incalculable consequences for their health in the future.

The war era was a time of personal as well as national stress, with families separated, people shifting jobs and residences, women often taking over men's duties, and bombs falling on the cities. Probably the hardest thing to deal with of all was the unknowable: the fate of loved ones in battle and the future beyond the war. Mental health statistics can only crudely measure the psychological toll of wartime, especially since four-fifths of Japan's psychiatric hospitals were shut down between 1941 and 1945 for lack of personnel to manage them. For this reason it is not surprising that their inpatients fell from 20,124 in 1941 to 4,389 in 1945, after a steadily rising trend in mental diseases in the 1930s. Deaths by suicide dropped from a yearly average of 14,000 in 1930–1935 to 9,851 in 1940 and 8,784 in 1943, then regained their prewar level by 1949. Full employment and general public participation in an all-consuming national effort may have helped individuals deflect or work out their anxieties so long as the war was still on. But the relatively immature recognition of mental disease at the time, together with poor record-keeping and inadequate care for the ill, make it risky to infer that wartime was less upsetting to most Japanese than the peaceful years before or since.

Health problems that intersect public morality generally plagued the major countries engaged in the war, but Japan seems to have suffered from relatively little drug abuse and even less venereal disease than before 1937. Little is known about illegal drug consumption during wartime, although rigid laws and strong social pressures apparently kept the number of addicts at the modest level of 3,600 after 1938. The government took a generally realistic approach to the problem of venereal disease, even though its fervent natalism contradicted efforts to distribute preventive devices. The separation of millions of men from their usual sexual partners, a consequence of war rather than official policy, probably had a greater bearing on both fertility and disease rates among civilians than the health and population programs of the state.

The government's policy was simple: it favored sex within marriage and made birth control in principle illegal. At the same time, it campaigned vigorously against love diseases through films and booklets and dispensed condoms regularly to the armed forces. Another sign of wartime realism was a frank, although unillustrated, manual called *Pure-blooded Public Health—Sex Education* by Dr. Kagawa Tetsuo, published with official endorsement in 1943. Although it contained some practical thoughts about sexual morality, the book mainly dealt with the nature and consequences of various illnesses in explicit detail. Still it seems that diminished opportunity rather than action by the authorities was the reason why venereal diseases declined.

As a potential menace to public health, sanitation worried local officials in the cities throughout the whole war. Neighborhood associations were helpful with burning rubbish, but sewage disposal became a problem when private contractors ran short of manpower to haul the accumulation to nearby farms, where it was used as fertilizer. By 1944 the head of sanitation in Tokyo told the *Asahi* newspapers that brokendown trucks, aging equipment, and gasoline shortages meant that city workers could not handle more than 70 percent of the sewage that was produced each day. The city government importuned private railways—notably Seibu and Tōbu—to haul sewage on "filth trains" in the dead of night to farmers in the surrounding prefectures. But because of manpower and transport difficulties, many tons ended up untreated in Tokyo Bay.

Although people living near the bay suffered as a result, the health and sanitation policies of the wartime government were practical, but very inadequate. More to the point was the plain adversity of living on a home front mobilized for a losing war. Poor clothing and shelter, crowded workplaces, and the scarcity of doctors and medical supplies were the results of a wartime footing that compromised a person's chances of staying well. Considering the fearsome capacity of a total war for disrupting life and limb, its full potential for making mischief with people's health in Japan happily went unfulfilled.

Fitful Leisure

Through its cabinet information board, its controls on the liquor industry, and its multiple police forces, the wartime Japanese state had more leverage over how its citizens used their spare time than over their marriage customs, reproductive habits, health patterns, or perhaps even their education, at least near the end of the war. Like every government responsible for directing a general mobilization, the Tōjō cabinet and its successors found that they had to balance their ideological disdain for frivolous entertainments and the organizational demands to conserve resources against the basic need for the weary public to have an occasional good time. The result was a mélange of inconsistent official prohibitions and desultory popular amusements until the last year of the war. Then the pinch of an impoverished economy and an understaffed entertainment industry meant that even during the off-hours life simply was no longer much fun.

Within a week of Pearl Harbor the information board cut the hours at movie theaters to keep civilians off the streets at night, but admissions jumped anyway because other amusements were disappearing. Radio programming understandably grew even more patriotic, with many lectures in early 1942 on topics such as "the history of America's and Britain's crimes" and "rubber in the East Asia Co-Prosperity Sphere." Philatelists quickly bought up a commemorative issue marking the fall of Singapore, smugly put on sale on February 16, 1942, the morning after the British surrendered. Despite the ambience of wartime, Robert Guillain reported, life in Tokyo's night quarters that year was still very good. The streets were dark, but the restaurants stayed open until eleven, when customers spilled out to catch the last train home. The war was going well abroad, and no one seemed to mind a little more sobriety at home, especially since it would be only temporary.

Despite rules against long trips, people still managed to

take trains to their favorite mountain hot springs in early 1943, the same year that coldhearted officials in one northeastern community burned a collection of blonde, blue-eyed dolls to guard local children from "Western infection." The summer season at Karuizawa, a mountain retreat for the rich, still featured its customary concerts, lectures on Asian culture, and tennis tournament—a high-altitude refuge impregnable even to total war.

Down in the cities the musical atmosphere was more clouded. By now the dance halls were closed and the education ministry had renamed the notes of the scale *ha, ni, ho, he, to, i,* and *ro,* the sequence of the Japanese phonetic syllabary. Jazz was banned from the air because it was considered decadent, and the tenor sax was called a tool of the enemy. Some coffeeshops apparently went on playing jazz anyway, on the presumption that the police could not tell Basie from Bach, until the military surprised everyone by changing the name of the rumba to the Gumba ("military horse"). Radio stations were prohibited from playing such random genres as Hawaiian and tango music, Dvorak's *New World* Symphony, and the songs of Stephen Foster, but German and Italian pop music was deemed praiseworthy. After a good deal of discussion, the authorities decided not to bar the common children's song "Hotaru no hikari," finding that the tune to which it was set, "Auld Lang Syne," was "almost Japanese."

Far fewer concerts of any type took place after 1941, because the information board ruled that half the selections had to be works by Japanese artists. This restriction helped along the careers of local composers and choreographers, but it impoverished the normally rich choice of dance and music for city audiences. Exceptions were made for certain German composers late in the war, particularly Beethoven whose works took up full programs in Tokyo's Hibiya Public Hall in January and February 1945. Even the ballet adapted itself to war in March 1944, when four artists performed a new dance called "Decisive Aerial Warfare Ballet," billed as "an artistic contribution to the national drive for heightening the air consciousness of the people."

By 1943 the nighttime sobriety seemed a good deal more

permanent. Belt tightening and a 50-percent tax on comestibles had cut business in the restaurants, and in Okayama those that stayed open past the legal curfew of 8 P.M. had to "turn down their lights low in each room by hand." In March the government added a 90-percent surcharge on theater admissions, not so much to raise revenue as to slash the hours they were open. Bookshops and toy stores closed down because their clerks had been drafted, and children even lost the fun of looking at exotic beasts when the air defense authorities, worried about a breakout during bombings, destroyed all the elephants, lions, tigers, and big snakes at Ueno zoo.

As more and more athletes were conscripted, Japan's professional baseball teams learned to make do with substitutes until partway through the 1944 season, when the Osaka Tigers were declared the champions to replace the Tokyo Giants, now renamed Kyōjin. The Waseda crew won the last intercollegiate men's eight-oar trophy in November 1943, and even the innocent pastime of fishing was less fun because anglers were supposed to sell their catch to the army or navy food centers. Sumo wrestling, the most popular of Japan's native sports, stayed nearly immune from the war until the May tournament of 1945. The bouts that month were moved to the outdoor stadium in Tokyo's Meiji park and cut back to a single week, because air raids had damaged the usual arena and killed the high-ranking wrestlers Toyoshima and Matsuuragata.

The state also broke up entertainment troupes, starting in 1943, and closed more than 10,000 geisha houses and other amusement centers. Prostitutes were egged into factory work, because in their former profession "they were accomplices of the Anglo-American ideological strategy"—a fifth column that might well have intrigued Churchill and Roosevelt, had they only known of it. The vitality and good spirits of 1942 had nearly vanished, and just a year later "to be a woman, basically, is not patriotic. . . . The kimono has disappeared, not only because its silk flaps would be encumbrances for wartime work but also because it would be happy and gay."

The official puritanism had a hollow ring to a people with an indulgent and highly secular view of nightlife. Depriving men of the supportive mothering they often sought (or settled for) in the amusement districts was a drastic action, one that was taken to meet the need for more war workers, not just to placate moralistic bureaucrats. Yet beyond piety and planning was the practical necessity of doing without, because food and drink were terribly scarce at the end of the fighting.

The government's last big step to curb the amusement industry affected high livers more than ordinary workers, a sign that not even the elite were exempt from adversity's blade. On February 25, 1944 the cabinet approved an "Outline of Decisive War Emergency Measures," which closed all the remaining expensive restaurants, geisha houses, stage shows, kabuki dramas, high-price bars, and top-line theaters—the latter soon to be converted for producing balloon bombs. Movie theaters were limited to three showings, all during daylight hours, and by now they were featuring almost nothing but war films and historical episodes. The state made these moves partly to shift entertainers to the factories but also partly to conserve fuel. Soon the streets of the big cities turned lifeless after dark, but the rich still had the solace of Karuizawa, where lectures on wood block prints and the annual summer tennis championships went on as usual in August 1944.

"Happy New Year," a notice from a community council in Tokyo's Nakanoku said on January 6, 1945. "In the face of warnings that the war situation is growing more severe, let's greet the new year with faith in inevitable victory and a determined fighting spirit, so that this will be the year we fight to the finish." A Kyushu farmer, Tanaka Ningo, suspected that it would be. He got up at 5 A.M. on January 1, prayed for victory and his son's safe return from battle at a shrine nearby, and took a long bath. The luxury of " a morning bath feels good," he wrote in his diary—and then he went off to join his air defense group.

Bathing was no small amenity by 1945, with fuel so scarce, yet there were few other pleasures still left. When ordinary bars and restaurants closed and hodgepodge dining halls became the only places for refreshment, the government decided to open "people's bars" in the big cities once or twice a week, selling a single shot of whiskey, a bottle of beer, or a few cups of low-grade sake—known as bombs (*bakudan*) because they made your mouth explode. The novelist Takami Jun wrote in his diary for February 7, 1945 about the mood of ordinary Tokyo residents as they huddled outside one establishment waiting for a drink:

> There's an intimate people's bar at Nitta in Asakusa. They say it opens at 5:30, but it was only 4:30 and already there was a line down the street in back—a double line. . . . the people all looked bedraggled. It looked like a column of old-time coolies. . . . Minute by minute the line grew longer.

(ASAHI SHINBUNSHA)

Neighborhood Tavern: Amid the ruins of an air raid in May 1945, the government opened a basement "people's bar" near Sugamo station, Tokyo.

People were quietly wedging themselves in behind friends in the middle of the line, and looking up ahead I saw that the number of people in front of me was getting bigger. "Don't butt in line," a furious voice shouted from the rear.

Whatever small lift the government's bars may have given public morale, the spartan climate of a losing war had reduced the entertainment centers to a handful of frugal taverns offering little refreshment and even less cheer.

Early in the 1970s a group of several hundred seventh-graders at Sennan junior high school in Suginamiku, Tokyo, were asked how much their parents had told them about what it was like growing up during the war. It turned out that more than three-quarters of them had discussed the war with their mothers, and a majority had talked it over with their fathers as well, typically in the later years of elementary school. Most of the children found that their parents could speak about the era openly, although a few mothers or fathers felt the topic was "too wretched" or "the memory unspeakable." When they were asked their strongest impression after hearing about the war, 75 percent of the students picked one of three answers: "I well appreciated my parents' hardships," "I well appreciated the cruelty, fearfulness, and sadness of war," or "War must not recur." To the generation that went to school barefoot, worked in the war plants as volunteers, searched out fitful amusements, and perhaps fell ill from rickets or TB, these must have been gratifying responses. For those parents, perhaps it was a little easier to live with the memory of adjusting to wartime because they knew someone still understood.

9

Fleeing

The rural people, who had not experienced air raids, were frosty.
Although there was no reason why we who had been burned out should have
any possessions, they wouldn't give us a thing to eat without goods in
exchange.

> —Torinoumi Shigeko, a Tokyo housewife
> who escaped to Chiba prefecture

We didn't care for this kind of [resettlement] work. It was a lot of trouble.
We just did it because we felt sorry, not as a pleasure. Tokyo people
had nothing new to tell us—they just brought their tales of horror
and bombing.

> —Head of a local women's association,
> Yamagata prefecture

Like a restless nightmare, the war's most dreadful episodes
for the Japanese people came at the end. But the last months
of the fighting were too horrid, and too real, to be merely a
bad dream. Most of the ravages were compressed into a
period from late November 1944, when the American bombings began in earnest, to the surrender on August 15, 1945.
By then no one could escape the ill effects of war's destruc-
tiveness on the already depleted modes of living in city and
country alike. The greatest of these effects were the movement of more than ten million urban residents to the countryside and the immense personal suffering when hundreds
of B–29s ruined the largest cities. Since the devastation affected everyone in some way, the Yamagata clubwoman is
probably right that Tokyo people had little new to tell her—

especially because each individual's experiences were so intensely personal and because so many who fled were too numbed by it all to know what to say.

Defending the Cities

As long as the war abroad was going well, both civil and military officials took a relaxed view of protecting the cities at home against air raids. Ever since 1928, Osaka and Tokyo had been holding desultory drills, and the air defense law of October 1937 ordered local governments to take precautions, usually no more than handing out manuals at poorly attended neighborhood exercises. These publications told citizens what to do in the event of a bombing: fight, don't run—in this case, the fires in the vicinity. As a report in Kawasaki admitted just before Pearl Harbor, "there are many defects and inadequacies in the current conditions of air defense in our country."

Not even the surprise raid by sixteen American B–25s, launched from the carrier *Hornet* on April 18, 1942, under Lt. Col. James H. Doolittle, had much effect on the state's planning for homeland defense. The army minister, General Sugiyama Gen, admitted his surprise at the attack but shrugged the incident off: "When several enemy planes come flying into our territory, there is just no way to prevent them." The cabinet's outlook may have been astigmatic, but no American bombers returned for more than two years. Meanwhile the navy suffered its first defeats in mid-1942 in the Coral Sea and at Midway, but despite the loss at Guadalcanal in February 1943, the empire actually began to contract only at the end of that year when Bougainville and the Gilbert Islands fell. Not surprisingly, the cabinet took its first concrete steps to help civilians deal with air raids that same autumn, anticipating the attacks that became possible after Sai-

Guarding Ginza: Neighborhood women dig a streetside bomb shelter, downtown Tokyo, 1943.

pan and other islands in the Marianas were conquered the following June.

In the interval between the Doolittle raid and the cabinet actions of late 1943, neighborhood associations were the main line of civilian air defense. Since many neighborhood units had helped to fight fires for decades, it was natural for them to hold bucket relay drills and see that every home had such primitive equipment as sand, buckets, shovels, brooms, ladders, and cisterns. The associations also observed the blackout rules in the cities very strictly. Ōya Akiko recalled that in 1942 the captain on her block would sometimes shout, "I can see light! That'll be a target for enemy planes! Put it out! Why don't you buy a blackout curtain?"

Many people can remember wearing iron air raid helmets and chanting "oh, one, two, oh, one, two" as they dug trenches in their yards or neighborhoods for refuge during bombardments—and then brightening them by planting flowers around the top. Shimizu Yoshihisa unearthed ten bucketfuls of rare Chinese coins while he was expanding his shelter in the Shinagawa district of Tokyo, and in a fit of patriotism he gave them all to the army. Others were not so lucky. Sometimes pedestrians broke their legs at night falling into the trenches dug in the flower beds along the unlighted city sidewalks, and many persons, such as the six whose bodies were discovered by workers building the new Tōzai subway in 1967, roasted to death in their poorly made shelters once the raids got under way.

A bucket of sand and a ditch in the back yard were better than no protection at all, but before 1944 the neighborhood groups relied mostly on ritualized morale-building to make citizens feel safer than they really were. On the one hand, neighbors took an "air defense oath of certain victory," publicly pledging to "follow orders," "refrain from selfish conduct," and "cooperate with one another in air defense." On the other hand, for those whose vows of mutual aid with their neighbors wore thin, the authorities used a psychology of immunity ("it can't happen again, or perhaps not at all") to keep people from fleeing the attacks: "Because bombs absolutely will not fall again in a place that has been hit, all residents are responsible for bravely rushing forth to take part in air defense. This is the safest method." Such assurances were totally unrealistic in light of the American firepower, but they apparently helped convince Miyahara Noriko that "no matter what sort of air raid comes, this neighborhood association will be safe." Even as late as 1945, Yabashi Yasuko comforted herself by thinking that "the bombs won't fall on this corner of such a huge plant," only to have her illusion exploded by a giant shell that hit the factory in May. By resorting once again to public ceremonial occasions to reinforce the individual's obligations to the group, the authorities used the collective tradition as a prop for morale—the only real defense available until the cabinet laid more practical plans starting in the fall of 1943.

The government strategy for protecting the cities, developed piecemeal as the war slowly degenerated, included four programs involving civilians: factory dispersal, creating firebreaks, strengthening air defense activities in the neighborhoods, and evacuating as many people as possible to the countryside. The first of these was logistically the hardest and got little attention, at least until the heavy American raids began a year later. Of the others, each of which was pursued actively for the rest of the war, resettlement in the rural areas undoubtedly had the greatest social consequences, a silent admission that the "fight, don't run" technique was an impractical way to safeguard ordinary citizens. Even so, planning by the state had far less to do with whether people fled the cities than the course of the war itself, since most of those escaping to the country left only after the greatest bombings began in March 1945.

When the home ministry set up an air defense general headquarters in November 1943 to help protect civilians, "there was by no means a uniformity of outlook between the air defense general headquarters and the military concerning the basic matter of what attitude to take toward human lives." But there was no bureaucratic dispute about what was decorously called "structure evacuation"—in other words, smashing down homes and other buildings for firebreaks. By December certain industrial zones from Tokyo to Kyushu had been marked for protection, and broad stripes of open land soon appeared around the edges of factories, transport centers, and military bases where ordinary houses and neighborhood shops had recently stood. On January 8, 1944, the government used the *Asahi* newspapers to tell people who had lost their homes that they would have to find new ones on their own: "Try harder. Talk it over with your friends and relatives. . . . Try putting up notices." As always, those with connections were more fortunate. Morii Sei, a shopkeeper in

Yokohama whose home was demolished in March 1944, persuaded the head of her community council to get the police to show her a list of vacant dwellings. Altogether 614,000 housing units were cleared away, usually by members of nearby neighborhood associations working with ropes and hand tools. One-fifth of all the housing destroyed by the war was lost in this manner, sending more than 3.5 million city residents out to hunt new places to live.

Besides ripping down buildings, the neighborhood associations were asked to take on more and more duties to help guard the people who stayed on in the cities. In February 1944 the home ministry ordered each unit of local government to stop asking the community councils and neighborhood groups to carry out "unnecessary activities" and instead to let them "use the fruits of their own experience." Evidently the councils and associations had become trapped in the routine of local administration during the three years since their incorporation under the new structure movement, and now the state needed to free them, in the case of Tokyo at least, for insuring "that victory was inevitable and defeat impossible and planning for the defense of the imperial capital."

That same month the cabinet information board reinforced the work of the local groups by rushing out a graphic instructional film, called *Bomb Blasts and Shell Fragments,* that showed experiments with captured American bombs to demonstrate their explosive power. The movie taught citizens how to board up office windows and take refuge in downtown shelters, but no amount of trumpet music or sandbagging of railway entrances could obscure how vulnerable the ordinary residential areas were. As a result, the neighborhood units held lecture meetings about ways to stop fires, distributed pamphlets, drilled far more frequently than earlier in the war, and recruited a civilian air defense corps to help military spotters. Yet the extra pairs of eyes did little good once the army's thin complement of fighters, searchlights, and anti-aircraft guns grew helpless in the face of bigger and bigger American attacks.

In late January 1945 the imperial general headquarters finally settled on a plan for defending the homeland, almost two months after the first B–29s thundered across the northwestern Pacific to hit industrial and military targets in Japan. The military planners called on community councils and neighborhoods to take charge of fire fighting, since ordinary fire companies were hopelessly understaffed. Families were expected to shroud their lights from sunset to 10 P.M. and not to use them at all after that hour, even though nearly all the night bombings before March 10 took place by radar, usually through thick clouds, from an altitude of 9,000 meters. Japanese monitors in the Bonin Islands normally gave the cities an

(KAGEYAMA KŌYŌ)

Women's Brigade: Prim matrons in well-to-do districts worked out with rifles as a part of their neighborhood association duties.

hour's notice before an attack, triggering sirens and factory whistles so loud that when they stopped people said, "Listen to the silence." By January the alerts were so frequent, and the houses so unheated, that most persons slept in their street clothes. No one doubted the bold editorialist who wrote the same month that "we are now entering upon that stage of the war wherein the truly decisive battle will be fought."

The first daytime incendiary raids by Maj. Gen. Curtis Le-May's Twenty-first Bomber Command took place on January 27 in Tokyo and February 4 in Kobe. Two days later Obata Tadayoshi, a statesman with close ties to the cabinet, declared bluntly that "the expression 'sure victory' is misleading" because it "is identical with sure death. . . . Our leaders should frankly reveal the real state of affairs, while our people on their part must be ready for any emergency." Soon this unexpected candor would seem prescient, yet until the cataclysmic destruction of Tokyo's low-lying riverside districts on March 10, the residential groups managed to snuff out most of the fires at once. It was only in the last five months of the war that the moral exhortations and primitive tools of the neighborhood associations became utterly inadequate for defending the cities.

The Cruelest Move

Of all the cabinet's policies for protecting its citizens, the most important was a decision on October 15, 1943, to begin evacuating persons from urban areas who were not needed in the war plants. The hope was that city leaders and the neighborhood associations could persuade the families of soldiers and conscripted laborers, mothers with small children, the elderly, and the infirm to resettle in the countryside, ideally with rural relatives. The revised air defense law of December 1943 carefully deferred to social custom when it stated that evacuation "will count on sending household units to the countryside whenever possible, and it will be led in such a way as not to violate the spirit of familism."

Yet so long as the danger of raids seemed remote and relocation was optional, fewer people responded than the government had hoped. There are no reliable figures on how many city residents voluntarily fled before the bombings started in late November 1944, but the cabinet's dismay was evident from Home Minister Andō Kisaburō's abashed remark to the Diet on March 22, 1944, that "I haven't come across much public sentiment for picking up and leaving." Since inducement seemed to be unavailing, the government decided to shock people into escaping through such propaganda movies as the shrill, menacing short called *Evacuation,* released in July. This thin and hortatory production showed whole neighborhoods ablaze from bombs, especially those leeward of a prevailing wind. But despite the official encouragements and pressures, the only systematic evacuation was perhaps the cruelest act of all—the forced removal of many thousands of primary schoolchildren from their families in the cities to group resettlement centers in the countryside.

So long as leaving for the rural areas remained voluntary, the government interposed itself very little in people's freedom to live where they wished. But when the cabinet announced an "Outline for Encouraging the Evacuation of Schoolchildren" on June 30, 1944, it abruptly violated the spirit of familism that the air defense law had pledged to respect six months earlier. Beneath the earnest guise of keeping the education system intact, the state's real motive was to protect the students as a human resource in the abstract, no matter how they or their parents felt about being separated from one another. As one crestfallen father later explained, it was no easy matter to see his daughter off to the country: "Eventually we were told that they would depart two days later. We took Ruriko on a walk from Nihonbashi to Ginza. Perhaps this would be goodbye forever. The final thing I wanted her to do was to eat something . . . but there wasn't a single shop selling bread the whole way." Not even the frightful air raids themselves were probably so traumatic as this compulsory detachment of young children from their homes.

Under the government plan, more than 350,000 third-through sixth-graders from the national schools in a dozen major cities were evacuated by school groups, starting in August 1944, to vacant inns, meeting halls, temples, and resorts in nearby prefectures. Already there were 300,000 urban schoolchildren in the villages as voluntary evacuees, including many from smaller cities not covered by the cabinet's program. Another 100,000 first- and second-graders sent out in March 1945 raised the number of students who relocated as groups to more than 450,000. The government budgeted 241,000 yen to pay the innkeepers, cooks, and helpers who fed and housed the children and their teachers.

Once they had settled in, the evacuees were expected to continue their schooling, but all of them had stiff labor obligations under the April 1944 order creating student volunteer corps. The schools in the host communities usually could not absorb the newcomers, so the children mostly studied in their lodgings. Their beleaguered instructors were given uncommon latitude to decide how to use the class periods, but school rarely lasted more than an hour or two each day. Most students spent their time outside class gathering food for the group or working on the nearby farms as labor volunteers. The schedule of duties for the Tatsuoka national school in Iida included treading wheat plants, opening new lands, cultivating silkworms, cutting rice plants, placing topsoil in paddies, and mowing weeds. The school's principal, Kinoshita Uji, reported that despite the hard work, students found "going on labor service one of their greatest pleasures because at a time when food was very scarce they would receive sweet potatoes for working on the farms."

The towns and villages that took in school groups welcomed the young newcomers less ambiguously than the adult refugees who later fled to the countryside. An Osaka fourth-grader whose class moved to the Kawano national school in Ehime prefecture wrote home that the local "children at this school are kind and strong. I think I'd like to become strong

Hungry Evacuees: Suppertime for a school group that resettled in a seaside inn late in the summer of 1944.

like that." Another boy in the same school wrote home happily that "I want to become good friends with the kids in this village." Students from Tokyo's Ikenoue national school were greeted just as warmly at their resettlement center in Nagano prefecture, where the local officials made Takeda Hikozaemon and his group feel at home immediately. The host-refugee relationship was cordial not only because the evacuees were young and their numbers relatively manageable but also because the government made special efforts, through entreaties and cash, to smooth hard feelings that might occur. The students had their own lodgings—perhaps the greatest irritant in any evacuation program—and they kept pretty much to themselves. Later in the war, when everyone was weary and twenty times as many homeless city people descended on the villages, the climate turned much chillier.

The students may have enjoyed playing with the local children or working for sweet potatoes, but on most other counts life away from home was dreary and depressing. Every one of twenty-two pupils from the Ochanomizu national school in

Tokyo lost weight between April and August 1945 after fleeing to Nagano prefecture, averaging more than two kilograms each. For many students who lived through evacuation in poor villages far from home, the only memory that lingered after the war was searching for edible weeds or eating boiled licorice greens, bracken ferns, and potato sprouts thinned by farmers. "It was pitiful," recalled a teacher accompanying the Daizawa national school group that evacuated from Tokyo to Asama hot springs in Nagano prefecture, "to see the children lament when they took off the covers of their lunch boxes, to find them only half-full."

Boring and skimpy meals certainly made the students lose weight, but there is little evidence that they fell sick as a direct result. The Minamizakura national school from Tokyo, which moved en masse to Kinugawa hot springs, Tochigi prefecture, experienced colds but no major contagious diseases. The Daizawa group and nearly 2,000 other displaced schoolchildren shared a single physician with the local residents in Asama, where far more pupils fell ill from improper diphtheria inoculations than from the disease itself. "If those had been ordinary times," Hamadate Kikuo noted, the incident "probably would have become a big problem, but it was hushed up."

Equally important was the emotional well-being of the young people, who almost universally felt homesick. Hamadate countered it by checking outgoing mail to detect the students' frame of mind and curtailing visitors for two months. One of the letters he inspected, written in late August 1944 by a sixth-grader, read:

Mother, please listen to Mitsuko's one great request. Mother, as soon as this letter arrives, please come to see me that very day. Please, mother.

Mother, every day Mitsuko goes on crying. Everyone teases me. When a lunch box was missing from our group, I was told by the teacher that I must have stolen it. Everyone tormented me and ostracized me.

Mother, Mitsuko might die if you don't come to see me. Please

bring a bowl with a little rice, I'm so hungry, I can't stand it. All we
ever get as a side dish is pumpkin every day. Mother, please. As
soon as this letter arrives, come right away, OK? By all means
come.

Mitsuko

Eventually parents were allowed to visit once again, and all
the food brought as presents was shared with the other children. Yet Hamadate felt at a loss, even after conferring with
nearby physicians, to cope with the students' loneliness and
distress: "We were sorry that no one could explain these psychological problems." However meddlesome, at least his approach was more realistic than that of Nagumo Yasue, one of
those who accompanied the Minamizakura group, who denied the problem by stating that "as food conditions worsened, their bodies naturally declined. . . . but psychologically
they were all fine." There is no gauge that can measure the
emotional damage when winsome children were separated
from their anxious families, but at least parents may have
been comforted, in the case of Hamadate's group, to know
that someone cared enough to be watchful about feelings as
well as physiques.

Escaping En Masse

Like most people in the teeth of disaster, the Japanese were
reluctant to leave their city homes, possessions, and familiar
environments, and they were also quite resentful that the
state had made their school-aged children do so. In a society
much taken with superstitions, it may well be that "people
overestimate their luck and do not evacuate, preferring to
believe that the danger is more serious for others." Only
when they are confronted with uniformed authority or the disaster itself, it seems, will many persons finally leave, yet even

then the Japanese experience in 1945 shows that a mass exodus does not have to involve disorderly panic.

One of history's great migrations took place in Japan during the last months of the war, comparable in scale to the southward flight of Han Chinese in the third century or the movement of rural black Americans to cities between 1940 and 1970. More than ten million Japanese, one-seventh of the national population, spilled out to the farms to find refuge—a few of them through inducement but most through fear. Their departure inevitably hurt the morale of those who stayed behind. At the end of the war the six largest cities had lost 58 percent of their 1940 populations, and the ones with more than a million persons lost two-thirds of their residents after February 1944. More than 4,200,000 persons left Tokyo during the last year of the war, four-fifths of them after the massive March 10 air raid. Only then did the war convince citizens to do what their government had not been able to—to flee for their lives.

Apart from the school groups, nearly all of this enormous flow of persons took place voluntarily, much of it outside the state's disaster planning. Britain, by comparison, in three days officially evacuated 1.5 million residents from the cities in September 1939, joining another two million who had left on their own account earlier that summer. Many drifted back to urban areas the following year, only to be reevacuated as a part of the 1.25 million who were officially moved out during the blitz of September 1940. Germany, which suffered its first Allied raids in 1942, followed a less systematic dispersal plan than Britain but reaccommodated twice as many bomb victims in its relatively sturdy urban housing as did Japan. The Germans lost 28 percent of all their dwellings to the air attacks, compared with 24 percent in Japan, yet only half as many persons relocated in the countryside (4.8 million, versus more than ten million in Japan). Even though they tore down more than 600,000 homes, the Japanese authorities were apparently more reluctant than the British to interfere forcibly with urban lifestyles by imposing a mandatory evacuation plan for adults. At the same time, Japanese city housing was already so crowded, and so many people had rural relatives or acquaintances, that the German pattern of urban reaccommodation was much less frequent in Japan. Lacking both the orderliness of the British and the housing elasticity of the Germans, Japan luckily avoided chaos when the B–29s finally drove millions of city residents to the hills.

What the exodus meant for the burned-out cities is almost beyond imagination. Starkly denuded lots, their rubble picked over by the homeless, stood empty alongside the melee outside train stations as civilians got ready to escape. It was as though all the vital energy that made Japanese cities so supremely human had suddenly been poured into a few transportation funnels, leaving the ruined districts arid and still. The animation practically disappeared from streets that shortly before had still been able to divert passersby with their people's bars and hodgepodge dining halls. The cities were literally wasted, unable to support the life that in happier times made them exceptionally vivacious communities.

After March 10 the government ran special refugee trains to the mountains from Tokyo and other main centers, to try to cope with the throngs who now needed no persuasion to flee. Kumagai Sachi recalled the bustle outside Shinjuku station after the March raid on Tokyo, with evacuees desperately trying to make sacrifice sales of pianos, gas ovens, and other items too large to carry on their backs—"but there were so few buyers." Others escaped in the beds of trucks if they were lucky enough to hire them. But most people, in the timeless pattern of war refugees everywhere, wordlessly left town riding bicycles, sitting atop oxcarts, or trudging on foot.

Still, some residents stayed on to face the unceasing American attacks. Sutō Ryōsaku, the neighborhood captain in Egota Yonchōme, Tokyo, wrote on April 20, 1945, that "we thought about evacuating" his family to Niigata prefecture, "but in mother's opinion it was impossible for her to leave." She didn't relish spending her few remaining years "caring for the children and living a life of hardships for a long time in another part of the country." Others on Sutō's block apparently agreed, because his careful monthly census of the

The Uprooted: Bomb victims fleeing Tokyo after the March 10, 1945, raid. Some have reason to smile—not only a free ride in a freightcar but also food to eat.

neighborhood showed that evacuation caused a drop from 56 to 35 residents between April 1 and June 1, 1945, after which the number rose to 51 on June 19 and stayed there right to the surrender. The increase happened because several technical school students and three families resettled in vacant houses in the vicinity after their original dwellings had been destroyed. Evidently Sutō's area was both more stable and more stretchable than most city neighborhoods, but in all the big cities local organizations such as his kept on helping people move in and out, despite the death and devastation around them, to the very end.

Because the great majority of civilians in the largest cities migrated, the rural population of Japan bloated from 42.0 million in February 1944 to 52.5 million in November 1945 (two-thirds of the newcomers were females). What this influx meant for schools, housing, and especially food supplies can be imagined from the case of Gunma prefecture, near Tokyo. In Kawaba village, 293 evacuees had moved in by November 1944 and another 192 up to the next March. Then when the great incendiary bombs began falling, 807 more city people took refuge in the village during the last five months of the war. By July 31, 1945, the prefecture as a whole had absorbed 222,880 outsiders, about a quarter of them persons who had lost their homes to fires and the other three-fourths people who had fled because they feared the same fate. Much more secure shelters, such as hilly Nagano and Niigata prefectures, soaked up many thousands more.

Minota village in Saitama prefecture gives an even sharper portrait of how outsiders were taken in by farming communities. A survey in June 1945 showed that evacuation had swollen the village's population by 30 percent since January 1944. As in Gunma, about a quarter of the new residents were direct bomb victims, and the rest had fled the cities as a precaution. Three-fourths of the host families were relatives of the refugees they housed, and proportionately as many poor homes accepted evacuees as rich ones. More than 77 percent of the visitors arrived after the huge city fire raids started in March 1945, higher even than the proportion in Gunma. Less than two-fifths of them were males, and almost none previously had any experience in the fields. Since the great majority were lodged with farm families, this handicap became a source of friction, not just in Minota but throughout the countryside.

Somehow they fitted the homeless in, but villagers were often testy and suspicious toward their guests. Refugee mothers with small children seemed particularly burdensome, as in the British evacuation, and the hospitality soon wore thin when too many cooks shared the same kitchen. Even ties of blood could not mask the cultural and emotional gaps between city and country relatives when they were thrown together under the extreme circumstances of mass flight. The government tried to shame farmers into cooperating with such arrogant slogans as "families that won't take people in are a disgrace." Eventually simple necessity crowded out all other considerations. The refugees were there, there were millions of them, and they had nowhere to stay nor anything to eat. Basic human cooperation took over in these emergency conditions, where official plans and pronouncements had not been enough.

It is hard to know whether host or guest was discomfited more when ten million outsiders piggybacked on forty-two million country people. Takahashi Aiko pinpointed the tension as early as January 4, 1944, when she observed that "city residents now seem to be saying flattering things to rural people, whereas before they never said a thing. When people's positions are suddenly reversed, it's hard to tell good feelings from bad ones. But come to think of it, it seems miserable that the two groups despise each other." Even though Takahashi probably used too bold a brush, no one disputes the recollection of Torinoumi Shigeko that relations were often frosty. Ishizuka Rui noted that "if villagers didn't recognize you, they were very hesitant to sell anything to evacuees." Hatano Isoko fought with her rural ration clerk over a pair of socks left over from a recent distribution, and even the public bathhouses gave first crack at the hot water to old customers. Usually the power of money buys war migrants the cooperation of local merchants, whether in factory boom towns or remote refugee camps, but by the end of World War Two Japan's rural economy of barter ruled out even this pecuniary entree for most of the displaced families.

The farmers in Minota and elsewhere understandably felt irked that most newcomers lacked the skills to help grow what they ate. Local people especially resented evacuees who "played idly" while the farmers struggled to keep up production. But most city residents apparently followed the example of Watanabe Toyoko, a Tokyo housewife who resettled in Yamamiyayama, Yamanashi prefecture. Although her husband stayed at his job in Tokyo and she was responsible for a family of thirteen, Watanabe learned to do farm chores such as using a hoe, cutting weeds, working land, and the ticklish task of thinning peaches. Yet in the end, even if Tokyo people had nothing new to tell the farmers, the two groups learned to get along because the wreckage of a lost war deprived them of any other choice.

Well before 1950 the cities of Japan had regained their normal size, as the ten million evacuees filtered back to reconstruct their lives after the numbing impoverishment of flight and survival. There they were joined by many of the 3.1 million Japanese civilians and 3.5 million troops who were repatriated from abroad after the surrender, far outnumbering the 1.2 million noncitizens who emigrated from Japan at the same time. The fate of 237,000 other Japanese in Siberia, 79,000 in Karafuto and the Kuriles, and 60,000 in Manchuria was less clear, but few of them presumably survived the war. For a time the wartime flight from Japan's big cities interrupted the long-term trend toward urbanization, but the great postwar movement of persons soon restored the normal pattern of city growth and congestion.

The mammoth dispersal of Japan's urban citizens during 1944–1945 was a heroic lesson in human cooperation at a time of fatigue, malnutrition, and desperation—but also urgent necessity. The evacuation was mainly voluntary but not chaotic. The state played its part by appealing to the collective nature of Japanese society, using school groups to relocate young people and neighborhood associations to ease the stress of moving in or out of town. Whatever the cultural distance between city and country, the most remarkable aspect of the entire migration is that most of those who fled were lodged with rural relatives—another sign of how durable the family remained even in total war.

10

Enduring

Like the subtle colors of sunset in an Edo woodblock print, the decisive turning points of history are often too evanescent to be appreciated until long after they are past. No one can say exactly when in the spectrum from bright pink to deep purple that twilight becomes night, or war becomes defeat. Often no single event in an incremental process stands out as the precise moment when a substantive change occurs, until suddenly it is apparent that a shift has taken place, a bridge crossed, that events have passed a point of no return.

In this sense both the beginning and the end of Japan's fruitless war with the United States were marked indistinctly. It is hard to tell exactly when war became inevitable in the long chain of actions leading to Pearl Harbor, and it is equally difficult to be sure just when Japan had been beaten. In many respects that point may already have been surpassed before the heaviest American bombings began in March 1945, but defeat did not become surrender until August 15. In the interval, the Japanese people managed to endure by bearing up under calamitous air raids and a futile last-minute mobilization armed with bamboo spears.

By early 1945 the U.S. naval blockade and the drain of all-out war production had sapped the Japanese economy to its core. Consumer expenditures were down to only 38 percent of the gross national product, compared with 67 percent in 1940. American submarines isolated Japan from her sources of raw materials so successfully that the level of gross national product in the first half of the 1945 fiscal year was estimated at 25 percent below the 1944 figure. Yet the farmers and factory laborers kept on working, and there is no way to tell how much longer the bitter chemistry of perseverance and sacrifice could have kept the home front from collapsing had the B–29s never come.

That same spring the imperial forces were critically weak but not yet exhausted. Japanese air and naval power were no longer offensive threats after meeting defeat in November 1944 at Leyte Gulf in the Philippines. The army was worn down by the long Philippine campaign that peaked in February 1945, just when a bloody month-long battle for the obscure island of Iwo Jima began far to the northeast. But the crucial Okinawa campaign, which started April 1, did not result in a clear American victory until June 21. Japan's military fate may actually have been settled as early as February 1943 at Guadalcanal, or possibly even at Midway the previous June, but the crippled army and navy were still very much in the fight when American bombers began burning city neighborhoods in March 1945. By then perhaps Japan had already lost the war, but citizens had to bear a gigantic cost before the firing ended five months later.

"Cut Open My Chest,
Let the Clean Air In"

For civilians the most violent phase of the eight-year war was
the strategic bombing of sixty-six Japanese cities by the Twentieth Air Force, especially from the time of the largest incendiary raid, on March 10, 1945, in Tokyo. These fearsome attacks are naturally unforgettable to anyone who experienced
them, and they take up a good many shelves in the library of
wartime lore. As horrible as they undoubtedly were, the fire
raids and explosive attacks on Japan involved fewer than one-
eighth the number of bombs dropped on Germany during
the war (160,000 tons, versus 1,360,000). Their effect was cat-
astrophic for the cities and towns that were strategic targets,
but the technology, logistics, terrain, and objectives in 1945
did not produce a level of destruction nearly so great as the
saturation bombings of Vietnam by American B–52s two decades later. Although conventional bombs killed nearly as
many people as the atomic attacks of August 1945, only the
most partisan or aggrieved could deny that Hiroshima and
Nagasaki were qualitatively different from all other explo-
sions, before or since.

Most of the casualty statistics for the raids are a product of
more art than science, but the best estimate is that a half-
million persons died from the American bombings of Japan
proper (the figure for Germany is 300,000). The Japanese attacks were lumped into the last months of the war when the
economy was already ravished, and only 22 percent of the
bombs were dropped on precision industrial targets. Japanese city dwellings were dense and very flammable, increasing the efficiency of the American weapons greatly. As a result, the much smaller tonnage that fell on Japan destroyed
almost as much of the housing supply as the Allied attacks on
German cities (24 percent, versus 28 percent in Germany),
where most of the bombings were directed at factories and

bases. The U.S. Navy also shelled the coastline in fourteen Japanese prefectures, but 99.5 percent of the civilian casualties resulted from air raids. Being outside the city during an attack was excellent insurance, since 86 percent of the bomb deaths occurred in six heavily urbanized prefectures plus Hiroshima and Nagasaki.

The raids burned out more than 160 square kilometers in five main cities, including twenty-five square kilometers in Tokyo the night of March 10. About 42 percent of Japan's urban industrial zones were demolished, further depressing output in factories that were already starved for resources. More than half of the country's manufacturing capacity in vacuum tubes, ammonium sulfate, and oil refining was destroyed in the war, as was a fourth of the aluminum and pig iron production capability. Half of the telephones and national railway repair shops were wrecked by the air raids, and the output of wheat flour dropped by 50 percent because of the bombings. Soon after the surrender, the Japanese government calculated that the Boeing Superfortresses had ruined 40 percent of Osaka and Nagoya, 50 percent of Tokyo, Kobe, and Yokohama, 90 percent of the prefectural capital of Aomori, and almost 100 percent of Hiroshima.

The U.S. turned to incendiary tactics, which are sometimes called area bombings, because the earlier precision raids on strategic and industrial sites had not had so much effect as was hoped. Now the aim was to cripple the cities and perhaps frighten people into giving up the fight. Before March 10 most attacks took place in midday with relatively small bomb loads, because the planes had to carry huge amounts of fuel to operate at high altitudes from bases in the Marianas. All this changed late on March 9 when General Curtis LeMay dispatched more than 300 B-29s, code named Meeting House, toward Japan. Each plane carried six tons of incendiaries and almost no fuel reserves, operating between 2,000 and 3,000 meters in order to cut gasoline use, confuse the Japanese radar operators, and keep the bombs from blowing off target. The goal was to destroy the packed residential districts along the Sumida River in eastern Tokyo. The result was a conflagration that burned an area as large as Manhattan Island from the Battery to Central Park.

As the sirens alerted families all over the capital that evening, Matsumura Hidetoshi, chief of the press section of the army general headquarters, broadcast a message on NHK saluting March 10 as Armed Forces Day. He ended by cheering the audience with the cliché, "The darkest hour is just before the dawn." Soon after Matsumura went off the air, a strong northwest wind blew flames hundreds of feet into the night sky as the American planes poured nearly 1,700 tons of fire bombs on the small homes and shops of Tokyo's riverside districts. Violent wind shears from the updraft bounced the B–29s hundreds of meters during their methodical bomb runs from all directions, almost unchallenged by the threadbare Japanese air defenses. After immolating the target for

(ASAHI SHINBUNSHA)

Janus: The two faces of war, Armed Forces Day, March 10, 1945, downtown Tokyo.

two and a half hours, the departing air crews could see flames from 250 kilometers out at sea. Some of the fires took four days to burn out. Later that morning, as thousands of people fled the ruins, some of them passed the imperial army band gravely parading down a broad thoroughfare to martial music in honor of Armed Forces Day.

The lanes, canals, and rivers of the low-lying districts trapped many thousands in the holocaust. Most of the dead suffocated because the flames consumed so much oxygen. Yamamoto Katsuko, a fifty-nine-year-old foster mother to eight children, literally kept her family bound together in the midst of the disaster. "We could hardly breathe, we couldn't see at all," she recalled, "and I figured that if we all fled right there in the midst of the fire, scattering in every direction, we'd all burn up and die." So she "felt a rope with my foot and used it to tie the whole family together. The eldest son led the way, and I carried the newborn baby." Yamamoto and the children reached safety in front of a neighborhood movie theater, but at another, the Meijiza, the bodies of suffocated victims were reportedly stacked more than two meters high.

Thousands of people escaped the flames by jumping into the rivers, only to drown in the melee. Dr. Kubota Shigenori, who headed a military rescue unit, drove up to the Ryōgoku bridge before dawn by picking his way through fallen telephone poles and loose wires. "In the black Sumida river," he later wrote, "countless bodies were floating, clothed bodies, naked bodies, all as black as charcoal. It was unreal. These were dead people, but you couldn't tell whether they were men or women. You couldn't even tell if the objects floating by were arms and legs or pieces of burnt wood." Residents who fled on land stampeded the few remaining bridges, where some of them hurried past carrying their possessions on their backs, oblivious that their belongings had caught fire from flying sparks.

"I can't tell you, it hurts so much I'm about to go crazy," one victim of the smoke told rescue workers at Dr. Kubota's emergency headquarters in the Honjo national school. Carbon monoxide poisoning and other forms of oxygen deficiency were obvious among the survivors. One man gasped, "It hurts so much I'd like to cut open my chest and let some clean air in." The ash and dust blocked many people's tear ducts, and some of them were permanently blinded by infections that went untreated. Dr. Kubota's unit consisted of nine physicians and eleven nurses, the only official medical personnel still available in Tokyo for disaster duty because so many doctors had been drafted and most of the rest had already moved their equipment and patients to the countryside. His group was aided by many Japan Red Cross teams at emergency first aid stations in the ruined area.

In the midst of the flames Taniguchi Masumi gave birth to her third child. On the evening of March 9, she recounted, her labor pains began and she entered a maternity hospital in Shitayaku. "I heard that they were using drugs to speed up deliveries," she wrote. "Suddenly there was the roar of enemy planes, and at the same moment a half-dozen flaming red objects came streaking down out in front of the hospital. . . . In a moment the head doctor appeared, saying 'This hospital has become dangerous, so let's all take shelter. Please follow me.' " He led Taniguchi and the others to the ruins of a building near the Asakusa International Theater. She lay down on the bare ground. "I was desperate. I simply had to give birth. Fortunately the three nurses there encouraged me. While they spurred me on, 'Now's the time, it'll be right away,' I bore down and in a few minutes I delivered a large baby boy." Since there was nothing to keep the infant warm, "I took my own slip and wrapped him up inside it." In temperatures only a few degrees above freezing, she lay and the others sat there on the earth, watching the fires and smoke "with no place to rest, waiting for dawn to come."

When it arrived there was no water pressure left in the broken mains and no gas or electric service for days. Block after block was burned flat, and "the lonesome telephone poles in the wasteland were like grave markers." The weather stayed cold after March 10, helping to preserve corpses, but a prisoner of war several kilometers from the Asakusa area, David H. James, wrote that "all day an acrid smell filled our nostrils in Omori camp. When the tide lapped our fences it cast up hundreds of charred bodies. We stared through the knot-holes at the men, women and children sprawled in the mud ... there to rot alongside others who floated in after other raids on the Capital."

Eastern Tokyo was obliterated. Nearly one-fifth of the city's industrial areas and an astounding 63 percent of its commercial districts had disappeared overnight. More than a quarter-million buildings burned down, driving at least a million survivors to the countryside or elsewhere in Tokyo to find places to stay. If their families did not retrieve the dead, they were carted to temples and parks, identified if possible, and cremated without delay. The ashes were to be buried in a potter's field if they were not claimed within a year. Some bodies were buried directly in mass graves. The U.S. Strategic Bombing Survey calculated that 83,793 persons died in the March 10 raid, but the actual figure was probably at least 90,000 and may have exceeded 100,000—greater than the 73,000 who died in the Kanto earthquake of September 1, 1923, and surpassed among modern Japanese disasters only by the agony at Hiroshima.

The Americans justified the fire bombings as a tactic to shorten the war and insure that industrial centers not identifiable by air reconnaissance were demolished. After the indifferent results of the high-explosive attacks from November to February, the March 10 raid by any military definition had succeeded royally. The American forces presumably fire-bombed Japan more than Germany because the closely built wooden houses burned very easily and because the precision attacks on German factories and bases had been much more effective. There is no reason to think that the U.S. would not have used incendiary tactics more frequently in Europe if conditions had warranted them.

Local people were the first to help resettle the victims after March 10, particularly through community councils and neighborhood associations. In the Suginami district of Tokyo, far from the target zone, Yoshizawa Hisako's council put up fifty-four refugees in a nearby Tenri sect church. Each neighborhood association was asked to contribute bedding and dishware to tide the survivors over until they could relocate more permanently somewhere else. The government sent out instructions on March 12 and 17 about emergency food distributions, but most of its relief actions related to longer-range evacuation plans, restoring transport, and giving loans and tax remissions to those who lost their assets. Apparently some people thought the state could have done more, because Yoshizawa wrote on April 8 that "there are many persons who are very angry at the government for not taking responsibility for the problems of daily living for the war victims." Without the help of countless ordinary residents, the central government and city authorities could not possibly have coped with the flood of evacuees immediately after the raids. Still, the only permanent answer was to take shelter in the countryside, where ties of blood kept people together while the cities burned.

Mr. Itō's Study

The B–29s returned to Saipan and Tinian, rearmed and refueled there, then flew off again to drop 1,790 tons of high explosives on Nagoya. Two days later they hit Osaka, then Kobe, then Nagoya again with incendiaries, dynamite, and jelly bombs. In ten days the Americans flew 1,595 sorties, unloaded two million bombs (9,373 tons), and burned down nearly fifty square kilometers of Tokyo, Nagoya, Osaka, and Kobe, at a cost of twenty-two planes. Officials in Kobe estimated that the March 17 fire raid there left more than 35,000 homeless. By mid-April, the government announced, three million persons had been forced to take refuge because fire raids had burned down their homes during the previous six weeks.

While bombers pounded the cities, Japan's army and navy were slowly being driven back in the Pacific. Iwo Jima fell at the height of the fire raids in mid-March, and two weeks later fighting began on Okinawa. Admiral Suzuki Kantarō, the miraculous survivor of a death plot in February 1936, replaced General Koiso as prime minister on April 7, 1945. Although Suzuki eventually presided over the ceasefire on August 15, Japan was still very much in the war when he took office. By the end of his brief rule, huge sections of the country's most important cities had been turned into ghost towns.

Where the desolation was not complete, neighborhood groups went on holding air defense drills, seeing conscripts off, and helping resettle bomb victims temporarily until they could escape to the country. Captains patrolled their blocks during night raids and took roll by the light of flares. Community councils distributed whatever fire-fighting equipment they could collect, and everyone processed endless forms as a part of the government's relief program for the homeless. Even in the midst of danger, Rev. Bruno Bitters observed, people behaved in a matter-of-fact manner as bombs exploded: "There is not much excitement. The only voices you hear, are those of mothers calling for their children, or children calling their parents." The refugees, Bitters said, "were silent and calm, but the horror they went through reflected in their faces."

One of the greatest fire raids took place early on May 26, when 500 Superfortresses dropped 4,000 tons of bombs on residential sections in northern and western Tokyo. As the planes headed southwest back toward the sea, Sutō Ryōsaku wrote in his diary, "I thought the air raids would be over for tonight after that, but for a long time no official cancellation of the alert came." Then another formation moved over Tokyo from the south, attacking part of Nakanoku. Between Egota Yonchōme and Numabukuro, "oil turning to fire rained down. Flames broke out all over and spread from house to house before my eyes. The shouts of people trying to escape the flames mixed together, and in an instant the quiet residential streets turned into a hellish scene of destruction.

"There was nothing we could do. We were in a wretched plight," Sutō continued. "The noise of the bombs faded away, and I climbed on the roof to look around. Down the road to the south was a sea of flames in which the high roofs were floating." His neighbor Yamazaki Seizaburō's home was burning, so "Yamazaki's family took refuge in their garden tool shed, but it filled with smoke and they were killed." Sutō quickly overcame his numbed feelings of helplessness and plunged into frantic activity. He noticed that the upstairs study where Itō Gorō gave lessons was in danger. "I assembled some people from the neighborhood association and set up a bucket relay to heave water on his second story clapboards. We kept it from catching fire."

Saving Mr. Itō's study was only a gesture amid the incineration on all sides, but it clearly mattered to Sutō: "Bucket relays did the job in actual fighting." Evidently he felt useful by carrying out this small task, justifying his having survived the flames and his role as the local leader. After daybreak Sutō gathered with other captains at the home of the community council chairman, where "the branches of the big oak in his garden were still smouldering." They immediately calculated how many victims each association could lodge and began sorting bedding and furniture. By the next morning four persons from his group had made precious rice balls and taken them around to the burned-out families. Very much like persons exposed to disasters anywhere, Sutō apparently found it personally meaningful to throw himself into building a new pattern of activity that could give him purpose and satisfaction in the unstructured emergency. The energetic vitalism that has long animated Japanese work habits and the organizational strength of the local associations were both great assets when men and women like Sutō confronted the destruction and began to overcome it.

Reacting to
the Bombers

The B–29s kept coming back to Japan with bigger and bigger loads, especially after Okinawa was captured in mid-June 1945. They bombarded Yokohama on May 29 and Osaka two days later, dropping 3,200 tons of high explosives on each city with damaging effect. The busiest day of the entire air operation against Japan was July 10, when 2,000 Superfortresses and fighters attacked cities from Kyushu to Tokyo. In the last weeks of the war many smaller communities became targets, once the main centers had been smashed so badly that they could not recover. Nowhere short of the mountains seemed safe.

To a nation already inured to exhausting war work, to grievous shortages of food and clothing, and to anxious separation from families and friends, the nine months of air raids were yet another heavy burden imposed by wartime—although a particularly cruel one. Part of the reason the bombings were not socially more disruptive may be that the Japanese had always lived with the threat of fire and earthquake, but more important was the fact that their impoverished style of life since at least early 1943 left few comforts to be plundered. Looting in Yokohama's great raid on May 29 was no problem, according to an observer, because there was almost nothing left to be stolen. The cities also remained fairly orderly because their neighborhoods were sufficiently coherent to avoid complete disorganization, except in the most extreme circumstances such as those on March 10. Another way citizens stayed calm under attack was to ascribe magical qualities to foods that were scarce but not totally lacking. Some superstitious people apparently believed that they could be protected by eating pickled plums or red beans with rice. But certainly the major comfort for most city residents

was the knowledge that they could escape to the countryside if things got bad enough.

There is little question that the bombings made people's spirits sag, however resolutely they kept on working. In January 1945 the Foreign Morale Analysis Division of the U.S. Office of War Information reported that public morale in Japan was already low, but the cabinet information board trumpeted that because of the March 10 raid Japan's fighting spirit would "become harder, stronger and more acute through this baptism of fire." After the surrender, Maj. Gen. Amano Masamichi said that the air attacks had "strengthened the people's enmity toward the United States and the will to carry the war through to a successful conclusion." About the same time Admiral Tomioka Sadatoshi noted that "the damage wrought was immense owing to the self-spreading nature of the incendiaries. Therefore, the people lost their desire for the continuation of the war." If the experience of Germany is a guide, both leaders were probably right. Strategic bombings seemed to lower the public's "passive morale," or inner feel-

Two Months Before Hiroshima: Central Osaka after suffering its third major air raid, June 7, 1945. Only telephone poles and stone pillars of the gates in front of homes remain upright.

ings, without necessarily making them more reluctant to stick to their jobs. But no one could have felt happy about seeing burnt bodies and ruined property, no matter how determined he or she may have been to keep up the fight.

Right after the war a U.S. Strategic Bombing Survey team, working through interpreters at a time when many Japanese were emotionally flat, concluded that well-educated civilians had been both less certain of victory and less willing to stop the war than other citizens. The fire bombs helped to convince even the most optimistic persons that Japan's position was desperate. Young people, and particularly individuals with a secondary school education or more, expressed the most consistent criticism of the country's war leaders. These findings seemed to confirm that people's hopes were dimmed by the bombings but also that they were willing to carry on the battle. Whether public morale had much influence on ending the war seems doubtful, since only the top political and military leaders, meeting in the imperial caves during the first two weeks of August, were in a position to choose surrender.

When they became deadlocked and failed to reach a decision, it was the emperor, not the exhausted public, who chose peace.

Spears and Awls

Before their government agreed to the terms announced by the Allies on July 26 at Potsdam, the Japanese had to endure one last mobilization—into "people's volunteer corps" for defending the country against a possible American landing. The U.S. had every intention of sending its troops ashore, first in Kyushu in November 1945 (Operation Olympic) and then in the Kanto plain near Tokyo (Operation Coronet) the following March. As its ultimate weapon against what might have become the bloodiest invasion by sea in history, the government organized civilian men under sixty-five and women under forty-five into volunteer corps (Kokumin Giyūtai) in their neighborhoods or places of work. On June 13 the moribund Imperial Rule Assistance Association and patriotic industrial groups were officially dissolved so that their members coud join volunteer units, which the Tokyo police aptly referred to as "the final people's movement." The army took command of most of the volunteer groups on June 23, but the generals were reluctant to let untrained civilians touch rifles or ammunition and put most of them to work digging shelters or clearing debris instead.

The cabinet expected the volunteers to be home-front equivalents of the Kamikaze pilots, who went into battle with meager weapons fully prepared to die. The civilian units were routed out weekly at 3 A.M. to worship at shrines and drill with bamboo staves, the residue of General Araki Sadao's prewar fantasy that "if we could have three million bamboo spears, we would be able to conquer Russia easily." Hatano Isoko was a good deal less confident, as she wrote on July 24,

1945: "The enemy will attack with bombs and guns; it is absurd to meet them with such weapons." The authorities also used volunteer corps to set up barbed wire, pill boxes, and primitive traps for armored vehicles along the Pacific shoreline to help resist an invasion. Happily, the surrender deprived volunteers of any chance to find out how useful their tactics might have been against the American firepower.

Even students were organized into volunteer fighting corps in June 1945, now that their labor was not needed so urgently in the war industries because raw materials were scarce. Like their adult counterparts, most of the student corps never saw action. One that did was a unit consisting mostly of girls, the Lily Brigade (Himeyuri Butai), which was totally wiped out in the battle for Okinawa and later exalted in a best-seller and a movie. Many school groups were sent to root out pine stumps from forests that had already been stripped bare for lumber. Like the fermented sweet potatoes produced by city neighborhoods, the pine resin was to be used for aviation fuel. As

(KIKUCHI SHUNKICHI)

"Spirit of Three Million Spears": Japanese soldier trains neighborhood women wielding bamboo staves for defending the homeland against American invasion, summer 1945.

the drill masters put it, "Two hundred pine stumps will keep an airplane flying for an hour."

High school girls in remote Shimane prefecture worked out with carpenter's awls and were told "to guard their honor like samurai without shame" against invading troops. Kasai Yukiko recalled her teacher's warning: "When they do, we must be ready to settle the war by drawing on our Japanese spirit and killing them. Even killing just one American soldier will do. You must prepare to use the awls for self-defense. You must aim at the enemy's abdomen. Understand? The abdomen! If you don't kill at least one enemy soldier, you don't deserve to die!" Kasai added wryly that the Japanese would have looked ridiculous facing the American flame throwers and machine guns with such tools—but she dutifully took part in the drills anyway.

Society was still well enough organized in mid-1945 to let the government set up such volunteer units, and the repeated air attacks did not prevent people from carrying on with their duties. But war weariness was unavoidable, as the cabinet acknowledged on June 8 in a report called "The Present State of National Power": "Criticism of the military and government has steadily increased. This trend is apt to shake faith in the leadership class. This is also a sign of the deterioration of public morality." The army monitored rumors, gossip, and public complaints carefully, and it used the community councils to spread messages that were supposed to help people keep their chins up.

Most persons kept their reservations to themselves or confided them to their diaries, such as Ezaki Tsuneko, an eighteen-year-old girl who wrote on July 21, 1945: "Everything considered, I wish I had ended up dying during the bombings. If only there weren't a war, we wouldn't have to pretend we were happy." When the Americans began dropping leaflets announcing bomb targets in advance, the public could see how powerless to protect them the state had become. War weariness grew even greater after the army admitted an American raid on Hiroshima: "As a result of an attack by a small number of enemy B–29s yesterday, August 6, the city of Hiroshima was considerably damaged. In this raid the enemy apparently used a new type of bomb. Details are now under investigation." When the government revealed a second raid on Nagasaki three days later, Sutō Ryōsaku wrote in his diary, "It is reported in today's paper that Japan's destiny has become the worst imaginable."

Civilians may have been fed up, and the volunteers may have felt foolish training with spears and awls, but nearly everyone on the home front kept up the fight to the very end. One reason for persisting, as Yoshikawa Hisako noted on January 12, 1945, was that no one wanted to be blamed for quitting. Another was that people were not fully aware of the grim situation in Okinawa, the Pacific, or even the Japanese cities unless they happened to be there. More war workers would have fled if they had not needed their wages. No doubt a natural patriotism, in the elemental sense of love for the homeland, impelled many persons to pick up spears to defend their territory, and others almost certainly felt an obligation to loved ones at the front. The Potsdam Declaration left the fate of Japan's political system in doubt, another reason to persevere until its future could be determined. The threat of force also kept many citizens on the job, because the army and police still monopolized the weapons of violence. But probably the biggest incentive to keep on battling was a basic fear of what would happen if people stopped—whether terror at "the sound of the shoes of Russian troops" once they joined the war on August 9 or a simple dread of the future whose shape could scarcely be known.

Release

From the Diary of Sutō Ryōsaku

Wednesday, August 15. The news on the radio was terrible. The imperial edict ending the war was announced. It was proclaimed to the people when the emperor himself read

High Noon: Weeping citizens bowing in the Imperial Palace plaza, Tokyo, Wednesday, August 15, 1945, after hearing emperor's broadcast announcing surrender.

it over the radio. . . . All of us sank into silence and didn't say a word. I felt in a daze, exasperated, and tears of resentment began to flow. I wonder what the emperor felt as he read it aloud? Ever since the China incident of 1937, eight long years of ceaseless hard work in wartime, with Japan's fate in the balance, have ended up in unconditional surrender. Every aspect of people's daily lives had been whipped into line on behalf of winning the war. They had been forcibly paraded about, compelled to persevere through unending tensions, hardships, and privations. The amount of controlled food that was distributed was very meager, making cooking difficult, and in fact there were things that were simply inedible. Both men and women managed to rally their undernourished bodies to carry out strenuous air defense work and fire prevention drills, the heavy job of digging air raid shelters, and all sorts of labor service such as ripping down buildings and repairing the roads. They cultivated vegetable gardens, laid in vegetables as substitute foodstuffs, working for long months and years, earnestly hoping and praying that the goals of the fatherland could be attained. But unfortunate is the only word to use for the end of the war. The woman on duty for the neighborhood association distribution came, so I asked her what she thought about the end of the war. She was surprisingly calm and bright-eyed—perhaps because the fear of air raids had disappeared and the bitter work of preventing fires had ended. Although most people think that defeat is extremely unfortunate, in their hearts they generally seem relieved. Everyone has different feelings, depending on his or her position. Leaders doubtless differ from those who are led. What will happen to Japan now? Will it become a colony under American guidance, like the Philippines? Everyone is no doubt feeling truly anxious, a mixture of worry, fear, and speculation. American planes are already flying around low, right in our faces. We have to listen to their terrible, harsh buzzing without lifting a finger in resistance. I keenly felt a sense of cruel grief. No matter what I thought, there was nothing to do but await the course of events. I got hold of myself and began to take care of the distribution of goods. Rice was distributed, seventy-five kilograms at 27.80 yen, and crackers were distributed, ninety-six kilograms at 26.88 yen.

Dazed, exasperated, resentful, relieved, anxious for the future—and then back to business as usual. Persistence had helped the Japanese people endure eight years of war, and now it would help them bear up in defeat.

11

War's Social Residue

"Even if we are routed in battle, the mountains and rivers will remain. The people will remain." With this pensive paraphrase of the Chinese classics, Yoshizawa Hisako reassured herself several months before the surrender that somehow the Japanese could survive defeat. Her instinct turned out to be quite right, since World War Two on all fronts ended up as a war of attrition but not one of social destruction. In spite of all the blows that were struck, Japan in August 1945 was quite recognizably the country that had started fighting the Chinese eight summers before. But it was certainly not the same country it would have been without the war.

There are three things that make it hard to weigh just what the era meant for the Japanese people. First and most important, they lost the war. Every personal and official response to the reconstruction after 1945 was colored in some way by the stubborn fact of unqualified defeat. Second, the winners occupied Japan militarily for six and one-half years and flooded its arid economy with more than two billion dollars. The Americans almost certainly made social changes more quickly than could have happened without an occupation. Third, the standard of living for most citizens rose very fast because of extraordinary economic growth after 1952, probably affecting their lives even more dramatically than the social engineering of 1945–1952. Defeat, occupation, and prosperity are naturally and unavoidably the lenses through which the war era is now perceived.

Groups and Dogmas: Getting Ready for War

As the Japanese government prepared the country for total war, the spiritual mobilization campaigns helped to make individuals more aware of the fighting, but very soon it became clear that civic associations were the best means to rally people. In some ways the wartime state resembled the Nazis in bending organizational needs to the demands of ideology. Just as Hitler's lieutenants dampened war output before 1942 to keep consumers happy, the Japanese government deferred to popular conventions about community solidarity, the roles of women, and the status of Koreans, even at the cost of a crisply rational labor plan. Like most other countries in battle, Japan found that technology and organizational forms changed somewhat faster than public attitudes. As a result, familiar symbols such as family, farm, and throne probably made it easier for some persons to adjust to tough times, although most civilians certainly accepted rather than denied the harsh realities of wartime living.

Ideology was nevertheless much less decisive than the concrete requirements of the war buildup. The state's employment planners may have been vexed by traditional outlooks, but poor shipping and meager resources, not a dearth of workers, are the real reasons why Japan's output rose by only one-fourth between 1940 and 1944, while production in the U.S. was climbing by two-thirds. When the authorities appealed to conservative communal doctrines, their goal was to rationalize new groups and associations that would guarantee wartime social stability and high farm yields. Even the public ceremonies and rituals, while paying obeisance to Japan's ideological aims in Asia, also had the very practical effect of drawing people into organized activities.

The pivot of Japanese ideology during 1937–1945 was the emperor, but he was important mostly as a symbol of the nation, not as a law-giver or object of worship. Because every large organization needs a set of principles to keep it from splintering, the state's imperial doctrines were useful for cementing Japan's innumerable social groupings into a mosaic that could sustain war. All the main countries which joined the fighting centralized their governments and economies enormously, regardless of ideological differences. To fortify the mobilization, what counted most was that Japan have a dogma, not its precise content. For historical and religious reasons the best choice was imperial loyalism, but the political, military, and economic apparatus it legitimized was indispensable for fighting the war. In effect, the organization became its own ideology.

Like soldiers and sailors everywhere, the twelve million Japanese who went on military duty served an institution, not just a doctrine. Getting civilians to participate in group events was likewise more imperative for a smooth buildup than converting them ideologically. The state at least made people accept the war, if not support it enthusiastically, by persuading them to join in collective activities. When faith happened to reinforce participation, the results were predictably even more impressive. But as the fighting wore on, fewer and fewer Japanese were susceptible to ideological deflection because the shrinking consumer economy made it harder to blind themselves to fact with sheer belief. At the very end, neither the dogmas nor the organizations were so important for avoiding chaos as the basic integrity of Japanese society and the simple need to cooperate in a crisis.

Social Changes: Accelerator or Brake?

Most of the guided changes in Japan between 1937 and 1945 were centralizing in intent and regimenting in consequence, slowing social trends that had been developing for several decades. In one way or another, labor conscription, press controls, altered school routines, fertility campaigns, and commodity rations all restricted the choices that modernization had begun to make available since the late nineteenth century. Except for the school-group evacuations, nearly all the government plans for tightening the social system were founded on visions of a conservative order predating the mass consumer economy. In this respect Japan resembled strong states elsewhere when it tried to fight a major war abroad by slowing the rate of social change at home.

But the official programs mattered much less than the effects of war itself. The fighting inspired few if any really new social trends, but it helped along many of the prewar changes accompanying urbanization. Because it made the big industries swell, wartime attracted even more farmers to the cities, speeding up the nuclearization of families and the decline of patriarchal authority. Through 1944, more and more Japanese were drawn to new urban modes of living, purchasing, traveling, and amusing themselves—and were exposed to perils such as crowding, tuberculosis, poor sanitation, and emotional estrangement from the countryside. As a whip for migration to the cities, war hurried up a process under way since the thirteenth century and intensely so since the 1890s.

Even though the cabinet shied away from fully mobilizing their labor, women were probably affected more measurably by wartime than any other social group. Coercion if they were single and economic necessity if they were married sent more of them into the labor force than ever before. Popular attitudes about work appropriate for females changed a good deal more slowly than their actual participation in the economy, which stayed permanently higher after the surrender. In 1944, the proportion of women in the labor force reached 42 percent, up from 35 percent before the war. The figure fell slightly in the spotty conditions of 1950 to 41 percent, then climbed to 43 percent in 1954. By then a record 18.1 million women were employed, a gain of 4.1 million since 1944. Industrial development and a labor shortage might have led women to take jobs even without a war, but the hurry-up mobilization and a military draft that removed male wage-earners from their families speeded up the likelihood greatly. Yet whether or not they went to work, women in homes with men absent found their duties as wives and mothers enormously unsettled, with uncountable consequences for themselves and their children.

The Larger the Organization, The Greater the Change

War probably prodded more social changes in Japan than it foiled, but its greatest result may have been a matter of scale, not speed or direction. As a rule, wartime transformed large social institutions much more thoroughly than small ones. The state itself was the largest and most altered of all. Its budget, taxing authority, and control over individual freedoms multiplied to a degree hardly imaginable before 1937. The web of attachments that joined it to the richest corporations grew thicker and more tangled because of military procurement. But even though the wartime state accumulated more power than any other Japanese regime before or since, it fell short of dictatorship or absolutism. The Diet still met, elections still took place, and informal community groups were vital for making local administration work. After the surrender, American planners renovated the state as completely as any component of society, but they were either powerless or unwilling to shave its bulk in relation to ordinary citizens.

The great manufacturing and trading combines doubled their share of corporate and partnership capital during 1941–1945 and swallowed up smaller companies, as in America, at an astounding rate. In 1930 more than half of industrial employees worked in small industries, but by 1942 the proportion had fallen to one-fifth. After they were partially dissolved during the occupation, most of the manufacturing giants soon surpassed their wartime output during the 1950s and 1960s and now stand as some of the most awesome clusters of corporate wealth and power anywhere.

Smaller organizations were very much affected while the war was on but generally were left alone once it was over. Schools were something of an exception, since the Americans tried to redo the whole system, but the changes they made in education were the first to be revoked when the Japanese regained self-rule in 1952. Perhaps it is more significant that war skewed the age structures of the schoolchildren for years to come and radicalized the teachers' union into a tedious struggle with the national education officials. Religious bodies, youth, farm, and women's groups, and other voluntary organizations were spared the yoke of the Imperial Rule Assistance Association after 1945 and free to resume their prewar activities without interference.

The smallest institution of all, the family, was the firmest source of continuity for the Japanese in wartime. Urban living and the neighborhood associations made people rely more on others nearby, but in the catastrophe of aerial bombardment it was the family that usually offered refuge through relatives in the villages. Wartime made little difference to Japan's long-term patterns of marriage, fertility, divorce, or juvenile crime, unlike America or Britain. Minoguchi Tokijirō made it plain in March 1943 that the cabinet would have been happy to muster married women faster than social attitudes would allow, yet the government decided "to accomplish the mobilization of Japanese women while simultaneously giving rise to their special qualities associated with the household."

One of the qualities was mothering, something the war re-emphasized among Japanese psycho-cultural values, even though fewer women were home all day to practice it. The spiritual mobilization in 1937–1940 depended mostly on women's organizations to make people more aware of the fight in China and the need for restraint, and patriotic women's groups comforted the lonely, the injured, and the bereaved for the entire war. The "thousand-stitch bands" worn by many soldiers in battle were emblems of the love and nurturance of home-front matrons, not sweethearts. With men absent, many public jobs involving announcements, directions, guidance, and crowd management were permanently taken over by clear-voiced women. The state's fertility campaign glorified motherhood as well as mothering, yet for any boy or girl whose father was away the mother's role in childrearing was made even more consequential, whether or not she agreed with Mrs. Tōjō that "having babies is fun." When the government finally put the bar girls to work in the war plants in 1943, it deprived men of surrogate mothering in the night quarters, but the authorities carefully avoided interfering with the genuine coddling and supportiveness provided by Japanese families.

The resilient primary group was a main reason why the social body could endure after its political head collapsed. When the Americans took charge after the surrender, they put through various legal reforms in favor of women, heirs, and young married persons, but sensibly avoided obtrusive changes in the one social unit that not even the wartime state was willing to disturb.

The War Takes Command

Once the fighting started to turn sour for Japan in mid-1943, its course slowly neutralized the government mobilization programs, and then air raids and the naval blockade made the controls over labor, prices, and food supplies go slack. The neighborhood associations and community councils, originally creatures of the state, carried on to the end because they answered people's needs while the national government was tormented by a losing war. They distributed food, clothing, and fuel, carried out health programs, fought fires, and found shelter for the homeless, usually with great ingenuity and always with aplomb. Taking part meant a degree of leveling, if only temporarily, and not merely rote obedience to authority. Because local elites staffed the councils, they were at least a partial check on centralized political power.

State propaganda and curricular revisions frayed the schools less seriously than did the ancillary programs brought about by the war, such as military drill, labor service, volunteer corps, and particularly the evacuations to escape the silver bombers. Although official summonses or police harassment may have driven them to take work, most laborers stuck it out because they needed the income in an economy suffering from a 20-percent rate of inflation and a drastic lack of goods. Textile shortages, not patriotic entreaties, put women in *monpe* when they'd rather have been wearing dresses, and separations enforced by the military draft, as well as poor nutrition, sliced the birth rate by a quarter—to the cabinet's chagrin. Despite the government's efforts, the war and bad weather made food production fall off so sharply at the end that the loathsome black market could no longer fill in the gap.

Even the world of entertainment and mass culture was more inhibited by wartime scarcities than by the prudishness of the state. Travel was restricted, movies flourished for want of alternatives, newsprint was very scarce, and athletes were off in the service. Restaurants stayed open, legally or not, only so long as they could get food and drink from their suppliers. In the arts there was a retreat from criticism like that in America and Europe, with strict media censorship, ludicrous controls on music, and a great deal of heroism in films and the dance. Writers, musicians, and the Kyoto school of philosophers made wartime an era of cultural nationalism, but avant garde painting remained thriving and unmolested. Like working, eating, studying, or bearing children, the public amusements were eventually reduced by a desiccated consumer economy to a few tawdry bars selling sake so rude it exploded in your mouth.

The Residue

World War Two made "people's spirits really gloomy," as Yoshizawa put it, and for nearly all of them its memory remained depressing long after it was over. Eighteen years after the surrender, a survey by a Tokyo television station found that 0.8 percent of the public thought the war was the best period of their lives—presumably a few old soldiers, impoverished landlords, and deracinated nationalists. Everyone else surely agreed that the war "was a bad thing."

It left Japan intact as a civilization but made it a different country after 1945 because of the fighting. The gruesome losses of people and property totaled about three million dead and $26 billion worth of national wealth destroyed. (World War Two as a whole killed ten times this many and cost at least ten times as much.) The defeat of Japanese imperialism liberated Taiwan, Korea, Manchuria, and the entire "co-prosperity sphere" in China, Southeast Asia, and the Pacific. For the first time in a half-century the nation retreated to its home islands and became a minor factor in world politics. The shooting disrupted foreign commerce and finance, which had already been snarled by the depression and trade wars of the 1930s. After the surrender Japan lived in an economic and diplomatic cocoon until the mid-1950s, when exports and imports turned more normal, but in an international market utterly different from the prewar period.

The defeat affected the exercise of power in Japanese society most obviously by hobbling the military for at least a generation. The armed services reached the apex of authority in 1940–1945, then tumbled into political gloom and constitutional confinement. At least as important were the economic repercussions of military spending. In wartime the army and navy consumed as much as 70 percent of the national budget, but after 1945 the defense burden fell mostly on the Americans and military costs stayed below 1 percent of the postwar Japanese gross national product. So many guns followed by so much butter had a mercurial effect on the choices available and the buying habits of consumers.

The other important group declassed by the war were the large landlords, provided they had not already put their money into urban investments. The government programs for rice purchasing, land sales, and insurance during 1937–1945 injured the big landowners by coincidence, and the land reforms of 1947 felled them by design. As a result, landlords lost most of their influence in electoral politics. The political parties were eclipsed during 1940–1945 but took on much greater authority after the surrender than they had ever enjoyed before, thanks partly to the occupation reforms. The powerful civil service was remarkably undisturbed by the fighting, even though several ministries were overhauled by the Americans. Big business was probably the prewar group that gained the most from the war, in spite of a purge of its top leaders after 1945. With landlords, generals, and admirals out of the way, the corporations that grew rich and influential during the war ended up sharing the postwar triangle of power with the parties and the bureaucracy.

Japan's wartime rulers deliberately nourished the family system and the small-group propensities of society, both in rhetoric and in program. The marriage improvement campaign, the earnest natalism of the welfare ministry, the neighborhood associations, and the civic organizations arrayed under the Imperial Rule Assistance Association all stiffened the hierarchy of status by which people had sorted themselves out for more than a century. The government's intent was socially regressive, but the military's ferocious appetite for guns and ships helped to corrode the old competitive order of unequal interest groups by turning big industries into giants. When a few great enterprises consumed most of the smaller ones and oligopoly usurped rivalry in the marketplace, social relations began to show some of the class frictions of present-day capitalism.

In the broadest sense, wartime buffeted Japanese society at three ascending levels of impact: structure, organization, and culture. Fierce and brutalizing though it was, the war scarcely affected the deep, underlying structures of society at all—particularly the family patterning of small groups. Such core values as loyalty, teamwork, harmony, and competence stayed untouched. Wartime had much more bearing on the organizational forms used for carrying out people's activities. Both during the fighting and after the institutional reforms of the American occupation, the biggest organizations were altered the most. But the greatest change of all was the profound and very permanent transformation of Japanese culture that took place because of the war.

The national crisis was a time for reaffirming familiar beliefs, not one for cultural innovation, and in this respect Japan was probably no more nor any less patriotic than its allies or enemies. But ordinary citizens outlasted the narrow chauvinsim and control schemes of their military government, and for them the long-term result of war was revolutionary. Because everyone on the home front worked in war plants, joined in fire drills, or took part in some fashion, people's lives would never be quite the same again: "The egg cannot be unscrambled."

In the decades after surrender, the public developed a new cultural style marked by cosmopolitanism at nearly every level of society—in foods, fashions, and the arts. Drawing on the long-standing Japanese habits of earnest striving and esthetic sensitivity, the people eventually created an ultramodern society of consumer conveniences, massive concentrations of information, highly technical levels of organization, and keen perceptions of the outside world—a cultural mode much closer to the twenty-first century than to the years before 1945.

Most important of all, people's outlooks on themselves and their country were fundamentally overturned by the dark valley of war and defeat. Hiroshima and Nagasaki, acorns and pumpkins, spears and awls—each is a symbol of how individual tastes, attitudes, and behavior were all different because of the eight-year encounter with total war. For persons who lived through that astringent era, war and peace became the dominant cultural motifs shaping their awareness of the past and their perception of the present. Soon enough, no doubt, those motifs will seem as remote and incredible to a generation unacquainted with war as the doctrines of imperialism seem today.

Notes

Numbers at opening of each note indicate page and line.

CHAPTER 1

2–14   For standard Japanese accounts of the Marco Polo Bridge incident, see Mainichi Newspapers, *Fifty Years of Light and Dark: The Hirohito Era*, 2nd ed. (Tokyo: Mainichi Newspapers, 1976), pp. 64–65; Kyōto Daigaku Bungakubu Kokushi Kenkyūshitsu, *Nihon kindaishi jiten* [Dictionary of modern Japanese history] (Tokyo: Tōyō Keizai Shinpōsha, 1958), pp. 640–41.

3–4   Jerome B. Cohen, *Japan's Economy in War and Reconstruction* (Minneapolis: University of Minnesota Press, 1949), pp. 3, 5; Iwao F. Ayusawa, *A History of Labor in Modern Japan* (Honolulu: East-West Center Press, 1966), p. 228; Takekazu Ogura, ed., *Agricultural Development in Modern Japan*, rev. ed. (Tokyo: Fuji Publishing Co., Ltd., 1967), p. 28; Katō Hidetoshi et al., *Meiji Taishō Shōwa sesōshi* [History of social conditions in the Meiji, Taishō, and Shōwa eras] (Tokyo: Shakai Shisōsha, 1967), pp. 257–58. The number of strikes in 1937 was 628, involving 123,730 workers. The wholesale farm price rise is for 1931–1936.

3–31   See Deborah A. McGlauflin, "Minority Status in Japan: The Koreans and the Burakumin" (B.A. thesis in Asian studies, Connecticut College, 1975), p. 4.

4–34   Eleanor M. Hadley, *Antitrust in Japan* (Princeton: Princeton University Press, 1970), p. 41. On social changes in Osaka in the Edo era, see William B. Hauser, *Economic Institutional Change in Tokugawa Japan* (Cambridge: Cambridge University Press, 1974).

5–14   Property became an absolute, recognized by law in 1872, as it had in England a century or more earlier. See Harold Perkin, *The Origins of Modern English Society, 1780–1880* (London: Routledge and Kegan Paul, 1969), pp. 52–57.

6–18   Yoshizawa Hisako, "Shūsen made" [To the end of the war], in Shōwa Sensō Bungaku Zenshū Henshū Iinkai, *Shōwa sensō bungaku zenshū,* vol. 13, *shimin no nikki* [Complete wartime literary works of the Shōwa era, vol. 13, City residents' diaries] (Tokyo: Shūeisha, 1965), p. 361.

6–29   Kitayama Mine, "Ningen no tama wa horobimai" [The spirit of mankind will not be destroyed], in Asahi Shinbunsha, *Tōkyō hibakuki* [Tokyo bombing victims' record] (Tokyo: Asahi Shinbunsha, 1971), p. 214.

CHAPTER 2

10–6   Hiroko Nakamoto, as told to Mildred Mastin Pace, *My Japan 1930–1951* (New York: McGraw-Hill Book Co., 1970), p. 22.

11–7   Donald Keene, "The Sino-Japanese War of 1894–95 and Its Cultural Effects in Japan," in *Landscapes and Portraits: Appreciations of Japanese Culture* (Tokyo: Kodansha International, Ltd., 1971), p. 274.

12–7   Sukekawa Hiroshi, ed., *Sōdōinhō taisei* [Administration of the general mobilization law] (Tokyo: Yūhikaku, 1940), pp. 1–2. On early wartime planning, see Chitoshi Yanaga, *Japan Since Perry* (New York: McGraw-Hill Book Co., 1949), p. 533.

13–5   Nihon Kindaishi Kenkyūkai, *Zusetsu kokumin no rekishi*, vol. 17, *kokumin seishin sōdōin* [Illustrated national history, vol. 17, The national spiritual mobilization] (Tokyo: Kokubunsha, 1965), pp. 86–87; Kisaka Jun'ichirō, "Nihon fuashizumu to jinmin shihai no tokushitsu" [Japanese fascism and special features of leading the people], *Rekishigaku kenkyū* [Historiographical studies], special number (October 1970), p. 120; Akimoto Ritsuo, *Sensō to minshū: Taiheiyō sensōka no toshi·seikatsu* [War and the people: City life during the Pacific war] (Tokyo: Gakuyō Shobō, 1974), p. 4; Fujiwara Akira, Imai Seiichi, and Ōe Shinobu, eds., *Kindai Nihonshi no kisō chishiki* [Basic knowledge about modern Japanese history] (Tokyo: Yūhikaku, 1972), p. 422. The basic documentary collections for the spiritual mobilization are Miura Tōsaku, ed., *Kokumin seishin sōdōin gengi* [Basic principles of the national spiritual mobilization] (Tokyo: Tōyō Tosho, 1937); Naikaku, Naimushō, and Monbushō, *Kokumin seishin sōdōin shiryō* [Materials on the national spiritual mobilization], 10 vols. (Tokyo: Naikaku, 1937–1938); and Kokumin Seishin Sōdōin Honbu, *Kokumin seishin sōdōin undō* [The national spiritual mobilization movement] (Tokyo: Kokumin Seishin Sōdōin Honbu, 1940). The latter volume, published by the movement's headquarters as successor to the central federation of the national spiritual mobilization, contains separate sections for each year from 1937 to 1940, compiled from the central federation's and the headquarters' records.

13–22   Nihon Kindaishi Kenkyūkai, ed., *Kokumin seishin sō-dōin*, p. 87. See Penelope D. Brown, "The Thought Control Program of Japan's Military Leaders, 1931–1941" (B.A. thesis in history, Connecticut College, 1972), pp. 62–69; Akimoto, *Sensō to minshū*, pp. 3–4; Akimoto Ritsuo, "Senjika no toshi ni okeru chiiki jūmin soshiki" [Local organization of city residents in wartime], *Shakai kagaku tokyū* [Social Science Review] 18, no. 2, consecutive no. 51 (February 1973): 69–70.

13–33   Hillis Lory, *Japan's Military Masters: The Army in Japanese Life* (New York: Viking Press, 1943), pp. 202, 207–208. See Kokumin Seishin Sōdōin Honbu, *Kokumin seishin sōdōin undō*, 1939 vol., p. 63.

14–17   *Kokka sōdōinhō* [National general mobilization law], 1938, quoted in Ishida Takeshi, *Nihon kindaishi taikei*, vol. 8, *hakyoku to heiwa* [Series on modern Japanese history, vol. 8, Cataclysm and peace] (Tokyo: Tōkyō Daigaku Shuppankai, 1968), p. 81. See Katō Hidetoshi et al., *Meiji Taishō Shōwa sesōshi* [History of social conditions in the Meiji, Taishō, and Shōwa eras] (Tokyo: Shakai Shisōsha, 1967), p. 253; Ishii Kin'ichirō, "Nihon fuashizumu to chihō seido" [Japanese fascism and local institutions], *Rekishigaku kenkyū* [Historiographical studies], no. 307 (December 1965): 1; Zdenka Vasiljevová, "The Industrial Patriotic Movement—A Study on the Structure of Fascist Dictatorship in War-Time Japan," in Vlasta Hilská and Zdenka Vasiljevová, *Problems of Modern Japanese Society* (Prague: Charles University, 1971), pp. 87–88; Yanaga, *Japan Since Perry*, p. 534; Charles B. Fahs, *Government in Japan: Recent Trends in Its Scope and Operation* (New York: International Secretariat, Institute of Pacific Relations, 1940), pp. 50–51.

14–37   Kiryū Yūyū, "Kokumin seishin to gunju kōgyō" [The national spirit and the munitions industries], *Tazan no ishi* [Food for thought], 1938, quoted in *Kindai Nihonshi*, ed. Fujiwara et al., p. 423. See Ishii, "Nihon fuashizumu," p. 2; Sakuraba Hiroshi, "Dainiji taisenka no sensō dōin soshiki o megutte" [Outline of mobilization organizations during World War Two], *Kanagawakenshi kenkyū* [Studies in the history of Kanagawa prefecture], no. 23 (February 1974): 20; Rekishigaku Kenkyūkai, *Taiheiyō sensōshi* [History of the Pacific war] (Tokyo: Aoki Shoten, 1972), 3:60; Anne S. Johnson, "The Emperor and the Imperial Institution in Modern Japan: A Study of Symbolism" (manuscript, Connecticut College, 1976).

15–13   Takeuchi Yoshimi, quoted in *Kindai Nihon shisōshi no kiso chishiki* [Basic knowledge about the history of modern Japanese

thought], ed. Hashikawa Bunzō, Kano Masanao, and Hiraoka Toshio (Tokyo: Yūhikaku, 1971), p. 457.

15–18   Yoko Matsuoka, *Daughter of the Pacific* (New York:
Harper and Brothers, 1952), p. 145; Takaaki Aikawa, *Unwilling Patriot* (Tokyo: The Jordan Press, 1960), p. 9.

16–6   Hideo Aragaki, "Japan's Home Front," *Contemporary
Japan* 7, no. 2 (1938): 291. See also ibid., pp. 292–93; Inumaru Giichi
and Nakamura Shintarō, *Monogatari Nihon kindaishi* [The story of
modern Japanese history] (Tokyo: Shin Nihon Shuppansha, 1971),
3:323; Katō et al., *Meiji*, pp. 253–54; Bunkyōku, *Bunkyōkushi*
[History of Bunkyōku] (Tokyo: Bunkyōku, 1969), 4:782; Fujiwara et al., eds., *Kindai Nihonshi*, p. 422; Lory, *Japan's Military Masters*, p. 209.

17–10   Aragaki, "Japan's Home Front," p. 289; Nagai Kafū,
Nagai Kafū zenshū [Complete works of Nagai Kafū] (Tokyo:
Chūō Kōronsha, 1948–1953), 21:353, quoted in Edward Seidensticker, *Kafū the Scribbler: The Life and Writings of Nagai Kafū,
1879–1959* (Stanford: Stanford University Press, 1965), p. 154. See
also Aragaki, "Japan's Home Front," p. 292; Fujiwara et al., eds.,
Kindai Nihonshi, p. 428.

17–26   Kazuko O. Amemiya interview, Tokyo, May 9, 1973. See
Aragaki, "Japan's Home Front," p. 291; Fujiwara et al., eds., *Kindai
Nihonshi*, p. 422; Fujiwara Akira, *Kokumin no rekishi*, vol. 23, *Taiheiyō
sensō* [National history, vol. 23, The Pacific war] (Tokyo: Bun'eidō,
1970), p. 188; Katō et al., *Meiji*, p. 256.

18–7   Matsuoka, *Daughter*, p. 181.

18–10   See T. A. Larson, *Wyoming's War Years, 1941–1945* (Laramie: The University of Wyoming, 1954), pp. 79–89.

19–5   Gwen Terasaki, *Bridge to the Sun* (Chapel Hill: University
of North Carolina Press, 1957), p. 113. See Wilfrid Fleisher, *Volcanic
Isle* (New York: Doubleday, Doran and Company, Inc., 1941),
p. 112; Katō et al., *Meiji*, pp. 256–57; Kurashi no Techōsha,
Tokushū Kurashi no techō, no. 96, *sensōchū no kurashi no kiroku*
[Special issue of *Notebook on Daily Living*, no. 96, Record of daily living during the war] (Tokyo: Kurashi no Techōsha, 1969), p. 20;
Joseph Newman, *Goodbye Japan* (New York: L. B. Fischer, 1942), p.
236.

20–12   Nakamoto, *My Japan*, pp. 20–21; Tsuji Toyoji, ed., *Aa
Toyokawa joshi teishintai* [The Toyokawa women's volunteer corps]
(Tokyo: Kōyō Shobō, 1963), pp. 44–45; Aikawa, *Unwilling Pa-
triot*, p. 74; Shimonaka Yasaburō, ed., *Yokusan kokumin undōshi* [His-

tory of the national imperial rule assistance movement] (Tokyo: Yokusan Undōshi Kankōkai, 1954), p. 1059; Hallett Abend, *Japan Unmasked* (New York: Ives, Washburn, Inc., 1941), p. 251; Hashikawa et al., eds., *Kindai Nihon shisōshi*, p. 458.

20–27   See Lucy D. Meo, *Japan's Radio War on Australia, 1941–1945* (Carlton: Melbourne University Press, 1968); Peter De Mendelssohn, *Japan's Political Warfare* (London: George Allen & Unwin, Ltd., 1944), pp. 11–15, 104–05; Arthur Marwick, *The Deluge: British Society and the First World War* (New York: W. W. Norton & Company, Inc., 1970), pp. 210–17; Gordon Wright, *The Ordeal of Total War, 1939–1945* (New York: Harper & Row, 1968), pp. 66–72; Peter Calvocoressi and Guy Wint, *Total War* (New York: Ballantine Books, 1973), vol. 1, *The War in the West*, pp. 549–63.

21–20   Quoted in Lory, *Japan's Military Masters*, p. 211. See Meo, *Radio War*, p. 19; Hashikawa et al., eds., *Kindai Nihon shisōshi*, p. 447; Fleisher, *Volcanic Isle*, p. 247; De Mendelssohn, *Political Warfare*, pp. 67–69; Fumiko H. Coyne, "Censorship of Publishing in Japan: 1868–1945" (M.A. thesis, Graduate Library School, University of Chicago, 1967), p. 55.

22–13   Coyne, "Censorship," pp. 55, 59; Carl Randau and Leane Zugsmith, *The Setting Sun of Japan* (New York: Random House, 1942), p. 10; Chalmers A. Johnson, *An Instance of Treason: Ozaki Hotsumi and the Sorge Spy Ring* (Stanford: Stanford University Press, 1964), p. 8; De Mendelssohn, *Political Warfare*, pp. 71–73; Meo, *Radio War*, pp. 30–31; Fleisher, *Volcanic Isle*, pp. 277–81.

22–30   Fleisher, *Volcanic Isle*, pp. 246, 290f; De Mendelssohn, *Political Warfare*, pp. 51–52; Fukawa Kakuzaemon, "Senji no shuppan tōsei" [Wartime publishing controls], *Bungaku* [Literature] 29, no. 5 (May 1961): 149.

23–26   Inumaru and Nakamura, *Monogatari*, p. 331. See Coyne, "Censorship," pp. 47, 57–60; Fukawa, "Senji," p. 139; De Mendelssohn, *Political Warfare*, p. 76; Foreign Affairs Association of Japan, *The Japan Year Book, 1946–48* (Tokyo: Foreign Affairs Association of Japan, 1948), pp. 538–39.

24–21   Konishi Shirō, "Senjika no kokumin seikatsu" [People's livelihoods in wartime], in *Taikei Nihonshi sōsho*, vol. 17, *seikatsushi*, pt. 3 [Series of works on Japanese history, no. 17, History of daily life, pt. 3], ed. Morimatsu Yoshiaki et al. (Tokyo: Yamakawa Shuppansha, 1969), p. 442; De Mendelssohn, *Political Warfare*, pp. 34–37; John F. Embree, *The Japanese Nation, a Social Survey* (New York: Rinehart & Co., 1945), pp. 144–45; Delmer M. Brown, *Nationalism in Japan: An Introductory Historical Analysis* (Berkeley: University of California Press, 1955), pp. 212–13; Stanley T. Fukawa, "Neighbourhood Associations in Japanese Cities and Their Political Implications" (M.A. thesis in sociology, London University, 1964), p. 113.

25–3   Lory, *Japan's Military Masters*, p. 208. See John Morris, *Traveler from Tokyo* (New York: Sheridan House, 1944), pp. 139–40; Joseph L. Anderson and Donald Richie, *The Japanese Film: Art and Industry* (New York: Grove Press, Inc., 1966), pp. 128–29; De Mendelssohn, *Political Warfare*, pp. 77–78.

26–18   Quoted in Lory, *Japan's Military Masters*, pp. 30–31. See Aikawa, *Unwilling Patriot*, pp. 5–7; Fujiwara et al., eds., *Kindai Nihonshi*, p. 444; Tottoriken, *Tottorikenshi, kindai,* vol. 4, *shakai bunkahen* [History of Tottori prefecture, modern, vol. 4, Society and culture] (Tottori: Tottoriken, 1960), pp. 235–36. Morris, a high school teacher before Pearl Harbor, observed that "I have no hesitation in saying that military training is the most unpopular feature of Japanese school life" (Morris, *Traveler*, p. 76).

26–29   Chaen Yoshio, *Gakuto kinrō dōin* [Student labor mobilization] (Tokushima: Tokushimaken Kyōikukai, 1969), p. 42; Fujiwara et al., eds., *Kindai Nihonshi*, pp. 444, 471.

28–5   Mitoji Nishmoto, *The Development of Educational Broadcasting in Japan* (Tokyo: Sophia University and Charles E. Tuttle Company, 1969), pp. 42–44, 58–63.

28–26   Tottoriken, *Tottorikenshi, kindai,* vol. 4, *shakai bunkahen,* p. 209; Ronald S. Anderson, *Japan: Three Epochs of Modern Education* (Washington, D.C.: U.S. Department of Health, Education and Welfare, 1959), pp. 40–41; Shima Tameo, *Meiji hyakunen kyōikushi* [Hundred-year history of education since Meiji] (Tokyo: Nihon Kyōto, 1968), 2:102–05; Monbushō, *Gakusei hachijūnenshi* [Eighty-year history of the education system] (Tokyo: Ōkurashō Insatsukyoku, 1954), p. 332; Nihon Seinenkan, *Dai Nihon Seishōnendanshi* [History of the greater Japan youth association] (Tokyo: Nihon Seinenkan, 1970), pp. 12, 85–86; Embree, *Japanese Nation,* p. 134; Kyōto Daigaku Bungakubu Kokushi Kenkyūshitsu, *Nihon Kindaishi jiten* [Dictionary of modern Japanese history] (Tokyo: Tōyō Keizai Shinpōsha, 1958), p. 317.

28–32   Quoted in Makoto Aso and Ikuo Amano, *Education and Japan's Modernization* (Tokyo: Ministry of Foreign Affairs, 1972), p. 57.

29–3   Monbushō, *Gakusei hachijūnenshi,* pp. 329–31. See Embree, *Japanese Nation,* pp. 136–39; Aso and Amano, *Education,* p. 58; Brown, *Nationalism in Japan,* pp. 221–22.

29–8   Fujiwara et al., eds., *Kindai Nihonshi,* pp. 444–45.

29–12   Shima, *Meiji hyakunen kyōikushi,* 2:87–92; Aikawa, *Unwilling Patriot,* pp. 11–15.

29–19   John G. Caiger, "Education, Values, and Japan's National Identity: A Study of the Aims and Contents of Courses in Japanese History, 1872–1963" (Ph.D. dissertation, Australian National University, 1966), p. 112; Harold J. Wray, "Changes and Continuity in Japanese Images of the *Kokutai* and Attitudes and Roles Toward the Outside World, A Content Analysis of Japanese Textbooks, 1903–1945" (Ph.D. dissertation in history, University of Hawaii, 1971), pp. 404–09.

29–33   A translation appears in Otto D. Tolischus, *Tokyo Record* (New York: Reynal & Hitchcock, 1943), pp. 405–27. See also ibid., pp. 186–88.

30–4   Lory, *Japan's Military Masters,* pp. 212–13.

30–17   Kawahara Hiroshi, "Senjika ni okeru kagaku gijutsuron" [On science and technology in wartime], in Waseda Daigaku Shakai Kagaku Kenkyūjo Fuashizumu Kenkyū Bukai, *Nihon no fuashizumu,* vol. 2, *sensō to kokumin* [Japanese fascism, vol. 2, War and the people] (Tokyo: Waseda Daigaku Shuppanbu, 1974), pp. 45–84; Aso and Amano, *Education,* pp. 58–59; Yanaga, *Japan Since Perry,* pp. 547–48; Jerome B. Cohen, *Japan's Economy in War and Reconstruction* (Minneapolis: University of Minnesota Press, 1949), p. 274.

30–24   "Supottoraito" [Spotlight], NHK, channel 1, Tokyo, September 16, 1976.

31–8   Iwateken Ichinoseki Kokumin Kyōiku Kenkyūkai, *Kyōshi no sensō taiken no kiroku* [Record of teachers' war experiences] (Tokyo: Rōdō Junpōsha, 1969), p. 191; Andō Masako, "Kinrō dōin no akekure" [Labor mobilization day and night], in Kusa no Mi Kai Daishichi Gurūpu, *Sensō to watakushi* [The War and I] (Tokyo: Kusa no Mi Kai, 1963), p. 18; Masuo Kato, *The Lost War: A Japanese Reporter's Inside Story* (New York: Alfred A. Knopf, 1946), p. 186; Minatokuritsu Mita Toshokan, *Senran to Minatoku* [War and Minatoku] (Tokyo: Minatokuritsu Mita Toshokan, 1969), p. 102.

31–27   Hashikawa et al., eds., *Kindai Nihon shisōshi,* p. 447; Araishishi Henshū Iinkai, *Araishishi* [History of Arai] (Niigataken, Araishi: Araishishi Henshū Iinkai, 1971), 2:575; Kato, *Lost War,* p. 186.

32–6   See Richard H. Mitchell, *Thought Control in Prewar Japan* (Ithaca: Cornell University Press, 1976), pp. 159–62.

CHAPTER 3

34–11   Fujiwara Akira, Imai Seiichi, and Ōe Shinobu, eds., *Kindai Nihonshi no kisō chishiki* [Basic knowledge about modern Japanese history] (Tokyo: Yūhikaku, 1972), p. 428.

35–6   Takekazu Ogura, ed., *Agricultural Development in Modern Japan*, rev. ed. (Tokyo: Fuji Publishing Co., Ltd., 1967), p. 48; Jerome B. Cohen, *Japan's Economy in War and Reconstruction* (Minneapolis: University of Minnesota Press, 1949), pp. 1–2, 5, 7. Cohen gives slightly different figures for military expenditures on p. 5.

35–21   T. A. Bisson, *Japan's War Economy* (New York: International Secretariat, Institute of Pacific Relations, 1945), p. 3.

35–33   Ogura, *Agricultural Development*, p. 48; Cohen, *Japan's Economy*, p. 97.

36–6   "Kakaku teishirei" [Price freeze order], September 19, 1939. See Akimoto Ritsuo, *Sensō to minshū: Taiheiyō sensōka no toshi seikatsu* [War and the people: City life during the Pacific war] (Tokyo: Gakuyō Shobō, 1974), pp. 158–59; Fujiwara et al., eds., *Kindai Nihonshi*, p. 429; Cohen, *Japan's Economy*, p. 357.

36–10   Araishishi Henshū Iinkai, *Araishishi* [History of Arai] (Niigataken, Araishi: Araishishi Henshū Iinkai, 1971), 2:567.

37–3   Dai Nihon Seinendan Honbu, *Seinendan nenkan, 1941* [Youth group annual, 1941] (Tokyo: Dai Nihon Seinendan Honbu, 1940), p. 53; Taikakai, ed., *Naimushōshi* [History of the Home Ministry] (Tokyo: Chihō Zaimu Kyōkai, 1971), 3:714–15.

37–8   "Kokumin seikatsu kōyō" [Outline of people's daily lives], August 11, 1939, quoted in Dai Nihon Seinendan Honbu, *Seinendan nenkan, 1941,* p. 53.

37–24   Details on the prewar history of these groups are drawn from Komori Ryūkichi, "Tōkyō ni okeru chōnaikai no hensen ni tsuite" [Changes in community councils in Tokyo], *Nihon rekishi* [Japanese history], no. 297 (February 1973): 82–93; Akimoto Ritsuo, "Senjika no toshi ni okeru chiiki jūmin soshiki" [Local organization of city residents in wartime], *Shakai kagaku tōkyū* [Social science review] 18, no. 2, consecutive no. 51 (February 1973): 66–68, 93; Ari Bokuji, "Chihō seido—burakukai chōnaikai seido" [Local institutions—The community council system], in *Kōza Nihon kindaihō hattatsushi* [Colloquium on the development of modern Japanese law], ed. Ukai Nobushige et al. (Tokyo: Keisō Shobō, 1959), 6:165–68, 201; Stanley T. Fukawa, "Neighbourhood

Associations in Japanese Cities and Their Political Implications"
(M.A. thesis in sociology, London University, 1964), pp. 103–04.

38–7   Tōkyō Shisei Chōsakai, *Tōkyōshi chōnaikai ni kansuru chōsa* [Investigation of community councils in the city of Tokyo]
(Tokyo: Tōkyō Shisei Chōsakai, 1925), p. 1; Tōkyō Shiyakusho, *Tōkyōshi chōnaikai no chōsa* [Investigation of community councils in the city of Tokyo] (Tokyo: Tōkyō Shiyakusho, 1934), pp.
5–10; Tōkyō Shisei Kakushin Dōmei, *Tōkyōshi no chōkai* [Com-
munity councils in the city of Tokyo] (Tokyo: Tōkyō Shisei Kakushin Dōmei, 1938), pp. 31–33; Taikakai, ed., *Naimushōshi* (1971),
1:232–66.

39–18   See Ari, "Chihō seido," pp. 196–99; Fukawa, "Neighbourhood Associations," pp. 114–17; Akimoto, "Soshiki," p. 74; Fujiwara et al., eds., *Kindai Nihonshi*, pp. 422–23, 440.

40–22   "Tōkyōshi chōkai seibi yōkō" [Outline of provisions for community councils in Tokyo], April 17, 1938, in *Kindai
Nihonshi*, ed. Fujiwara et al., pp. 440–41. See Akimoto, "Soshiki,"
pp. 73–74, 79.

40–34   See Tōkyō Shisei Chōsakai, *Godai toshi chōnaikai ni
kansuru chōsa* [Investigation of community councils in five large ci-
ties] (Tokyo: Tōkyō Shisei Chōsakai, 1944), p. 2; Tōkyō
Shisei Kakushin Dōmei, *Tōkyōshi no chōkai*, appendix, p. 1.

41–8   Fujiwara Akira, *Kokumin no rekishi*, vol. 23, *Taiheiyō sensō*
[National history, vol. 23, The Pacific war] (Tokyo: Bun'eidō, 1970),
pp. 198–99.

41–21   See Akimoto, *Sensō to minshū*, pp. 19, 24–27, 35.

41–31   Ari, "Chihō seido," pp. 201–02.

42–5   John F. Embree, "Japanese Administration at the Local
Level," *Applied Anthropology* 3, no. 4 (1944): 11–18. See Akimoto,
"Soshiki," pp. 64–69.

42–21   Sakuraba Hiroshi, "Dainiji taisenka no sensō dōin
soshiki o megutte" [Outline of mobilization organizations during
World War Two], *Kanagawakenshi kenkyū* [Studies in the history of
Kanagawa prefecture], no. 23 (February 1974): 23–24; Kokumin
Seishin Sōdōin Honbu, *Kokumin seishin sōdōin chihō taikei narabi
jissenmō seibi jōkyō chōsa* [Investigation of the local system of the na-
tional spiritual mobilization and current conditions of provisions for
practical implementation] (Tokyo: Kokumin Seishin Sōdōin
Honbu, 1940), p. 2. For a somewhat different interpretation, see
Akimoto, "Soshiki," pp. 81–82.

43– *Tōkyōshi chōkai jihō* [Tokyo community council news], no. 3 (1939), quoted in Ari, "Chihō seido," p. 192. See Akimoto, "Soshiki," pp. 78–79.

43–22 Kokumin Seishin Sōdōin Honbu, *Kokumin seishin sōdōin chihō taikei*, p. 2; Tōkyō Shisei Chōsakai, *Nihon toshi nenkan, Shōwa jūgonen'yō* [Japan city annual, 1940] (Tokyo: Tōkyō Shisei Chōsakai, 1940), pp. 112–13. See Fukawa, "Neighbourhood Associations," pp. 98–101, 120–22.

44–15 Kazuo Okochi, *Labor in Modern Japan* (Tokyo: The Science Council of Japan, 1958), pp. 67–71.

44–27 Iwao F. Ayusawa, *A History of Labor in Modern Japan* (Honolulu: East-West Center Press, 1966), p. 228. See Robert A. Scalapino, "Labor and Politics in Postwar Japan," in *The State and Economic Enterprise in Japan*, ed. William W. Lockwood (Princeton: Princeton University Press, 1965), pp. 679–80.

44–31 Kisaka Jun'ichirō, "Nihon fuashizumu to jinmin shihai no tokushitsu" [Japanese fascism and special features of leading the people], *Rekishigaku kenkyū* [Historiographical studies], special number (October 1970): 121. The suggestion that the army refused to deal with the unions and backed the patriotic industrial movement is found in Cohen, *Japan's Economy*, p. 283.

45–10 Kisaka Jun'ichirō, "Taisei Yokusankai no seiritsu" [Establishment of the imperial rule assistance association], *Iwanami kōza Nihon rekishi*, vol. 20, *kindai*, pt. 7 [Iwanami colloquium on Japanese history, vol. 20, Modern, pt. 7] (Tokyo: Iwanami Shoten, 1976), p. 280. See Asanuma Kazunori, "Nihon fuashizumu no seiji katei" [The political process of Japanese fascism], *Takushoku Daigaku ronshū* [Takushoku University reports], no. 79 (1971): 15; Fujiwara et al., eds., *Kindai Nihonshi*, p. 442; Zdenka Vasiljevová, "The Industrial Patriotic Movement—A Study on the Structure of Fascist Dictatorship in War-Time Japan," in Vlasta Hilská and Zdenka Vasiljevová, *Problems of Modern Japanese Society* (Prague: Charles University, 1971), pp. 99–105.

45–23 Shimonaka Yasaburō, ed., *Yokusan kokumin undōshi* [History of the national imperial rule assistance movement] (Tokyo: Yokusan Undōshi Kankōkai, 1954), p. 965.

46–21 See Samuel Dumas and K. O. Vedel-Petersen, *Losses of Life Caused by War* (Oxford: Clarendon Press, 1923), pp. 25–47, 80–111; Ales Hrdlicka, "The Effects of War on the American People," *Scientific Monthly* 8 (1919): 542–45.

47–9 Chitoshi Yanaga, *Japan Since Perry* (New York: McGraw-Hill Book Co., 1949), p. 533; Tottoriken, *Tottorikenshi, kindai*, vol. 4, *shakai bunkahen* [History of Tottori prefecture, modern, vol. 4, Society and culture] (Tottori: Tottoriken, 1969), pp. 235–36; F. Ohtani, ed., *One Hundred Years of Health Progress in Japan* (Tokyo: International Medical Foundation of Japan, 1971), p. 64; Kyōto Daigaku Bungakubu Kokushi Kenkyūshitsu, *Nihon kindaishi jiten* [Dictionary of modern Japanese history] (Tokyo: Tōyō Keizai Shinpōsha, 1958), p. 173; Hillis Lory, *Japan's Military Masters: The Army in Japanese Life* (New York: Viking Press, 1943), p. 22.

47–16   Ienaga Saburō, *Taiheiyō sensō* [The Pacific war] (Tokyo: Iwanami Shoten, 1968), p. 261; Charles B. Fahs, *Government in Japan: Recent Trends in Its Scope and Operation* (New York: International Secretariat, Institute of Pacific Relations, 1940), p. 56; Ayusawa, *Labor in Japan,* p. 230; Foreign Affairs Association of Japan, *The Japan Year Book, 1946–48* (Tokyo: Foreign Affairs Association of Japan, 1948), p. 495.

47–32   Kyōto Daigaku Bungakubu Kokushi Kenkyūshitsu, *Nihon kindaishi jiten,* p. 189; Ohtani, *Health Progress,* pp. 62–63; Foreign Affairs Association of Japan, *The Japan Year Book, 1946–48,* p. 263; Ayusawa, *Labor in Japan,* p. 231; Yanaga, *Japan Since Perry,* p. 533; Ienaga, *Taiheiyō sensō,* p. 261. The figures for 1938 and 1942 are Ohtani's; welfare ministry data show 170 associations with 601,568 members for 1938 and 6,490 associations with 22,884,779 members for 1942.

48–15   Hayashi Toshikazu, *Nōson igaku josetsu* [Introduction to rural medicine] (Tokyo: Itō Shoten, 1944), pp. 353–54; Ohtani, *Health Progress,* p. 65; Fukuiken, *Taishō Shōwa Fukuikenshi* [History of Fukui prefecture in the Taishō and Shōwa periods] (Fukui: Fukuiken, 1956), 1:40–41.

48–30   Hayashi, *Nōson,* p. 417; Foreign Affairs Association of Japan, *The Japan Year Book, 1946–48,* p. 513; Maejima Tadao, "Senchū sengo no iryō" [Medicine during and after the war], in Iida Bunkazai no Kai, *Dainiji taisen no koro* [The World War Two period] (Iida: Minami Shinshū Shinbunsha, 1972), p. 34.

49–5   Foreign Affairs Association of Japan, *The Japan Year Book, 1946–48,* p. 271; Fahs, *Government in Japan,* p. 57; Yanaga, *Japan Since Perry,* pp. 547–48, 604; Kawahara Hiroshi, "Senjika ni okeru kagaku gijutsuron" [On science and technology in wartime], in Waseda Daigaku Shakai Kagaku Kenkyūjo Fuashizumu Kenkyū Bukai, *Nihon no fuashizumu,* vol. 2, *sensō to kokumin* [Japanese fascism, vol. 2, War and the people] (Tokyo: Waseda Daigaku Shuppanbu, 1974), pp. 45–84.

50–9   Fujiwara et al., eds., *Kindai Nihonshi,* pp. 428–29; Yanaga, *Japan Since Perry,* p. 539; Hallett Abend, *Japan Unmasked* (New

York: Ives, Washburn, Inc., 1941), p. 246: Kumagai Sonoko, "Senji tōsei to sonraku shakai" [Wartime controls and village society], *Shakaigaku hyōron* [Sociology review] 20, no. 3 (January 1970): 38–39; Ebihara Haruyoshi, "Sensō no shinkō to kyōiku" [Progress of the war and education], in *Nihon kindai kyōkushi* [History of modern Japanese education], ed. Kaigo Muneomi (Tokyo: Iwanami Shoten, 1962), p. 296.

50–20   Wilfrid Fleisher, *Volcanic Isle* (New York: Doubleday, Doran and Company, Inc., 1941), p. 113. See Katō Hidetoshi et al., *Meiji Taishō Shōwa sesōshi* [History of social conditions in the Meiji, Taishō, and Shōwa eras] (Tokyo: Shakai Shisōsha, 1967), p. 259; Abend, *Japan Unmasked*, p. 251; Cohen, *Japan's Economy*, p. 363.

50–33   Araishishi Henshū Iinkai, *Araishishi*, 2:566. See Abend, *Japan Unmasked*, pp. 248, 253–54; Fleisher, *Volcanic Isle*, pp. 16–17; Cohen, *Japan's Economy*, p. 362; Richard R. Lingeman, *Don't You Know There's a War On?* (New York: Paperback Library, 1971), p. 296.

51–5   Abend, *Japan Unmasked*, p. 248. See ibid., pp. 245–49; Akimoto, *Sensō to minshū*, pp. 160–63.

52–2   Fleisher, *Volcanic Isle*, p. 113. See James R. Young, *Behind the Rising Sun* (New York: Doubleday, Doran and Company, Inc., 1941), p. 323; Abend, *Japan Unmasked*, p. 249.

52–13   Abend, *Japan Unmasked*, p. 257; Young, *Rising Sun*, p. 245.

52–21   Akimoto, *Sensō to minshū*, p. 162; Araishishi Henshū Iinkai, *Araishishi*, 2:575.

CHAPTER 4

53–13   Carl Randau and Leane Zugsmith, *The Setting Sun of Japan* (New York: Random House, 1942), pp. 53–54, 58–59. See Iwasaki Akira. "Tōsei teikō tōhi—senji no Nihon eiga" [Control, resistance, flight—Wartime Japanese movies], *Bungaku* [Literature] 29, no. 5 (May 1961): 66–75; Chitoshi Yanaga, *Japan Since Perry* (New York: McGraw-Hill Book Co., 1949), p. 549; Otto D. Tolischus, *Tokyo Record* (New York: Reynal & Hitchcock, 1943), p. 151.

54–11   Kisaka Jun'ichirō. "Taisei yokusankai no seiritsu" [Establishment of the imperial rule assistance association], *Iwanami kōza Nihon rekishi*, vol. 20, *kindai*, pt. 7 [Iwanami colloquium on Japanese history, vol. 20, Modern, pt. 7] (Tokyo: Iwanami Shoten, 1976), p. 296. See also ibid., pp. 297–98.

55–29   Kisaka, "Taisei," pp. 297–98, 305–07; Ishida Takeshi, *Nihon kindaishi taikei,* vol. 8, *hakyoku to heiwa* [Series on modern Japanese history, vol. 8, Cataclysm and peace] (Tokyo: Tōkyō Daigaku Shuppankai, 1968), p. 11; Mainichi Newspapers, *Fifty Years of Light and Dark: The Hirohito Era,* 2nd ed. (Tokyo: Mainichi Newspapers, 1976), p. 89.

56–1   Kyōto Daigaku Bungakubu Kokushi Kenkyūshitsu, *Nihon kindaishi jiten* [Dictionary of modern Japanese history] (Tokyo: Tōyō Keizai Shinpōsha, 1958), p. 346; Willis Lamott, *Nippon: The Crime and Punishment of Japan* (New York: John Day Company, 1944), p. 73.

56–7   Ienaga Saburō, *Taiheiyō sensō* [The Pacific war] (Tokyo: Iwanami Shoten, 1968), p. 137; Richard Yasko, "Hiranuma Kiichiro and the New Structure Movement 1940–1941."*Asian Forum* 5, no. 2 (April–June 1973): 121–29.

56–35   Kisaka, "Taisei," p. 280. See Shimonaka Yasaburō, ed., *Yokusan kokumin undōshi* [History of the national imperial rule assistance movement] (Tokyo: Yokusan Undōshi Kankōkai, 1954), pp. 964–67; Ishida, *Nihon kindaishi taikei,* p. 68; Zdenka Vasiljevová, "The Industrial Patriotic Movement—A Study on the Structure of Fascist Dictatorship in War-Time Japan," in Vlasta Hilská and Zdenka Vasiljevová, *Problems of Modern Japanese Society* (Prague: Charles University, 1971), p. 116; Fujiwara Akira, Imai Seiichi, and Ōe Shinobu, eds., *Kindai Nihonshi no kisō chishiki* [Basic knowledge about modern Japanese history] (Tokyo: Yūhikaku, 1972), pp. 442–43; Jerome B. Cohen, *Japan's Economy in War and Reconstruction* (Minneapolis: University of Minnesota Press, 1949), p. 285.

57–12   Ishida, *Nihon kindaishi taikei,* p. 68; Vasiljevová, "Patriotic Movement," pp. 141–49.

57–16   Iwao F. Ayusawa, *A History of Labor in Modern Japan* (Honolulu: East-West Center Press, 1966), p. 228. See Andrew Roth, *Dilemma in Japan* (Boston: Little, Brown, 1945), pp. 221–25.

58–6   Nihon Seinenkan, *Dai Nihon Seishōnendanshi* [History of the greater Japan youth association] (Tokyo: Nihon Seinenkan, 1970), p. 3. See also ibid., pp. 4–8, 50–53, 314–15; Monbushō, *Gakusei hachijūnenshi* [Eighty-year history of the education system] (Tokyo: Ōkurashō Insatsukyoku, 1954), p. 333; Shimonaka, ed., *Yokusan kokumin undōshi,* pp. 1036–56.

58–37   Shimonaka, ed., *Yokusan kokumin undōshi,* p. 1063; *Japan Times & Advertiser,* February 5, 1942, morning ed., p. 3. See Shimonaka, ed., *Yokusan kokumin undōshi,* pp. 1057–62; Kyōto Diagaku Bungakubu Kokushi Kenkyūshitsu, *Nihon kindaishi jiten,* pp. 4,

350–51, 353; Inoue Kiyoshi, *Nihon joseishi* [History of Japanese women], rev. ed. (Tokyo: San'ichi Shobō, 1967), pp. 289–90.

59–11   Shimonaka, ed., *Yokusan kokumin undōshi,* pp. 1057, 1072–74.

59–24   Kubota Ai, "Sensō tōji no fujin dantai no ugoki" [Movements of wartime women's groups], in Iida Bunkazai no Kai, *Dainiji taisen no koro* [The World War Two period] (Iida: Minami Shinshū Shinbunsha, 1972), p. 48; Taisei Yokusankai, *Kokumin sōjōkaishi— daisankai chūō kyōryoku kaigi sōjōkai kaigiroku (zen)* [Record of national general meeting—Record of discussions at the third general meeting of the Central Cooperation Conference (Complete)] (Tokyo: Taisei Yokusankai, 1942), pp. 613–14. See Shimonaka, ed., *Yokusan kokumin undōshi,* p. 1070.

59–31   See Inoue, *Nihon joseishi,* p. 291; Shimonaka, ed., *Yokusan kokumin undōshi,* pp. 1069–70; Fujiwara et al., eds., *Kindai Nihonshi,* p. 443.

60–15   On the adult association, see Shimonaka, ed., *Yokusan kokumin undōshi,* pp. 901–10; Fukuiken, *Taishō Shōwa Fukuikenshi* [History of Fukui prefecture in the Taishō and Shōwa periods] (Fukui: Fukuiken, 1956), 1:213; Fujiwara et al., eds., *Kindai Nihonshi,* p. 443; Kyōto Daigaku Bungakubu Kokushi Kenkyūshitsu, *Nihon kindaishi jiten,* pp. 354, 611–12; Yanaga, *Japan Since Perry,* p. 605; Ishida, *Nihon kindaishi taikei,* pp. 11–12; Kisaka Jun'ichirō, "Nihon fuashizumu to jinmin shihai no tokushitsu" [Japanese fascism and special features of leading the people], *Rekishigaku kenkyū* [Historiographical studies], special number (October 1970): 125–26.

60–31   Shimonaka, ed., *Yokusan kokumin undōshi,* p. 239. See Akimoto Ritsuo, *Sensō to minshū: Taiheiyō sensōka no toshi seikatsu* [War and the people: City life during the Pacific war] (Tokyo: Gakuyō Shobō, 1974), pp. 117–21; Ishida, *Nihon kindaishi taikei,* pp. 11, 64–67.

61–13   See Yanaga, *Japan Since Perry,* pp. 612–13; Roth, *Dilemma,* pp. 155–59; Masuo Kato, *The Lost War: A Japanese Reporter's Inside Story* (New York: Alfred A. Knopf, 1946), p. 186; Akimoto, *Sensō to minshū,* p. 125; Ienaga, *Taiheiyō sensō,* p. 137.

61–26   See Angus Calder, *The People's War: Britain—1939–1945* (New York: Pantheon Books, 1969), pp. 501–13; Arthur Marwick, *War and Social Change in the Twentieth Century* (London: Macmillan, 1974), pp. 128–30; Cohen, *Japan's Economy,* p. 53f.

62–15   Lucy D. Meo, *Japan's Radio War on Australia, 1941–1945* (Carlton: Melbourne University Press, 1968), pp. 18, 26. See Fujiwara et al., eds., *Kindai Nihonshi*, p. 468; Yanaga, *Japan Since Perry*, p. 468; Hashikawa Bunzō, Kano Masanao, and Hiraoka Toshio, eds., *Kindai Nihon shisōshi no kisō chishiki* [Basic knowledge about the history of modern Japanese thought] (Tokyo: Yūhikaku, 1971), p. 447.

62–28   Tolischus, *Tokyo Record*, p. 89. See Hashikawa et al., eds., *Kindai Nihon shisōshi*, p. 447; Meo, *Radio War*, p. 22.

63–3   Futagawa Yoshifumi, *Genron no dan'atsu* [Suppression of discussion] (Tokyo: Hōsei Daigaku Shuppanbu, 1959), p. 227; Peter De Mendelssohn, *Japan's Political Warfare* (London: George Allen & Unwin, Ltd., 1944), p. 52; Foreign Affairs Association of Japan, *The Japan Year Book, 1946–48* (Tokyo: Foreign Affairs Association of Japan, 1948), p. 519; Fumiko H. Coyne, "Censorship of Publishing in Japan: 1868–1945" (M.A. thesis, Graduate Library School, University of Chicago, 1967), p. 63.

63–12   Hashikawa et al., eds., *Kindai Nihon shisōshi*, p. 469.

63–21   Ishida, *Nihon kindaishi taikei*, p. 95. See Coyne, "Censorship," p. 71; Asahi jānaru, *Shōwashi no shunkan* [Moments in Shōwa history] (Tokyo: Asahi Shinbunsha, 1966), 2:58.

63–26   *Bungei shunjū* (April 1943), quoted in *Kindai Nihon shisōshi*, ed. Hashikawa et al., p. 449.

64–8   De Mendelssohn, *Political Warfare*, p. 55; Claude A. Buss, "Inside Wartime Japan," *Life*, January 24, 1944, p. 86; Yanaga, *Japan Since Perry*, pp. 607–08; Meo, *Radio War*, pp. 22–24.

64–36   Quoted in Coyne, "Censorship," p. 70. See Ishida, *Nihon kindaishi taikei*, p. 95; Rekishigaku Kenkyūkai, *Taiheiyō sensōshi* [History of the Pacific war] (Tokyo: Aoki Shoten, 1973), 5:134; Foreign Affairs Association of Japan, *The Japan Year Book, 1946–48*, p. 528; Coyne, "Censorship," p. 73; Sukagawashi Kyōiku Iinkai, *Sukagawashishi, gendai,* pt. 2 [History of Sukagawa, modern, pt. 2] (Fukushimaken, Sukagawashi: Sukagawashi Kyōiku Iinkai, 1972), p. 88.

65–10   Togawa Sadao, quoted in Hirano Ken, "Nihon Bungaku Hōkokukai no seiritsu" [Founding of the Japan patriotic literary association], *Bungaku* [Literature] 29, no. 5 (May 1961): 1. See Hashikawa et al., eds., *Kindai Nihon shisōshi*, p. 448; Asahi jānaru, ed., *Shōwashi no shunkan,* 2:58; Donald Keene, "Japanese Writers and the Greater East Asia War," in *Landscapes and Portraits: Appreciations of Japanese Culture* (Tokyo: Kodansha International, Ltd., 1971), p. 302; Foreign Affairs Association of Japan, *The Japan Year Book, 1946–48*, p. 539.

65–17   Rekishigaku Kenkyūkai, *Taiheiyō sensōshi* (1972), 4:257. See Ishida, *Nihon kindaishi taikei*, p. 98.

65–29   Hiraide Hiizu, *Senjika no genron tōsei* [Press controls in wartime], 2nd ed. (Tokyo: Kashiwaba Shoin, 1944), p. 7.

66–2   Fujiwara et al., eds., *Kindai Nihonshi*, pp. 468–69; Coyne, "Censorship," p. 64; Foreign Affairs Association of Japan, *The Japan Year Book, 1946–48*, p. 526; Ienaga Saburō, *Kindai Nihon no shisōka* [Modern Japanese thinkers], new ed. (Tokyo: Yūshindō, 1970), pp. 248–49.

66–24   See Asahi jānaru, *Shōwashi no shunkan*, 2:52–56; Hashikawa et al., eds., *Kindai Nihon shisōshi*, p. 444; Fujiwara et al., eds., *Kindai Nihonshi*, pp. 467–69, which gives the figure six deaths; Mimisaka Tarō, Fujita Chikamasa, and Watanabe Kiyoshi, *Genron no haiboku* [Collapse of free speech] (Tokyo: San'ichi Shobō), pp. 113–32; Kuroda Hidetoshi, *Chi nurareta genron* [Bloodied free speech] (Tokyo: Gakufū Shoin, 1951), pp. 1–6; Hatanaka Shigeo, "Shuppan dan'atsu" [Repression of the press], in Nihon Janārisuto Renmei, *Genron dan'atsushi* [History of repression of the press] (Tokyo: Ginkyō Shobō, 1949), pp. 75–138. The Japanese have never managed to quiet the unconfirmed and highly improbable rumor that Ozaki escaped execution by fleeing the country.

66–32   Quoted in Roth, *Dilemma*, p. 158.

66–35   Quoted in Asahi jānaru, *Shōwashi no shunkan*, 2:52.

67–4   Quoted in Joseph L. Anderson and Donald Richie, *The Japanese Film: Art and Industry* (New York: Grove Press, Inc., 1966), p. 135.

67–13   *Japan Times & Advertiser*, December 4, 1941, p. 3; ibid., December 11, 1941, p. 4. See Randau and Zugsmith, *Setting Sun*, p. 23.

67–32   Iwasaki, *Tōsei teikō tōhi*, p. 67. See ibid., p. 70; Rekishigaku Kenkyūkai, *Taiheiyō sensōshi*, 5:135; Anderson and Richie, *Japanese Film*, pp. 131–32, 137–40, 142–45.

68–9   Foreign Affairs Association of Japan, *The Japan Year Book, 1946–48*, pp. 549–50; Ienaga, *Taiheiyō sensō*, p. 150.

68–29   Rekishigaku Kenkyūkai, *Taiheiyō sensōshi*, 5:136–38; Kodama Yukita et al., eds., *Zusetsu Nihon bunkashi taikei*, vol. 12, *Taishō Shōwa jidai* [Illustrated series on the history of Japanese culture, vol. 12, The Taishō and Shōwa periods], rev. ed. (Tokyo: Shōgakukan, 1967), pp. 198–200; Eric W. Gosden, *Night Came to Japan* (London: Marshall, Morgan and Scott, 1951), pp. 88–94; Hashikawa et al., eds., *Kindai Nihon shisōshi*, pp. 462–63.

69-7   Hashikawa et al., eds., *Kindai Nihon shisōshi,* pp. 462–63; Kasahara Yoshimitsu, "Kojin Kirisutosha no teikō" [Resistance by individual Christians], in Dōshisha Daigaku Jinbun Kagaku Kenkyūjo, *Senjika teikō no kenkyū* [Studies of wartime resistance] (Tokyo: Misuzu Shobō, 1969), pp. 41–99; Kodama et al., eds., *Zusetsu Nihon bunkashi,* pp. 199–200; Rekishigaku Kenkyūkai, *Taiheiyō sensōshi,* 5:137–38.

69-15   *Japan Times & Advertiser,* January 8, 1942, evening ed., p. 2; Randau and Zugsmith, *Setting Sun,* pp. 13–15.

69-22   Ronald S. Anderson, "Nishi Honganji and Japanese Buddhist Nationalism, 1862–1945" (Ph.D. dissertation in history, University of California, Berkeley, 1956), pp. 138–45; *Nippon Times,* March 28, 1944, morning ed., p. 3.

70-8   Rekishigaku Kenkyūkai, *Taiheiyō sensōshi,* 5:117.

70-15   Naimushō Keihokyoku Hoanka, *Fuon gendō no jōkyō* [Current conditions of inflammatory words and conduct] (August 1945), quoted in Saitō Hideo, "Kūshū to minshū" [Air raids and the people], *Rekishi hyōron* [History review], no. 268 (October 1972): 11; Hashikawa et al., eds., *Kindai Nihon shisōshi,* p. 472.

70-29   Rekishigaku Kenkyūkai, *Taiheiyō sensōshi,* 5:117; Hashikawa et al., eds., *Kindai Nihon shisōshi,* p. 463; Nakanishi San'yō, "Senjika no higōhō katsudō" [Illegal wartime activity], *Rekishi hyōron* [History review], no. 269 (November 1972): 80–88; Patricia G. Steinhoff, "*Tenkō:* Ideology and Societal Integration in Prewar Japan" (Ph.D. dissertation in social relations, Harvard University, 1969), pp. 217–18, 237–39, 253–54; Inumaru Giichi and Nakamura Shintarō, *Monogatari Nihon kindaishi* [The story of modern Japanese history] (Tokyo: Shin Nihon Shuppansha, 1971), 3:373–74; Edward Seidensticker, *Kafū the Scribbler: The Life and Writings of Nagai Kafū, 1879–1959* (Stanford: Stanford University Press, 1965), pp. 157–59; Kamiyama Shigeo, "Gokuchū Taiheiyō sensōshi" [Prison history of the Pacific war], in *Jitsuroku Taiheiyō sensō* [True record of the Pacific war], ed. Itō Masanori et al. (Tokyo: Chūō Kōronsha, 1960), 7:257–75.

71-17   Bruno Bettelheim, *The Informed Heart: Autonomy in a Mass Age* (Glencoe, Ill.: The Free Press, 1960); Naimushō Keihokyoku, "Chian taisaku yōkō" [Outline of measures to preserve order] (January 1943), quoted in Rekishigaku Kenkyūkai, *Taiheiyō sensōshi,* 5:113–14; Naimushō Keihokyoku, "Chian iji no konpon hōshin" [Basic policies for preserving order], quoted ibid., p. 114; Roth, *Dilemma,* p. 159; Isoko Hatano and Ichiro Hatano, *Mother and*

Son: The Wartime Correspondence of Isoko and Ichiro Hatano (Boston: Houghton Mifflin, 1962), pp. 75–76.

71–22   Ienaga, *Taiheiyō sensō,* pp. 235–55.

CHAPTER 5

73–3   Kumagai Jirō, ed., *Tonarigumi tokyhon* [A reader for neighborhood associations] (Tokyo: Hibonkaku, 1940), pp. 276–77, 291.

73–8   Akimoto Ritsuo, *Sensō to minshū: Taiheiyō sensōka no toshi seikatsu* [War and the people: City life during the Pacific war] (Tokyo: Gakuyō Shobō, 1974), p. 78.

74–16   Kumagai Sonoko, "Senji tōsei to sonraku shakai" [Wartime controls and village society], *Shakaigaku hyōron* [Sociology review] 20, no. 3 (January 1970): 43. See Ishida Takeshi, *Nihon kindaishi taikei,* vol. 8, *hakyoku to heiwa* [Series on modern Japanese history, vol. 8, Cataclysm and peace] (Tokyo: Tōkyō Daigaku Shuppankai, 1968), p. 73.

75–23   Naimushō, "Burakukai chōnaikaitō seibi yōryō" [Essentials of providing for community councils], September 11, 1940, in Jichi Daigakkō, *Sengo jichishi,* vol. 1, *tonarigumi oyobi chōnaikai burakukaitō no haishi* [History of postwar self-rule, vol. 1, The abolition of neighborhood associations and community councils] (Tokyo: Jichi Daigakkō, 1960), pp. 2–3.

75–35   See Jichi Daigakkō, *Sengo jichishi,* 1:1–6; Ishida, *Nihon kindaishi taikei,* p. 72; Ari Bokuji, "Chihō seido—burakukai chōnaikai seido" [Local institutions—The community council system], in *Kōza Nihon kindaihō hattatsushi* [Colloquium on the development of modern Japanese law], ed. Ukai Nobushige et al. (Tokyo: Keisō Shobō, 1959), 6:200–06; Akimoto Ritsuo, "Senjika no toshi ni okeru chiiki jūmin soshiki" [Local organizations of city residents in wartime], *Shakai kagaku tōkyū* [Social science review] 18, no. 2, consecutive no. 51 (February 1973): 76–77; Akimoto, *Sensō to minshū,* p. 46; Stanley T. Fukawa, "Nieghbourhood Associations in Japanese Cities and Their Political Implications" (M.A. thesis in sociology. London University, 1964), pp. 125–29; Ralph J. D. Braibanti, "Neighborhood Associations in Japan and Their Democratic Potentialities," *Far Eastern Quarterly* 7, no. 2 (February 1948): 141; Fujiwara Akira, Imai Seiichi, and Ōe Shinobu, eds., *Kindai Nihonshi no kiso chishiki* [Basic knowledge about modern Japanese history] (Tokyo: Yūhikaku, 1972), p. 423.

76–33   Komori Ryūkichi, "Tōkyō ni okeru chōnaikai no hensen ni tsuite" [Changes in community councils in Tokyo], *Nihon rekishi* [Japanese history], no. 297 (February 1973): 95.

77–6   Computed from Shimonaka Yasaburō, ed., *Yokusan kokumin undōshi* [History of the national imperial rule assistance movement] (Tokyo: Yokusan Undōshi Kankōkai, 1954), pp. 413–15; Tōkyō Shisei Chōsakai, *Nihon toshi nenkan, Shōwa jūhachinen'yō* [Japan city annual, 1943] (Tokyo: Tōkyō Shisei Chōsakai, 1943), pp. 111–14.

77–12   Akimoto, *Sensō to minshū*, pp. 45–46. See Fukawa, "Neighbourhood Associations," pp. 95–97, 160; Braibanti, "Neighborhood Associations in Japan," pp. 146–52; Konishi Shirō, "Senjika no kokumin seikatsu" [People's livelihoods in wartime], in *Taikei Nihonshi sōsho*, vol. 17, *seikatsushi*, pt. 3 [Series of works on Japanese history, vol. 17, History of daily life, pt. 3], ed. Morimatsu Yoshiaki et al. (Tokyo: Yamakawa Shuppansha, 1969), p. 440; Fujiwara et al., eds., *Kindai Nihonshi*, p. 441.

77–22   Akimoto, *Sensō to minshū*, pp. 95–96.

77–35   Kennosuke Sato, "How the Tonarigumi Operates," *Contemporary Japan* 13, nos. 7–9 (July-September 1944), p. 780.

78–29   Shimonaka, ed., *Yokusan kokumin undōshi*, p. 413. See Jichi Daigakkō, *Sengo jichishi*, 1:13–14; Fukawa, "Neighbourhood Associations," pp. 156–57; Akimoto, "Soshiki," p. 92.

79–3   *Asahi shinbun*, August 15, 1942, quoted in Akimoto, *Sensō to minshū*, p. 126.

79–25   Kagoshimashishi Hensan Iinkai, *Kagoshimashishi* [History of Kagoshima] (Kagoshima: Kagoshimashishi Hensan Iinkai, 1970), 2:146–49; Ari, "Chihō seido," pp. 199–200.

79–36   Jichi Daigakkō, *Sengo jichishi*, 1:9; Fukawa, "Neighbourhood Associations," pp. 142–43.

80–19   Naimushō, Nōrinshō, Shōkōshō, Kōseishō, "Chōnaikai shōhi keizai shisetsu seibi ni kansuru ken" [Regulations concerning providing consumer economy facilities in community councils], October 29, 1942, in Jichi Daigakkō, *Sengo jichishi*, 1:14–16; Braibanti, "Neighborhood Associations in Japan," p. 51; Akimoto, *Sensō to minshū*, p. 55.

81–4   Taikakai, *Naimushōshi* [History of the Home Ministry] (Tokyo, Chihō Zaimu Kyōkai, 1970), 2:531–32; Jichi Daigakkō, *Sengo jichishi*, 1:18–19; Ishida, *Nihon kindaishi taikei*, p. 74; Akimoto, *Sensō to minshū*, pp. 143–44, 147–48; Ari, "Chihō seido," pp. 206–08.

81–8   Ōsaka mainichi, October 10, 1943, quoted in Ishii Kin'ichirō, "Nihon fuashizumu to chihō seido" [Japanese fascism and local institutions], Rekishigaku kenkyū [Historiographical studies], no. 307 (December 1965):9.

81–19   Quoted in Akimoto, "Soshiki," p. 89.

81–29   Sakuraba Hiroshi, "Dainiji taisenka no sensō dōin soshiki o megutte" [Outline of mobilization organizations during World War Two], Kanagawakenshi kenkyū [Studies in the history of Kanagawa prefecture], no. 23 (February 1974): 23–24; Kokumin Seishin Sōdōin Honbu, Kokumin seishin sōdōin chihō taikei narabi jissenmō seibi jōkyō chōsa [Investigation of the local system of the national spiritual mobilization and current conditions of provisions for practical implementation] (Tokyo: Kokumin Seishin Sōdōin Honbu, 1940), p. 2; Kumagai, "Senji tōsei," pp. 38–54, which argues instead that the chairmen sold out village interests to those of the state—an improbable situation for landlords still resident in the villages.

81–32   Tōkyōfu Sōmubu Shinkōka, Tonarigumi fujin tokuhon [A reader for neighborhood association women] (Tokyo: Tōkyōfu Sōmubu Shinkōka, 1941), pp. 108–09.

81–35   Akimoto, Sensō to minshū, pp. 58–60, 131–32; Fukawa, "Neighbourhood Associations," p. 138.

82–4   The figures in this paragraph are derived from data in Akimoto, "Soshiki," pp. 82–85.

82–27   Sutō Ryōsaku, Tonarigumichō no shuki [A neighborhood captain's notes] (Fokyo: privately printed, 1970), p. 4.

83–6   Akimoto, Sensō to minshū, pp. 58–63; Fukawa, "Neighbourhood Associations," pp. 135–40; Rekishigaku Kenyūkai, Taiheiyō sensōshi [History of the Pacific war] (Tokyo: Aoki Shoten, 1973), 5:118; Takaaki Aikawa, Unwilling Patriot (Tokyo: The Jordan Press, 1960), p. 50; Karl D. Hartzell, The Empire State at War: World War II (Albany: The State of New York, 1949), pp. 126–27.

83–19   Katō Hidetoshi et al., eds., Meiji Taishō Shōwa sesōshi [History of social conditions in the Meiji, Taishō, and Shōwa eras] (Tokyo: Shakai Shisōsha, 1967), p. 260.

84–14   Sutō, Tonarigumichō no shuki, pp. 14, 27; Braibanti, "Neighborhood Associations in Japan," pp. 154–55; Fukawa, "Neighbourhood Associations," pp. 147–49; Fortune, April 1944, p. 204.

84–21   Shisei shūhō [City Administration Weekly], no. 206 (April 1943), quoted in Bunkyōku, Bunkyōkushi [History of Bunkyōku], (Tokyo: Bunkyōku, 1969), 4:747–48; Sutō, *Tonarigumichō no shuki*, p. 8.

85–4   Sakuraba, "Dainiji," pp. 25–27. See Jichi Daigakkō, *Sengo jichishi*, 1:11–12; Fukawa, "Neighbourhood Associations," p. 152; Akimoto, *Sensō to minshū*, pp. 87–91.

85–16   Akimoto, *Sensō to minshū*, pp. 128–29; Fukawa, Neighbourhood Associations," p. 162.

85–34   Ari, "Chihō seido," p. 191; Akimoto, *Sensō to minshū*, pp. 75–77.

86–22   Sumie S. Mishima, *The Broader Way* (London: Victor Gollancz, 1954), p. 11. See Akimoto, *Sensō to minshū*, p. 46.

88–4   Takahashi Aiko, "Sensō kara no nikki" [Diary from the war], in Shōwa Sensō Bungaku Zenshū Henshū Iinkai, *Shōwa sensō bungaku zenshū*, vol. 14, *shimin no nikki* [Complete wartime literary works of the Shōwa era, vol. 14, City residents' diaries] (Tokyo: Shūeisha, 1965), p. 329; *Ashai shinbun*, May 14, 1944, quoted in Akimoto, *Sensō to minshū*, pp. 64–65.

88–7   Inoue Kiyoshi, *Nihon joseishi* [History of Japanese women], rev. ed. (Tokyo: San'ichi Shobō, 1967), p. 291; Akimoto, "Soshiki," pp. 82–85; Masuo Kato, *The Lost War: A Japanese Reporter's Inside Story* (New York: Alfred A. Knopf, 1946), p. 188.

88–28   Tōkyō Teikoku Daigaku Shakai Kagaku Kenkyūkai, *Tachiagaru hitobito* [People who are springing back] (Tokyo: Gakusei Shobō, 1946), pp. 16–17, 33–35. On local organizations after the surrender, see Jichi Daigakkō, *Sengo jichishi*, 1:71, 75–78, 81.

88–32   Sōrifu Kokuritsu Seron Chōsajo, *Chihō jichi seron chōsa—chōnaikai, burakukai, tonarigumi ni tsuite* [Opinion survey of local self-rule—Concerning community councils and neighborhood associations](Tokyo: Sōrifu, 1952), pp. 104–10.

89–15   Alexis de Tocqueville, *Democracy in America*, in *War: Studies from Psychology, Sociology, and Anthropology*, ed. L. Bramson and G. W. Goethals (New York: Basic Books, 1964), pp. 332–44; John A. Armstrong et al., *Soviet Partisans in World War II* (Madison: University of Wisconsin Press, 1964), pp. 3–5.

CHAPTER 6

90–9   Naimushō Keihokyoku Hoanka, *Tokkō geppō* [Special higher police monthly reports] (Tokyo: Seikei Shuppansha, 1972) (March 1943), 4:63; Tanaka Ningo, "Hyakushō nikki" [Farmer's diary], in Kurashi no Techōsha, *Tokushū* Kurashi no techō, no. 96, *sensōchū no kurashi no kiroku* [Special issue of *Notebook on Daily Living*, no. 96, Record of daily living during the war] (Tokyo: Kurashi no Techōsha, 1969): 240–41.

91–18   See Jerome B. Cohen, *Japan's Economy in War and Reconstruction* (Minneapolis: University of Minnesota Press, 1949), pp. 48–51, 58, 387–88; Okayamashishi Henshū Iinkai, *Okayamashishi, sensai fukkōhen* [History of Okayama, volume on recovery from war damage](Okayama: Okayama Shiyakusho, 1960), p. 60; T. A. Bisson, *Japan's War Economy* (New York: International Secretariat, Institute of Pacific Relations, 1945), pp. 4–11, passim; International Labor Organization, "A Survey of Economic and Social Conditions in Japan," *International Labor Review* 60, no. 1 (July 1949): 8; Ishida Takeshi, *Nihon kindaishi taikei*, vol. 8, *hakyoku to heiwa* [Series on modern Japanese history, vol. 8, Cataclysm and peace] (Tokyo: Tōkyō Daigaku Shuppankai, 1968), p. 82; U.S. Bureau of the Budget, War Records Section, *The United States at War: Development and Administration of the War Program by the Federal Government,* Bureau of the Budget, Historical Reports on War Administration, no. 1 (Washington, D.C.: U.S. Government Printing Office, 1946), pp. 514–15. Kyōchōkai Chōsabu, *Senji rōdō jijō* [Wartime labor conditions] (Tokyo: Kyōchōkai, 1944), discusses the economic planning of early 1942 in detail.

92–11   *Zaisei keizai tōkei nenpō* [Annual statistical report on finance and economics], p. 589, quoted in Kajinishi Mitsuhaya et al., *Nihon shihonshugi no botsuraku* [The collapse of Japanese capitalism] (Tokyo: Tōkyō Daigaku Shuppankai, 1964), 4:1131; U.S. Strategic Bombing Survey, Over-all Economic Effects Division, *The Effects of Strategic Bombing on Japan's War Economy* (Washington, D.C., 1946), p. 31.

92–22   Otto D. Tolischus, *Tokyo Record* (New York: Reynal & Hitchcock, 1943), p. 160. See Ōhara Shakai Mondai Kenkyūjo, *Taiheiyō sensōka no rōdōsha jōtai* [Workers' conditions during the Pacific war] (Tokyo: Tōyō Keizai Shinpōsha, 1964), pp. 65–66; Cohen, *Japan's Economy,* pp. 318, 328.

93–16   Fujiwara Akira, Imai Seiichi, and Ōe Shinobu, eds., *Kindai Nihonski no kisō chishiki* [Basic knowledge about modern Japanese history] (Tokyo: Yūhikaku, 1972), p. 470; Cohen, *Japan's Economy,* pp. 317–18, 348; Takahashi Saburō, "Shūmatsuki no kokumin shisō" [People's thought at the end], in *Kindai Nihon seiji shisōshi* [History of modern Japanese political thought], ed. Hashikawa Bunzō and Matsumoto Sannosuke (Tokyo: Yūhikaku, 1970), 2:421–22; Kazuo Okochi, *Labor in Modern Japan* (Tokyo: The

Science Council of Japan, 1958), p. 72; Fujiwara Akira, *Kokumin no rekishi,* vol. 23, *Taiheiyō sensō* [National history, vol. 23, The Pacific war] (Tokyo: Bun'eidō, 1970), p. 191; U.S. Strategic Bombing Survey, *Japan's War Economy,* p. 31.

93–31   Ohara Shakai Mondai Kenkyūjo, *Rōdōsha jōtai,* pp. 65–66; Rekishigaku Kenkyūkai, *Taiheiyō sensōshi* [History of the Pacific war] (Tokyo: Aoki Shoten, 1973), 5:124.

94–3   Tōyama Shigeki, Imai Seiichi, and Fujiwara Akira, *Shōwashi* [History of the Shōwa era], rev. ed. (Tokyo: Iwanami Shoten, 1959), p. 224; Saburo Shiomi, *Japan's Finance and Taxation, 1940–1956,* trans. Shotaro Hasegawa (New York: Columbia University Press, 1957), pp. 6, 17, 53–59; Masuo Kato, *The Lost War: A Japanese Reporter's Inside Story* (New York: Alfred A. Knopf, 1946), pp. 175–76.

94–15   Sakuraba Hiroshi, "Dainiji taisenka no sensō dōin soshiki o megutte" [Outline of mobilization organizations during World War Two], *Kanagawakenshi kenkyū* [Studies in the history of Kanagawa prefecture], no. 23 (February 1974): 28; Bruce F. Johnston, with Mosaburo Hosoda and Yoshio Kusumi, *Japanese Food Management in World War II* (Stanford: Stanford University Press, 1953), p. 167; *Nippon Times,* May 10, 1944, morning ed., p. 1; ibid., January 27, 1945, morning ed., p. 3; ibid., March 8, 1945, morning ed., p. 3. The national savings plan raised 10.2 billion yen in 1939 and an astounding 43.4 billion yen in 1944.

94–36   Takekazu Ogura, ed., *Agricultural Development in Modern Japan,* rev. ed. (Tokyo: Fuji Publishing Co., Ltd., 1967) p. 47; Cohen, *Japan's Economy,* p. 97; Ōhara Shakai Mondai Kenkyūjo, *Rōdōsha jōtai,* pp. 125–28; Gunmaken, *Gunmaken hyakunenshi* [Hundred-year history of Gunma prefecture] (Maebashi: Gunmaken, 1971), 2:575.

95–16   Johnston, *Food Management,* p. 165. See Bisson, *War Economy,* p. 201; *U.S. at War,* p. 509; Cohen, *Japan's Economy,* p. 56; Alan S. Milward, *The German Economy at War* (London: University of London, 1965), p. 47; Richard Polenberg, *War and Society: The United States, 1941–1945* (Philadelphia: J. B. Lippincott Company, 1972), pp. 11–31; International Labor Organization, "Survey," p. 8. For different figures, see Cohen, *Japan's Economy,* pp. 415–16.

96–4   Naimushō Keihokyoku, "Chōyō kōin no dōkō" [Trends among conscripted workers], *Shakai undō no jōkyō* [Condition of the social movement] (Tokyo, 1942), quoted in Ichikawa Ryōichi, "Senjika minshū ishiki kenkyū nōto" [Research notes on people's outlooks in wartime], *Hitotsubashi ronsō* [Hitotsubashi collection] 70, no. 6 (1973): 72. See Naimushō Keihokyoku, "Chian iji no konpon hōshin" [Basic policies for preserving order], quoted in Rekishigaku Kenkyūkai, *Taiheiyō sensōshi*, 5:114; Iwao F. Ayusawa, *A History of Labor in Modern Japan* (Honolulu: East-West Center Press, 1966), p. 228. Ienaga Saburō, *Taiheiyō sensō* [The Pacific war] (Tokyo: Iwanami Shoten, 1968), p. 240, lists 417 strikes for 1943.

96–18   Naimushō Keihokyoku Hoanka, ed., *Tokkō geppō* (December 1943), 4:66.

96–36   Andrew Roth, *Dilemma in Japan* (Boston: Little, Brown, 1945), pp. 227–30; Ichikawa, "Senjika," p. 73; U.S. Strategic Bombing Survey, Morale Division, *The Effects of Strategic Bombing on Japanese Morale* (Washington, D.C., 1947), p. 65; Cohen, *Japan's Economy*, p. 275.

98–1   Kajinishi et al., *Nihon shihonshugi*, 4:1131; Ogura, *Agricultural Development*, p. 52; Cohen, *Japan's Economy*, p. 294; Johnston, *Food Management*, p. 97; Kawazu Katsu, ed., *Sagamiharashishi* [History of Sagamihara] (Yokohama: Kanagawa Shinbunsha, 1971), 4:766; Kōriyamashi, *Kōriyamashishi*, vol. 5, *kindai*, pt. 2 [History of Kōriyama, vol. 5, Modern, pt. 2] (Kōriyama: Kōriyamashi, 1971), p. 453.

98–15   Ogura, *Agricultural Development*, pp. 50–53, 60–61, 197; Kumagai Sonoko, "Senji tōsei to sonraku shakai" [Wartime controls and village society], *Shakaigaku hyōron* [Sociology review] 20, no. 3 (January 1970): 39; Inumaru Giichi and Nakamura Shintarō, *Monogatari Nihon kindaishi* [The story of modern Japanese history] (Tokyo: Shin Nihon Shuppansha, 1971), 3:372; Kajinishi et al., *Nihon shihonshugi*, 4:1090–91; Niigataken, *Niigataken hyakunen no ayumi* [Hundred-year history of Niigataken] (Niigata: Niigataken, 1971), p. 435; Mori Takemaro, "Senjika nōson no kōzō henka" [Changes in the structure of wartime villages], in *Iwanami kōza Nihon rekishi*, vol. 20, *kindai*, pt. 7 [Iwanami colloquium on Japanese history, vol. 20, Modern, pt. 7] Tokyo: Iwanami Shoten, 1976), p. 355; Johnston, *Food Management*, pp. 97–99, 105–107.

99–17   Ogura, *Agricultural Development*, pp. 54–58, 114, 135–141, 200, 278–279; Kajinishi et al., *Nihon shihonshugi*, 4:1101; Johnston, *Food Management*, pp. 119–21; Ronald P. Dore, *Land Reform in Japan* (London: Oxford University Press, 1959), pp. 108–11; Kubota Ai, "Sensō tōji no fujin dantai no ugoki" [Movements of wartime women's groups], in Iida Bunkazai no Kai, *Dainiji taisen no koro* [The World War Two period] (Iida: Minami Shinshū Shinbunsha), p. 47.

99–28   Watanabe Kiyoshi, "Mura no senchū nikki (zoku)" [Wartime village diary (continued)], *Wadatsumi no koe* [Neptune's voice], January 1967, quoted in Ienaga, *Taiheiyō sensō*, p. 153.

100–3　　　Naimushō Keihokyoku Hoanka, *Tokkō geppō* (March 1943), 4:62. See also ibid. (July 1943), p. 73; Ogura, *Agricultural Development*, p. 60.

100–12　　Quoted in Frank Gibney, *Five Gentlemen of Japan* (New York: Farrar, Straus and Young, 1953), p. 167.

101–10　　Kajinishi et al., *Nihon shihonshugi*, 4:1082–85, 1118, 1122–26; Dore, *Land Reform*, p. 114; Ogura, *Agricultural Development*, pp. 56–60, 174–75; Mori, "Senjika nōson," pp. 319, 321, 325.

101–21　　U.S. Strategic Bombing Survey, *Japan's War Economy*, p. 31; Cohen, *Japan's Economy*, pp. 298–304.

102–21　　Joseph Newman, *Goodbye Japan* (New York: L. B. Fischer, 1942), p. 217; Hiroko Nakamoto, as told to Mildred Mastin Pace, *My Japan, 1930–1951* (New York: McGraw-Hill Book Co., 1970), p. 39; *Nippon Times*, February 16, 1943, evening ed., p. 1; ibid., May 13, 1943, morning ed., p. 2; ibid., April 1, 1944, morning ed., p. 3; ibid., March 8, 1945, morning ed., p. 3; ibid., March 19, 1945, morning ed., p. 1; Kurashi no Techōsha, *Sensōchū no kurashi no kiroku*, p. 88; John Toland, *The Rising Sun* (New York: Random House, 1970), pp. 523–24.

102–28　　Jōhōkyoku, *Shūhō* [Weekly report], no. 325 (January 6, 1943), p. 14.

103–9　　　Fujiwara, *Taiheiyō sensō*, p. 198; Minatokuritsu Mita Toshokan, *Senran to Minatoku* [War and Minatoku] (Tokyo: Minatokuritsu Mita Toshokan, 1969), p. 98; Araishishi Henshū Iinkai, *Araishishi* [History of Arai] (Niigataken, Araishi: Araishishi Henshū Iinkai, 1971), 2:575–76; Urabe Takeyo, "Shirami" [Lice], in Izumi no Kai, *Shufu no sensō taikenki* [Record of housewives' war experiences] (Nagoya: Fūbaisha, 1965), p. 145; Okayamashishi Henshū Iinkai, *Okayamashishi, sensai fukkōhen*, p. 69; Tsuji Toyoji, ed., *Aa Toyokawa joshi teishintai* [The Toyokawa women's volunteer corps] (Tokyo: Kōyō Shōbō, 1963), p. 44; Takahashi Ichiharu, "Senjika no kokutetsu" [The national railways in wartime], in Chibaken Sensō Taiken Kiroku Undō Susumeru Kai, *Sensō taiken no kiroku* [Record of war experiences], no. 1 (Chiba: Chibaken Sensō Taiken Kiroku Undō Susumeru Kai, 1972), p. 63; Kurashi no Techōsha, *Sensōchū no kurashi no kiroku*, pp. 96–97.

103–32　　Urabe, "Shirami," p. 146. See Monbushō, *Gakusei hachijūnenshi* [Eighty-year history of the education system] (Tokyo: Ōkurashō Insatsukyoku, 1954), pp. 396, 400; Konishi Shirō, "Senjika no kokumin seikatsu" [People's livelihoods in wartime], in *Taikei Nihonshi sōsho*, vol. 17, *seikatsushi, pt. 3* [Series of works on Japanese history, vol. 17, History of daily life, pt. 3], ed. Morimatsu Yoshiaki et al. (Tokyo: Yamakawa Shuppansha, 1969), p. 444; Takaaki Aikawa, *Unwilling Patriot* (Tokyo: The Jordan Press, 1960), p. 57; Cohen, *Japan's Economy,* pp. 322–23; Tanaka, "Hyakushō nikki," p. 242.

104–3   Irene B. Taeuber, *The Population of Japan* (Princeton: Princeton University Press, 1958), p. 337.

104–18   Cohen, *Japan's Economy,* pp. 326–27; Hideo Totsuka, "Korean Immigration in Prewar Japan," *Annals of the Institute of Social Science,* no. 17 (1976): 92, 98; Rekishigaku Kenkyūkai, *Taiheiyō sensōshi,* 5:130–31; Eugene M. Kulischer, *Europe on the Move: War and Population Changes, 1917–1947* (New York: Columbia University Press, 1948), pp. 262–66; Edward W. Wagner, *The Korean Minority in Japan, 1904–1950* (Vancouver: University of British Columbia Publications Centre, 1951), p. 25; Peter Calvocoressi and Guy Wint, *Total War* (New York: Ballantine Books, 1973), vol. 1, *The War in the West,* pp. 271–91.

106–2   Rekishigaku Kenkyūpkai, *Taiheiyō sensōshi,* 5:130. See Wagner, *Korean Minority,* pp. 25–26, 36–38; Polenberg, *War and Society,* pp. 99, 243.

106–17   Inumaru and Nakamura, *Monogatari Nihon,* p. 371; Rekishigaku Kenkyūkai, *Taiheiyō sensōshi,* 5:129–31; Ōmutashishi Henshū Iinkai, *Ōmutashishi* [History of Ōmuta] (Ōmuta: Ōmutashishi Henshū Iinkai, 1966), 2:852.

107–4   Taeuber, *Population of Japan,* p. 218; Inoue Kiyoshi, *Nihon joseishi* [History of Japanese women], rev. ed. (Tokyo: San'ichi Shobō, 1967), p. 277. See also Taeuber, *Population of Japan,* pp. 117–18, 217, 339.

107–25   U.S. Strategic Bombing Survey, *Japan's War Economy,* p. 31; Kajinishi et al., *Nihon Shihonshugi,* 4:1131; William H. Chafe, *The American Woman: Her Changing Social, Economic, and Political Role, 1920–1970* (New York: Oxford University Press, 1972), p. 135; Gordon Wright, *The Ordeal of Total War, 1939–1945* (New York: Harper & Row, 1968), pp. 51, 59; Cohen, *Japan's Economy,* p. 290; Milward, *German Economy,* p. 47. The jump in the percentage of working female Germans resulted mostly from a drop in the number of men remaining in the nonmilitary work force rather than from a significant rise in the employment of women.

108–15   Fujiwara et al., eds., *Kindai Nihonshi,* p. 470; Ōya Akiko, "Binbō monogatari" [Tale of poverty], in Izumi no Kai, *Shufu no sensō taikenki,* p. 163.

108–26   Koizumi Chikahiko, speech to the Diet, February 1942, quoted in Yoneda Sayoko, *Kindai Nihon joseishi* [History of modern

Japanese women] (Tokyo: Shin Nihon Shuppansha, 1972), 2:66; Tōjō Hideki, quoted ibid. See Inoue, *Nihon joseishi*, p. 294.

109-1   Sakaguchi Takenosuke, speech of September 1942, quoted in Taisei Yokusankai, *Kokumin sōjōkaishi—daisankai chūō kyōryoku kaigi sōjōkai kaigiroku (zen)* [Record of national general meeting—Record of Discussions at the third general meeting of the central cooperation conference (complete)] (Tokyo: Taisei Yokusankai, 1942), p. 97.

109-14   Minoguchi Tokijirō, "Joshi dōinron" [On mobilizing women], *Kaizō* [Reconstruction] (March 1943): 40, 42.

109-33   *Nippon Times,* October 28, 1943, morning ed., p. 1. See Cohen, *Japan's Economy,* p. 315; Yoneda, *Kindai Nihon joseishi,* 2:64–68.

110-14   Nihon Seinenkan, *Dai Nihon Seishōnendanshi* [History of the greater Japan youth association] (Tokyo: Nihon Seinenkan, 1970), pp. 780–87; Cohen, *Japan's Economy,* pp. 315, 317, 321; Fujiwara et al., eds., *Kindai Nihonshi,* p. 471; Rōdōshō *Rōdō gyōseishi* [History of labor administration], vol. 1 quoted in Rekishigaku Kenkyūkai, *Taiheiyō sensōshi,* 5:121; U.S. Strategic Bombing Survey, *Japan's War Economy,* p. 31.

110-30   *Teikoku kokuryoku no genjō* [Current condition of the empire's strength], August 11, 1944, in Hara Shobō Henshūbu, *Haisen no kiroku—sanbō honbu shozō* [Record of defeat—General staff documents] (Tokyo: Hara Shobō, 1967), p. 132.

111-14   Nakamoto, *My Japan,* pp. 48–51.

111-36   Urabe, "Shirami," pp. 144–46; Kurashi no Techōsha, *Sensōchū no kurashi no kiroku,* p. 139.

112-6   Tsuji, ed., *Aa Toyokawa,* pp. 117–19.

112-13   Tomita Kimiko, "Kokubōshoku no seishun" [Youth in khaki], in Izumi no Kai, *Shufu no sensō taikenki,* p. 129.

112-32   Cohen, *Japan's Economy,* p. 292.

113-2   Taeuber, *Population of Japan,* p. 337.

CHAPTER 7

114-5   Fujiwara Akira, Imai Seiichi, and Ōe Shinobu, eds., *Kindai Nihonshi no kisō chishiki* [Basic knowledge about modern Japanese history] (Tokyo: Yūhikaku, 1972), p. 458.

116–8   See Akimoto Ritsuo, *Sensō to minshū: Taiheiyō sensōka no toshi seikatsu* [War and the people: City life during the Pacific war] (Tokyo: Gakuyō Shobō, 1974), pp. 106–07; Gwen Terasaki, *Bridge to the Sun* (Chapel Hill: University of North Carolina Press, 1957), p. 108; Takahashi Aiko, "Sensō kara no nikki" [Diary from the war], in Shōwa Sensō Bungaku Zenshū Henshū Iinkai, *Shōwa sensō bungaku zenshū,* vol. 14, *shimin no nikki* [Complete wartime literary works of the Shōwa Era, vol. 14, City residents' diaries] (Tokyo: Shūeisha, 1965), pp. 332–33; Ōsaka Shiyakusho, *Ōsaka sensai fukkōshi* [History of Osaka's recovery from war damage] (Osaka: Ōsaka Shiyakusho, 1958), p. 44.

116–37   Bunkyōku, *Bunkyōkushi* [History of Bunkyōku] (Tokyo: Bunkyōku, 1969), 4:766–67; Akimoto, *Sensō to minshu,* p. 103; Jerome B. Cohen, *Japan's Economy in War and Reconstruction* (Minneapolis: University of Minnesota Press, 1949), pp. 374–75; Bruce F. Johnston, with Mosaburo Hosoda and Yoshio Kusumi, *Japanese Food Management in World War II* (Stanford: Stanford University Press, 1953), pp. 168–70, 196–98; Suzuki Yoshiko, "Kiga no omoi" [Thoughts about hunger], in Izumi no Kai, *Shufu no sensō taikenki* [Record of housewives' war experiences] (Nagoya: Fūbaisha, 1965), pp. 154–55; Ōhara Shakai Mondai Kenkyūjo, *Taiheiyō sensōka no rōdōsha jōtai* [Workers' conditions during the Pacific war] (Tokyo: Tōyō Keizai Shinpōsha, 1964), pp. 134–35; Terasaki, *Bridge,* p. 107.

117–8   Takahashi, "Sensō kara no nikki," pp. 333–34.

117–24   Kurashi no Techōsha, *Tokushū* Kurashi no techō, no. 96, *sensōchū no kurashi no kiroku* [Special issue of *Notebook on Daily Living,* no. 96, Record of daily living during the war] (Tokyo: Kurashi no Techōsha, 1969), p. 38; Akimoto, *Sensō to minshū,* pp. 100–102; *Nippon Times,* March 4, 1945, morning ed., p. 3; Tōkyō Kūshū o Kirokusuru Kai, *Tōkyō daikūshū—sensaishi* [The great Tokyo air raids—Record of war damage] (Tokyo: Tōkyō Kūshū o Kirokusuru Kai, 1974), 5:83.

118–6   Masuo Kato, *The Lost War: A Japanese Reporter's Inside Story* (New York: Alfred A. Knopf, 1946), p. 93; *Japan Times & Advertiser,* December 17, 1941, p. 5; ibid., January 9, 1942, morning ed., p. 2; ibid., June 30, 1942, evening ed., p. 2; Tōkyō Kūshū o Kirokusuru Kai, *Tōkyō daikūshū,* 5:122; Terasaki, *Bridge,* p. 111; Konishi Shirō, "Senjika no kokumin seikatsu" [People's livelihoods in wartime], in *Taikei Nihonshi sōsho,* vol. 17, *seikatsushi,* pt. 3 [Series of works on Japanese history, vol. 17, History of daily life, pt. 3], ed. Morimatsu Yoshiaki et al. (Tokyo: Yamakawa Shuppansha, 1969), p. 443; Ienaga Saburō, *Taiheiyō sensō* [The Pacific war]

(Tokyo: Iwanami Shoten, 1968), p. 224; Akimoto, *Sensō to minshū,* p. 111; Kawakami Hajime, *Jijoden* [Autobiography] (Tokyo: Iwanami Shoten, 1952), 5:193; Kurashi no Techōsha, *Sensōchū no kurashi no kiroku,* p. 39.

118–27   Konishi, "Senjika," p. 445; Carl Randau and Leane Zugsmith, *The Setting Sun of Japan* (New York: Random House, 1942), p. 20; *Nippon Times,* March 8, 1944, morning ed., p. 1; Robert Guillain, *Le peuple japonais et la guerre: choses vues, 1939–1946* (Paris: R. Julliard, 1947), pp. 137–39; Mainichi Newspapers, *Fifty Years of Light and Dark: The Hirohito Era,* 2nd ed. (Tokyo: Mainichi Newspapers, 1976), p. 123; Sutō Ryōsaku, *Tonarigumichō no shuki* [A neighborhood captain's notes] (Tokyo: privately printed, 1970), pp. 1–2, 21–22; *Nippon Times,* January 24, 1945, morning ed., p. 3.

120–8   Konishi, "Senjika," p. 442; Akimoto, *Sensō to minshū,* pp. 103–04; Cohen, *Japan's Economy,* p. 403; Ōhara Shakai Mondai Kenkyūjo, *Rōdōsha jōtai,* p. 155.

120–22   Cohen, *Japan's Economy,* pp. 412–14; *Japan Times & Advertiser,* January 21, 1942, morning ed., p. 2; Kurashi no Techōsha, *Sensōchū no kurashi no kiroku,* pp. 24–25; Sutō, *Tonarigumichō no shuki,* pp. 2, 24–25.

120–36   Ueda Kōchirō, speech of September 1942, quoted in Taisei Yokusankai, *Kokumin sōjōkaishi—daisankai chūō kyōryoku kaigi sōjōkai kaigiroku (zen)* [Record of national general meeting— Record of discussions at the third general meeting of the central co-operation conference (complete)] (Tokyo: Taisei Yokusankai, 1942), p. 331; "Senji iseikatsu kansoka jisshi yōkō" [Outline for implementing simplified wartime clothing habits], June 1943, quoted in Konishi, "Senjika," p. 442; Rekishigaku Kenkyūkai, *Taiheiyō sensōshi* [History of the Pacific war] (Tokyo: Aoki Shoten, 1973), 5:101.

121–25   "Senchū sengo tonarigumi nikki" [Wartime and postwar neighborhood association diary], in Hirosakishishi Hensan Iinkai, *Hirosakishishi, Meiji Taishō Shōwahen* [History of Hirosaki, volume on the Meiji, Taishō, and Shōwa eras] (Hirosaki: Hirosakishishi Hensan Iinkai, 1964), pp. 680–81; Sutō, *Tonarigumichō no shuki,* pp. 20–21; Ōhara Shakai Mondai Kenkyūjo, *Rōdōsha jōtai,* p. 156; *Fortune,* April 1944, p. 148; Tōkyō Kūshū o Kirokusuru Kai, *Tōkyō daikūshū,* 5:75.

122–5   Cohen, *Japan's Economy,* pp. 408–09; Konishi, "Senjika," p. 443; Kurashi no Techōsha, *Sensōchū no kurashi no kiroku,* pp. 180, 186.

122–28   Akimoto, *Sensō to minshū,* pp. 102–03; Joseph Newman, *Goodbye Japan* (New York: L. B. Fischer, 1942), p. 203; Yoko

Matsuoka, *Daughter of the Pacific* (New York: Harper and Brothers, 1952), p. 170; *Fortune*, April 1944, pp. 147–48; Tawara Motoaki, *Shiba kagu no hyakunenshi* [Hundred-year history of the Shiba furniture business] (Tokyo, 1966), quoted in Minatokuritsu Mita Toshokan, *Senran to Minatoku* [War and Minatoku] (Tokyo: Minatokuritsu Mita Toshokan, 1969), p. 97; Okayamashishi Henshū Iinkai, *Okayamashishi, sensai fukkōhen* [History of Okayama, volume on recovery from war damage] (Okayama: Okayama Shiyakusho, 1960), p. 64; Ōya Akiko, "Binbō monogatari" [Tale of poverty], in *Izumi no Kai, Shufu no sensō taikenki*, p. 165; *Nippon Times*, May 8, 1945, morning ed., p. 3; Kurashi no Techōsha, *Sensō chū no kurashi no kiroku*, pp. 76–77; Sutō, *Tonarigumichō no shuki*, p. 8.

123–25   Tōkyō Kūshū o Kirokusuru Kai, *Tōkyō daikūshū*, 5:47, 61–68, 80–81, 108; Sutō, *Tonarigumichō no shuki*, pp. 2–7, 12–24; Kurashi no Techōsha, *Sensōchū no kurashi no kiroku*, pp. 19, 181–83; *Nippon Times*, November 1, 1944, morning ed., p. 2; ibid., January 28, 1945, morning ed., p. 1; ibid., February 4, 1945, morning ed., p. 3; ibid., April 13, 1945, morning ed., p. 3; Akimoto, *Sensō to minshū*, p. 187; "Senchū sengo tonarigumi nikki," pp. 676–77.

124–26   Kiyosawa Kiyoshi, *Ankoku nikki* [Diary of darkness] (Tokyo: Tōyō Keizai Shinpōsha, 1954), quoted in Akimoto, *Sensō to minshū*, p. 178; Otto D. Tolischus, *Tokyo Record* (New York: Reynal & Hitchcock, 1943), p. 163; Nakajima Kenzō, *Shōwa jidai* [The Shōwa period] (Tokyo: Iwanami Shoten, 1957), p. 176; Rekishigaku Kenkyūkai, *Taiheiyō sensōshi*, 5:109; Isoko Hatano and Ichiro Hatano, *Mother and Son: The Wartime Correspondence of Isoko and Ichiro Hatano* (Boston: Houghton Mifflin, 1962), p. 33.

125–16   Ishimura report, quoted in Okayamashishi Henshū Iinkai, *Okayamashishi, sensai fukkōhen*, pp. 57–60; Akimoto, *Sensō to minshū*, pp. 179–181.

125–30   Johnston, *Food Management*, pp. 161–63; Rekishigaku Kenkyūkai, *Taiheiyō sensōshi*, 5:109–10; Sutō, *Tonarigumichō no shuki*, pp. 4–6.

126–8   Ōhara Shakai Mondai Kenkyūjo, *Rōdōsha jōtai*, pp. 127, 148; Cohen, *Japan's Economy*, p. 385; Kōbeshi, *Kōbeshishi*, vol. 3, pt. 2, *shakai bunkahen* [History of Kobe, vol. 3 pt. 2, Society and culture] (Kobe: Kōbeshi, 1965), p. 18.

126–33   Fred C. Iklé, *The Social Impact of Bomb Destruction* (Norman: University of Oklahoma Press, 1958), pp. 143, 149; Akimoto, *sensō to minshū*, pp. 181–84; Katō Hidetoshi et al., *Meiji Taishō Shōwa sesōshi* [History of social conditions in the Meiji, Taishō, and

Shōwa eras] (Tokyo: Shakai Shisōsha, 1967), p. 272; Kurashi no Techōsha, *Sensōchū no kurashi no kiroku*, p. 108; Okayamashishi Henshū Iinkai, *Okayamashishi, sensai fukkōhen*, p. 62; Hashikawa Bunzō, ed., *Nihon no hyakunen*, vol. 3, *hateshinaki sensen* [Japan's hundred years, vol. 3, The endless war front] (Tokyo: Chikuma Shobō, 1962), pp. 226–28; Andrew Roth, *Dilemma in Japan* (Boston: Little, Brown, 1945), pp. 158, 226; *Nippon Times*, July 4, 1945, morning ed., p. 3.

127–14   Terasaki, *Bridge*, p. 144; Tanaka Ningo, "Hyakushō nikki" [Farmer's diary], in Kurashi no Techōsha, *Sensōchū no kurashi no kiroku*, p. 220.

128–9   Cohen, *Japan's Economy*, pp. 380–82; Johnston, *Food Management*, pp. 151–53, 157; Kato, *Lost War*, p. 174; Ishii Tominosuke, "Taiheiyō sensōka no 'kessen' shokuseikatsu" [Eating habits during the "decisive battle" of the Pacific war], *Kanagawakenshi kenkyū* [Studies in the history of Kanagawa prefecture], no. 23 (February 1974): 34–35.

128–34   Yoshizawa Hisako, "Shūsen made" [To the end of the war], in Shōwa Sensō Bungaku Zenshū Henshū Iinkai, *Shimin no nikki*, p. 373; Tōkyō Kūshū o Kirokusuru Kai, *Tōkyō daikūshū*, 5:108–18; Sutō, *Tonarigumichō no shuki*, pp. 6, 15, 19.

129–14   *Nippon Times*, April 3, 1945, morning ed., p. 3; ibid., June 30, 1945, morning ed., p. 3; ibid., July 3, 1945, morning ed., p. 3; Tōkyō Kūshū o Kirokusuru Kai, *Tōkyō daikūshū*, 5:101; Sutō, *Tonarigumichō no shuki*, pp. 15, 17.

130–2   *Nippon Times*, June 30, 1945, morning ed., p. 3; ibid., July 5, 1945, morning ed., p. 1; ibid., July 6, 1945, morning ed., p. 3; ibid., July 31, 1945, morning ed., p. 3; Kurashi no Techōsha, *Sensōchū no kurashi no kiroku*, pp. 108–11; Kato, *Lost War*, p. 174; Sutō, *Tonarigumichō no shuki*, pp. 17–18.

131–1   Johnston, *Food Management*, pp. 129–30; Ōhara Shakai Mondai Kenkyūjo, *Rōdōsha jōtai*, pp. 148–49; Cohen, *Japan's Economy*, p. 386; Konishi, "Senjika," p. 449.

131–21   *Teikoku kokuryoku no genjō* [Current condition of the empire's strength], August 11, 1944, in Hara Shobō Henshūbu, *Haisen no kiroku—sanbō honbu shozō* [Record of defeat—General staff documents] (Tokyo: Hara Shobō, 1967), p. 132.

132–12   Ōhara Shakai Mondai Kenkyūjo, ed., *Rōdōsha jōtai*, pp. 140–41, 148; Kōbeshi, *Kōbeshishi*, vol. 3, pt. 2, *shakai bunkahen*, p. 2; Cohen, *Japan's Economy*, p. 354.

132–22   Cohen, *Japan's Economy*, pp. 461–64; Inoue Kiyoshi, *Gendai Nihon joseishi* [History of modern Japanese women] (Tokyo: San'ichi Shobō, 1962), p. 16. Sutō, *Tonarigumichō no shuki*, p. 39, notes that "directly after the war it was very difficult to maintain distributions at the same level as during the war."

CHAPTER 8

134–2   Quoted in Kurashi no Techōsha, *Tokushū* Kurashi no techō, no. 96, *sensōchū no kurashi no kiroku* [Special issue of *Notebook on Daily Living*, no. 96, Record of daily living during the war] (Tokyo: Kurashi no Techōsha, 1969), p. 137.

135–1   Irene B. Taeuber, *The Population of Japan* (Princeton: Princeton University Press, 1958), pp. 223, 234, 334; Sōrifu Tōkeikyoku, *Nihon tōkei nenkan, tekiyōhan* [Japan statistical yearbook, summary] (Tokyo, 1950), p. 21.

135–17   Nihon Seinenkan, *Dai Nihon Seishōnendanshi* [History of the Greater Japan Youth Association] (Tokyo: Nihon Seinenkan, 1970), p. 314. See Richard Polenberg, *War and Society: The United States, 1941–1945* (Philadelphia: J. B. Lippincott Company, 1972), pp. 146–53.

135–37   Joseph Newman, *Goodbye Japan* (New York: L. B. Fischer, 1942), pp. 237–39; Carl Randau and Leane Zugsmith, *The Setting Sun of Japan* (New York: Random House, 1942), pp. 66–68.

136–19   *Japan Times & Advertiser,* June 12, 1942, morning ed., p. 3; *Japan Times Advertiser,* October 26, 1942, morning ed., p. 3; *Nippon Times,* April 14, 1943, evening ed., p. 2; ibid., May 1, 1943, evening ed., p. 2.

137–3   Taeuber, *Population of Japan,* pp. 223, 232, 354–55; Setsuko Hani, *The Japanese Family System, As Seen from the Standpoint of Japanese Women* (Tokyo: Japan Institute of Pacific Studies, 1948), p. 39; Fukuiken, *Taishō Shōwa Fukuikenshi* [History of Fukui prefecture in the Taishō and Shōwa periods] (Fukui: Fukuiken, 1956), 1:34.

137–11   Tōyama Shigeki, Imai Seiichi, and Fujiwara Akira, *Shōwashi* [History of the Shōwa era], rev. ed. (Tokyo: Iwanami Shoten, 1959), pp. 224, 226.

137–26   Eugene M. Kulischer, *Europe on the Move: War and Population Changes, 1917–1947* (New York: Columbia University Press, 1948), pp. 274–77; Taeuber, *Population of Japan,* pp. 340, 356, 358.

137–31   Sōrifu Tōkeikyoku, *Nihon tōkei nenkan, tekiyōhan,* p. 21.

137–36   Arthur Marwick, *The Deluge: British Society and the First World War* (New York: W. W. Norton & Company, Inc., 1970), pp. 105–13; Polenberg, *War and Society*, pp. 138–48.

138–15   Ōmutashishi Henshū Iinkai, *Ōmutashishi* [History of Ōmuta] Ōmuta: Ōmutashishi Henshū Iinkai, 1968), 3:666–73.

138–27   Hashikawa Bunzō, Kano Masanao, and Hiraoka Toshio, ed., *Kindai Nihon shisōshi no kisō chishiki* [Basic knowledge about the history of modern Japanese thought] (Tokyo: Yūhikaku, 1971), p. 459; Fujiwara Akira, Imai Seiichi, and Ōe Shinobu, eds., *Kindai Nihonshi no kisō chishiki* [Basic knowledge about modern Japanese history] (Tokyo: Yūhikaku, 1972), p. 471; Makoto Aso and Ikuo Amano, *Education and Japan's Modernization* (Tokyo: Ministry of Foreign Affairs, 1972), p. 60; *Nippon Times*, January 16, 1943, evening ed., p. 2.

139–10   George A. De Vos, *Socialization for Achievement: Essays on the Cultural Psychology of the Japanese* (Berkeley and Los Angeles: University of California Press, 1973), pp. 337, 343; Hashikawa et al., eds., *Kindai Nihon shisōshi*, p. 459; Hokkaidō Keisatsu Honbu, *Hokkaidō keisatsushi* [History of the Hokkaido police] (Sapporo: Hokkaidō Keisatsu Honbu, 1968), 2:329. See also ibid., pp. 330–31; Kōbeshi, *Kōbeshishi*, vol. 3, pt. 2, *shakai bunkahen* [History of Kobe, vol. 3, pt. 2, Society and culture] (Kobe: Kōbeshi, 1965), p. 190; Mori Teru, *Kaze wa sugiyuku—watakushi no senchū nōto* [The passing wind—My wartime notes] (Tokyo: Rinjinsha, 1967), p. 136; Keimu Kyōkai Shihō Hogo Jigyō Kenkyūjo, *Senjika no shōnen hanzai to sono bōshi* [Juvenile crime in wartime and its prevention] (Tokyo: Daidō Shobō, 1942), p. 1; Polenberg, *War and Society*, pp. 149–50; T. A. Larson, *Wyoming's War Years, 1941–1945* (Laramie: The University of Wyoming, 1954), pp. 147–64.

139–30   Foreign Affairs Association of Japan, *The Japan Year Book, 1946–48* (Tokyo: Foreign Affairs Association of Japan, 1948), p. 468; Robert K. Hall, *Education for a New Japan* (New Haven: Yale University Press, 1949), p. 2; *Japan Times & Advertiser*, September 12, 1942, morning ed., p. 3; Kurashi no Techōsha, *Sensōchū no kurashi no kiroku*, pp. 30–31.

140–4   Andō Masako, "Kinrō dōin no akekure" [Labor mobilization day and night], in Kusa no Mi Kai Daishichi Gurūpu, *Sensō to watakushi* [The war and I] (Tokyo: Kusa no Mi Kai, 1963), p. 17. See Hashikawa et al., eds, *Kindai Nihon shisōshi*, p. 459; Aso and Amano, *Education*, p. 60; Fujiwara et al., eds., *Kindai Nihonshi*, p. 471.

141–4   Tōdai Jūhachi Shikai, *Gakuto shutsujin no kiroku* [Record of student mobilization] (Tokyo: Chūō Kōronsha, 1968), pp.

i–ii; Hashikawa et al., eds., *Kindai Nihon shisōshi*, p. 456; Takahashi Aiko, "Sensō kara no nikki" [Diary from the war], in Shōwa Sensō Bungaku Zenshū Henshū Iinkai, *Shōwa sensō bungaku zenshū*, vol. 14, *shimin no nikki* [Complete wartime literary works of the Shōwa era, vol. 14, City residents' diaries] (Tokyo: Shūeisha, 1965), p. 335; Tōyama et al., *Shōwashi*, p. 222; T. J. Pempel, "The Politics of Enrollment Expansion in Japanese Universities," *Journal of Asian Studies* 33, no. 1 (November 1973): 67–68.

141–26   Dejima Motoko, "Gakuto dōin" [Student mobilization], in *Hikisakarete—haha no sensō taiken* [Separated—Mothers' war experiences], ed. Tsurumi Kazuko and Makise Kikue (Tokyo: Chikuma Shobō, 1959), pp. 96, 99; Kurashi no Techōsha, *Sensōchū no kurashi no kiroku*, pp. 94–95; Takaaki Aikawa, *Unwilling Patriot* (Tokyo: The Jordan Press, 1960), p. 60. See Saitō Isamu, "Shōgatsu o mukaete" [Greeting the new year], in Gakuto Kinrō Dōin no Kiroku Henshūkai, *Kurenai no chi wa moyuru* [Crimson blood on fire] (Tokyo: Yomiuri Shinbunsha, 1971), p. 208; Fukuda Bunji, *Waga machi no senki—chōchō memo* [Our town's war records—Mayor's memo] (Gunmaken, Ojimamachi: privately printed, 1970), pp. 29–30.

142–6   Hoshi Imae, "Sensō makki no shōgakkō" [Grade school at the end of the war], in Iida Bunkazai no Kai, *Dainiji taisen no koro* [The World War Two period] (Iida: Minami Shinshū Shinbunsha, 1972), p. 25; Iwateken Ichinoseki Kokumin Kyōiku Kenkyūkai, *Kyōshi no sensō taiken no kiroku* [Record of teachers' war experiences] (Tokyo: Rōdō Junpōsha, 1969), p. 121.

142–24   *Tatakau shōkokumin* [Fighting young citizens], shown at National Film Center, Kyōbashi, Tokyo, March 26, 1973. See Tōkyō Kokuritsu Kindai Bijutsukan Fuirumu Sentā, *FC fuirumu sentā* [FC Film Center], no. 13 (March 8, 1973): 20; Kurashi no Techōsha, *Sensōchū no kurashi no kiroku*, p. 26; Hall, *New Japan*, p. 8; Nagai Kenji, *Aa kokumin gakkō* [National schools] (Tokyo: Asahi Shinbunsha, 1972), pp. 13–14; *Nippon Times*, June 29, 1945, morning ed., p. 3; Fujiwara et al., eds., *Kindai Nihonshi*, p. 445; Aso and Amano, *Education*, p. 60.

143–20   Jichi Daigakkō, *Sengo jichishi*, vol. 1, *tonarigumi oyobi chōnaikai burakukaitō no haishi* [History of postwar self-rule, vol. 1, The abolition of neighborhood associations and community councils] (Tokyo: Jichi Daigakkō, 1960), pp. 16–17; *Nippon Times*, April 14, 1943, evening ed., p. 2.

143–33   Takahashi, "Sensō kara no nikki," p. 337; Tōkyō Kūshū o Kirokusuru Kai, *Tōkyō daikūshū—sensaishi* [The great Tokyo air raids—Record of war damage] (Tokyo: Tōkyō Kūshū o Kirokusuru Kai, 1974), 5:41–46.

144–10   Ōhara Shakai Mondai Kenkyūjo, *Taiheiyō sensōka no rōdōsha jōtai* [Workers' conditions during the Pacific war] (Tokyo: Tōyō Keizai Shinpōsha, 1964), p. 164; Foreign Affairs Association of Japan, *The Japan Year Book, 1946–48,* p. 508. See Ienaga Saburō, *Taiheiyō sensō* [The Pacific war] (Tokyo: Iwanami Shoten, 1968), pp. 221–22.

144–13   Nihon Igaku Hyakunenshi Kankōkai, *Nihon igaku hyakunenshi* [Hundred-year history of Japanese medicine] (Tokyo: Rinshō Igakusha, 1957), p. 226. Japan's TB death rate in 1899 was 152 per 100,000 and in 1940 was 210. In the same period the rate fell by two-thirds in France, Great Britain, and Italy, and by three-quarters in Germany and the U.S.

144–18   F. Ohtani, ed., *One Hundred Years of Health Progress in Japan* (Tokyo: International Medical Foundation of Japan, 1971), pp. 66–67. See Bruce F. Johnston, with Mosaburo Hosoda and Yoshio Kusumi, *Japanese Food Management in World War II* (Stanford: Stanford University Press, 1953), pp. 163–64.

145–4   Foreign Affairs Association of Japan, *The Japan Year Book, 1946–48,* p. 507; Johnston, *Food Management,* p. 164; Fukuiken, *Taishō Shōwa Fukuikenshi,* 1:40; Kurashi no Techōsha, *Sensōchū no kurashi no kiroku,* pp. 83, 117.

145–17   Foreign Affairs Association of Japan, *The Japan Year Book, 1946–48,* p. 507; Amagasakishi, *Amagasakishishi* [History of Amagasaki] (Amagasaki: Amagasakishi, 1970), 3:668; Maejima Tadao, "Senchū sengo no iryō" [Medicine during and after the war], in Iida Bunkazai no Kai, *Dainiji taisen no koro,* p. 35.

145–32   Foreign Affairs Association of Japan *The Japan Year Book, 1946–48,* p. 508; Newman, *Goodbye Japan,* pp. 212–13.

146–14   Sōrifu Tōkeikyoku, *Nihon tōkei nenkan, tekiyōhan,* pp. 23, 162; Sōrifu Tōkeikyoku, *Nihon tōkei nenkan* [Japan statistical yearbook] (Tokyo, 1949), 1:974–75; ibid. (1951), 3:401.

147–8   Maejima, "Senchū," p. 35; Frederick T. Merrill, *Japan and the Opium Menace* (New York: Institute of Pacific Relations and Foreign Policy Association, 1942), p. 74; Randau and Zugsmith, *Setting Sun,* pp. 66–68; Kagawa Tetsuo, *Jōketsu kenmin—sei no kyōiku* [Pure-blooded public health—Sex education] (Tokyo: Hokkō Shobō, 1943), esp. pp. 146–56.

147–25   Mori, *Kaze wa sugiyuku,* pp. 188–97; Bunkyōku, *Bunkyōkushi* [History of Bunkyōku] (Tokyo: Bunkyōku, 1969), 4:782–83.

148–31   *Japan Times & Advertiser,* December 16, 1941, p. 3; ibid., January 25, 1942, morning ed., p. 4; ibid., March 20, 1942, morning ed., p. 2; ibid., October 1, 1942, morning ed., p. 4; Robert Guillain, *Le peuple japonais et la guerre: choses vues, 1939–1946* (Paris: R. Julliard, 1947), p. 58.

149–7   Akimoto Ritsuo, *Sensō to minshū: Taiheiyō sensōka no toshi seikatsu* [War and the people: City life during the Pacific war] (Tokyo: Gakuyō Shobō, 1974), p. 164; David W. Plath, *The After Hours* (Berkeley and Los Angeles: University of California Press, 1964), pp. 136–38; *Fortune,* April 1944, p. 153; *Nippon Times,* October 6, 1943, p. 3.

149–25   Katō Hidetoshi et al., *Meiji Taishō Shōwa sesōshi* [History of social conditions in the Meiji, Taishō, and Shōwa eras] (Tokyo: Shakai Shisōsha, 1967), pp. 261–63, 270; John Morris, *Traveler from Tokyo* (New York: Sheridan House, 1944), p. 208; Masuo Kato, *The Lost War: A Japanese Reporter's Inside Story* (New York: Alfred A. Knopf, 1946), pp. 190–91; Rekishigaku Kenkyūkai, *Taiheiyō sensōshi* [History of the Pacific war] (Tokyo: Aoki Shoten, 1973), 5:135–36.

149–37   Foreign Affairs Association of Japan, *The Japan Year Book, 1946–48,* pp. 559–60; *Japan Times & Advertiser,* March 19, 1942, morning ed., p. 4; *Nippon Times,* October 3, 1943, morning ed., p. 2; ibid., March 8, 1944, morning ed., p. 3; ibid., January 24, 1945, morning ed., p. 3; ibid., February 25, 1945, morning ed., p. 3.

150–12   Okayamashishi Henshū Iinkai, *Okayamashishi, sensai fukkōhen* [History of Okayama, volume on recovery from war damage] (Okayama: Okayama Shiyakusho, 1960), p. 63; Hashikawa Bunzō, ed., *Nihon no hyakunen,* vol. 3, *hateshinaki sensen* [Japan's hundred years, vol. 3, The endless war front] (Tokyo: Chikuma Shobō, 1962), p. 229; Kōbe Kūshū o Kirokusuru Kai, *Kōbe daikūshū* [The great Kobe air raids] (Kobe: Nojigiku Bunko, 1972), pp. 138–44; Toshikazu Kase, *Journey to the Missouri,* ed. David N. Rowe (New Haven: Yale University Press, 1950), p. 67.

150–27   Foreign Affairs Association of Japan, *The Japan Year Book, 1946–48,* pp. 565, 572; *Japan Times Advertiser,* November 20, 1942, morning ed., p. 3; Hiroko Nakamoto, as told to Mildred Mastin Pace, *My Japan, 1930–1951* (New York: McGraw-Hill Book Co., 1970), p. 47; *Nippon Times,* April 13, 1945, morning ed., p. 3; ibid., May 8, 1945, morning ed., p. 3.

150–38   Kase, *Journey,* p. 67; Fukuda, *Waga machi no senki,* p. 4; Gullain, *Le peuple japonais,* p. 141.

151–25   "Kessen hijō sochi yōkō" [Outline of decisive war emergency measures], February 25, 1944, quoted in Rekishigaku

Kenkyūkai, *Taiheiyō sensōshi,* 5:135; Akimoto, *Sensō to minshū,* p. 187; Saburō Hayashi and Alvin D. Coox, *Kōgun: The Japanese Army in the Pacific War* (Quantico, Va.: Marine Corps Association, 1959), p. 118; *Nippon Times,* February 28, 1944, morning ed., p. 1; ibid., March 1, 1944, morning ed., p. 2; ibid., August 10, 1944, morning ed., p. 3; Okayamashishi Henshū Iinkai, *Okayamashishi, sensai fukkōhen,* pp. 65–66.

151–35   Tōkyō Kūshū o Kirokusuru Kai, *Tōkyō dai-kūshū,* 5:61; Tanaka Ningo, "Hyakushō nikki" [Farmer's diary], in Kurashi no Techōsha, *Sensōchū no kurashi no kiroku,* p. 220.

153–4   Takami Jun, *Haisen nikki* [Diary of defeat] (Tokyo: Bungei Shunjū Shinsha, 1959), quoted in Akimoto, *Sensō to minshū,* p. 186; Nakanoku, *Nakanokushi,* vol. 1, *Shōwahen,* [History of Nakanoku, vol. 1, Shōwa era] (Tokyo: Nakanoku, 1971), p. 521.

153–23   Kobayashi Keizaburō, ed., *Kikigaki: senka ni ikita fubotachi* [Transcript: Parents who lived during the war flames] (Tokyo: Taihei Shuppansha, 1972), p. 245.

CHAPTER 9

154–10   Torinoumi Shigeko, "Shōidan o abite" [In the midst of incendiary bombs], in Kusa no Mi Kai Daishichi Gurūpu, *Sensō to watakushi* [The War and I] (Tokyo: Kusa no Mi Kai, 1963), p. 36; U.S. Strategic Bombing Survey, Morale Division, *The Effects of Strategic Bombing on Japanese Morale* (Washington, D.C., 1947), p. 87.

155–15   Kawasakishi, *Kawasakishishi* [History of Kawasaki] (Kawasaki: Kawasakishi, 1968), 1:526–27. See Taikakai, *Naimushōshi* [History of the Home Ministry] (Tokyo: Chihō Zaimu Kyōkai, 1971), 3:490–92; Saitō Hideo, "Kūshū to minshū" [Air raids and the people], *Rekishi hyōron* [History review], no. 268 (October 1972): 1–3; Akimoto Ritsuo, *Sensō to minshū: Taiheiyō sensōka no toshi seikatsu* [War and the people: City life during the Pacific war] (Tokyo: Gakuyō Shobō, 1974), pp. 201–04.

155–22   Quoted in Taikakai, *Naimushōshi,* 3:493. See Carroll V. Glines, *Doolittle's Tokyo Raiders* (Princeton: D. Van Nostrand Company, Inc., 1964); John Morris, *Traveler from Tokyo* (New York: Sheridan House, 1944), pp. 196–99.

157–2   Ōya Akiko, "Binbō monogatari" [Tale of poverty], in Izumi no Kai, *Shufu no sensō taikenki* [Record of housewives' war experiences] (Nagoya: Fūbaisha, 1965), p. 163. See Taikakai, *Naimushōshi,* 3:493; Masuo Kato, *The Lost War: A Japanese Reporter's Inside Story* (New York: Alfred A. Knopf, 1946), pp. 202–03.

157–16   Akimoto, *Sensō to minshū*, p. 210; "Senchū sengo tonarigumi nikki" [Wartime and postwar neighborhood association diary], in Hirosakishishi Hensan Iinkai, *Hirosakishishi, Meiji Taishō Shōwahen* [History of Hirosaki, volume on the Meiji, Taishō, and Shōwa eras] (Hirosaki: Hirosakishishi Hensan Iinkai, 1964), pp. 679–80; Gwen Terasaki, *Bridge to the Sun* (Chapel Hill: University of North Carolina Press, 1957), p. 126; *Nippon Times*, December 30, 1944, morning ed., p. 2; Saotome Katsumoto, *Tokyō daikūshū* [The great Tokyo air raids] (Tokyo: Iwanami Shoten, 1971), p. 3; Lars Tillitse, "When Bombs Rained on Us in Tokyo," *Saturday Evening Post*, January 12, 1946, p. 34; Kato, *Lost War*, p. 203.

157–36   Saitō, "Kūshū to minshū," p. 3; *Asahi nenkan* [Asahi yearbook] (Tokyo, 1942), quoted ibid., p. 2; *Funabashi Seibu Fujinkai kaihō*, no. 10, *tokushū—kurushikatta sensō no omoide* [Memoirs of the Funabashi Seibu Fujinkai, no. 10, special issue—Memories of the difficult war] (March 1967): 26; Yabashi Yasuko, "Musume ni kataru" [Telling my daughter], in Izumi no Kai, *Shufu no sensō taikenki*, p. 134.

159–4   Taikakai, *Naimushōshi*, 3:511; *Asahi shinbun*, January 8, 1944, quoted in Akimoto, *Senō to minshū*, p. 225; Fujiwara Akira, *Kokumin no rekishi*, vol. 23, *Taiheiyō sensō* [National history, vol. 23, The Pacific War] (Tokyo: Bun'eidō, 1970), p. 248; Asahi jānaru, ed., *Shōwashi no shunkan* [Moments in Shōwa history] (Tokyo: Asahi Shinbunsha, 1966), 2:99; Saitō, "Kūshū to minshū," pp. 3–4; Kurashi no Techōsha, *Tokushū Kurashi no techō, no. 96, sen-sōchū no kurashi no kiroku* [Special issue of *Notebook on Daily Living*, no. 96, Record of daily living during the war] (Tokyo: Kurashi no Techōsha, 1969), pp. 142–43; Jerome B. Cohen, *Japan's Economy in War and Reconstruction* (Minneapolis: University of Minnesota Press, 1949), p. 407. See also Akimoto, *Sensō to minshū*, pp. 220–23.

159–21   Jichi Daigakkō, *Sengo jichishi*, vol. 1, *tonarigumi oyobi chōnaikai burakukaitō no haishi* [History of postwar self-rule, vol. 1, The abolition of neighborhood associations and community councils] (Tokyo: Jichi Daigakkō, 1960), pp. 21–22; Akimoto, *Sensō to minshū*, p. 97.

159–34   *Bakufū to danpen* [Bomb blasts and shell fragments], shown at National Film Center, Kyōbashi, Tokyo, March 28, 1973. See Tōkyō Kokuritsu Kindai Bijutsukan Fuirumu Sentā, *FC fuirumu sentā* [FC Film Center], no. 13 (March 8, 1973), p. 21; "Senchū sengo tonarigumi nikki," pp. 680–81; Akimoto, *Sensō to minshū*, pp. 252–53; Kato, *Lost War*, pp. 204–05.

161–7   Jichi Daigakkō, *Sengo jichishi*, 1:22; *Nippon Times*, December 31, 1944, morning ed., p. 3; ibid., January 8, 1945, morning ed., p. 2; ibid., January 21, 1945, morning ed., p. 3; Terasaki, *Bridge*, p. 142; Yoko Matsuoka, *Daughter of the Pacific* (New York: Harper and Brothers, 1952), p. 194.

161–15   *Nippon Times*, February 9, 1945, morning ed., p. 3; Tōkyō Kūshū o Kirokusuru Kai, *Tōkyō daikūshū—sensaishi* [The great Tokyo air raids—Record of war damage] (Tokyo: Tōkyō Kūshū o Kirokusuru Kai, 1974), 5:32–83.

162–3   "Bōkūho" [Air defense law], December 21, 1943, quoted in Akimoto, *Sensō to minshū*, p. 230. See also ibid., pp. 224–29; Asahi jānaru, ed., *Shōwashi no shunkan*, 2:98.

162–17   *Asahi shinbun*, March 23, 1944, quoted in Akimoto, *Sensō to minshū*, p. 237; *Sokai* [Evacuation], shown at National Film Center, Kyōbashi, Tokyo, March 26, 1973. See Tōkyō Kokuritsu Kindai Bijutsukan Fuirumu Sentā, *FC fuirumu sentā*, no. 13, p. 20.

162–38   Kurashi no Techōsha, *Sensōchū no kurashi no kiroku*, p. 50.

163–14   "Gakudō sokai sokushin yōkō" [Outline for encouraging the evacuation of schoolchildren], June 30, 1944, quoted in Monbushō, *Gakusei hachijūnenshi* [Eighty-year history of the educational system] (Tokyo: Ōkurashō Insatsukyoku, 1954), p. 403. See also ibid., pp. 404–06; Hashikawa Bunzō, Kano Masanao, and Hiraoka Toshio, eds., *Kindai Nihon shisōshi no kisō chishiki* [Basic knowledge about the history of modern Japanese thought] (Tokyo: Yūhikaku, 1971), p. 460; Akimoto, *Sensō to minshū*, pp. 230–39; Fred C. Iklé, *The Social Impact of Bomb Destruction* (Norman: University of Oklahoma Press, 1958), p. 88; Foreign Affairs Association of Japan, *The Japan Year Book, 1946–48* (Tokyo: Foreign Affairs Association of Japan, 1948), p. 468; *Nippon Times*, March 17, 1945, morning ed., p. 3.

163–32   Kurashi no Techōsha, *Sensōchū no kurashi no kiroku*, p. 129; *Nippon Times*, September 1, 1944, morning ed., p. 3; Kato, *Lost War*, p. 13; Monbushō, *Gakusei hachijūnenshi*, p. 405; Kinoshita Uji, "Senjichū no gakkō kyōiku no ichijirei" [One example of wartime school education], in Iida Bunkazai no Kai, *Dainiji taisen no koro* [The World War Two period] (Iida: Minami Shinshū Shinbunsha, 1972), pp. 159–60.

164–13   Takasuka Kōsei, "Taiheiyō sensōka no gakudō sokai to bunsan jugyō" [Student evacuation and dispersed teaching during the Pacific war], *Iyo shidan* [Iyo historical discussions], no. 200 (January 1971): 80; Hori Shichizō, ed., *Tōkyō Joshi Kōtō Shihan Gakkō gakudō no sokai* [Student evacuation from Tokyo women's higher normal school] (Tokyo: privately printed, 1965), p. 6; Takeda Hikozaemon, "Sokai gakudō no ukeire" [The reception of student evacuees], in Iida Bunkazai no Kai, *Dainiji taisen no koro*, pp. 117–20; Minatokuritsu Mita Toshokan, *Senran to Minatoku* [War and Minatoku] (Tokyo: Minatokuritsu Mita Toshokan, 1969), p. 115.

165–11   Sukagawashi Kyōiku Iinkai, *Sukagawashishi*, vol. 2, *gendai* [History of Sukagawa, vol. 2, Modern] (Fukushimaken, Sukagawashi: Sukagawa Kyōiku Iinkai, 1972), p. 94; Joseph Newman, *Goodbye Japan* (New York: L. B. Fischer, 1942), pp. 212–13; Hori, ed., *Tōkyō Joshi Kōtō Shihan Gakkō*, pp. 132–33; Kurashi no Techōsha, *Sensōchū no kurashi no kiroku*, p. 117; Gekkōhara Shōgakkō, *Gakudō sokai no kiroku* [Record of student evacuation] (Tokyo: Miraisha, 1960), p. 202; Hamadate Kikuo, *Gakudō shūdan sokai* [Student group evacuation] (Tokyo: Taihei Shuppansha, 1971), p. 76.

165–23   Minatokuritsu Mita Toshokan, *Senran to Minatoku*, pp. 114–15; Hamadate, *Gakudō*, p. 78.

166–16   Monbushō, *Gakusei hachijūnenshi*, p. 405; Minatokuritsu Mita Toshokan, *Senran to Minatoku*, p. 114.

167–2   Hideaki Ohta, "Evacuating Characteristics of Tokyo Citizens," *Proceedings of the Japan–United States Disaster Research Seminar: Organizational and Community Responses to Disasters* (Columbus: Disaster Research Center, The Ohio State University, 1972), p. 176. See also ibid., pp. 175–79; Iklé, *Social Impact*, pp. 101–02; Dennis Wenger, "DRC Studies of Community Functioning," *Proceedings of the Japan–United States Disaster Research Seminar*, p. 54.

167–16   Irene B. Taeuber, *The Population of Japan* (Princeton: Princeton University Press, 1958), pp. 167, 342, 353; Takahashi Saburō, "Shūmatsuki no kokumin shisō" [People's thought at the end], in *Kindai Nihon seiji shisōshi* [History of modern Japanese political thought], ed. Hashikawa Bunzō and Matsumoto Sannosuke (Tokyo: Yūhikaku, 1970), 2:418; Cohen, *Japan's Economy*, pp. 407–08.

168–3   Richard M. Titmuss, *Problems of Social Policy* (London: Longmans, Green and Co., 1950), pp. 101–09, 355–69; U.S. Strategic Bombing Survey, Morale Division, *The Effects of Strategic Bombing on German Morale* (Washington, D.C., 1947), 1:2–9; Eugene M. Kulischer, *Europe on the Move: War and Population Changes, 1917–1947* (New York: Columbia University Press, 1948), pp. 258–61; Cohen, *Japan's Economy*, p. 407; Iklé, *Social Impact*, pp. 61–62.

168–26   Kurashi no Techōsha, *Sensōchū no kurashi no kiroku*, pp. 142–43.

170–4 Sutō Ryōsaku, *Tonarigumichō no shuki* [A neighborhood captain's notes] (Tokyo: privately printed, 1970), pp. 1, 4, 6, 13–14, 16, 22.

170–11 Tōkyō Kūshū o Kirokusuru Kai, *Tōkyō daikūshū*, 5:98–108; *Nippon Times*, March 16, 1945, morning ed., p. 1; ibid., March 31, 1945, morning ed., p. 3; ibid., May 10, 1945, morning ed., p. 3; ibid., June 23, 1945; morning ed., p. 3.

170–25 U.S. Strategic Bombing Survey, *Japanese Morale*, p. 75; Saitō, "Kūshū to minshū," p. 4; Gunmaken, *Gunmaken hyakunenshi* [Hundred-year history of Gunma prefecture] (Maebashi: Gunmaken, 1971), 2:588–90.

171–2 Zenkoku Nōgyōkai Chōsabu, *Sokaisha ni kansuru chōsa* [Inquiry concerning evacuees] (n.p.: Zenkoku Nōgyōkai, 1946), pp. 1–4.

171–16 Titmuss, *Social Policy*, pp. 110–25; Iklé, *Social Impact*, pp. 90–96, 119, 197; Taeuber, *Population of Japan*, p. 343; *Fortune*, April 1944, p. 211; Asahi jānaru, *Shōwashi no shunkan*, 2:104.

171–37 Takahashi Aiko, "Sensō kara no nikki" [Diary from the war], in Shōwa Sensō Bungaku Zenshū Henshū Iinkai, *Shōwa sensō bungaku zenshū*, vol. 14, *shimin no nikki* [Complete wartime literary works of the Shōwa era, vol. 14, City residents' diaries] (Tokyo: Shūeisha, 1965), pp. 336–37; Ishizuka Rui, "Hokkaidō Uragawa ni sokaishite" [Evacuating to Uragawa in Hokkaido], in Kusa no Mi Kai Daishichi Gurūpu, *Sensō to watakushi*, p. 155; Isoko Hatano and Ichiro Hatano, *Mother and Son: The Wartime Correspondence of Isoko and Ichiro Hatano* (Boston: Houghton Mifflin, 1962), p. 50; *Mainichi shinbun*, February 2, 1945, quoted in Konishi Shirō, "Senjika no kokumin seikatsu" [People's livelihoods in wartime], in *Taikei Nihonshi sōsho*, vol. 17, *seikatsushi*, pt. 3 [Series of works on Japanese history, vol. 17, History of daily life, pt. 3], ed. Morimatsu Yoshiaki et al. (Tokyo: Yamakawa Shuppansha, 1969), p. 454.

172–15 Inoue Kiyoshi, *Gendai Nihon joseishi* [History of modern Japanese women] (Tokyo: San'ichi Shobō, 1962), p. 18; Kurashi no Techōsha, *Sensōchū no kurashi no kiroku*, p. 141.

172–28 Taeuber, *Population of Japan*, pp. 343–45.

CHAPTER 10

175–14 U.S. Strategic Bombing Survey, Over-all Economic Effects Division, *The Effects of Strategic Bombing on Japan's War Economy*

(Washington, D.C., 1946), pp. 32, 42f; Jerome B. Cohen, *Japan's Economy in War and Reconstruction* (Minneapolis: University of Minnesota Press, 1949), pp. 56, 58. I am grateful to Anne S. Johnson for comments on the inevitability of Pearl Harbor.

175–32   See Gordon Daniels, "The Great Tokyo Air Raid, 9–10 March 1945," in *Modern Japan: Aspects of History, Literature and Society*, ed. W. G. Beasley (Berkeley and Los Angeles: University of California Press, 1975), p. 115.

176–7   Documentary collections exist for at least eighteen cities apart from Hiroshima and Nagasaki, including ten titles on Tokyo alone. Five other books treat air raids on Japan as a whole.

176–10   David MacIssac, "The United States Strategic Bombing Survey, 1944–1947" (Ph.D. dissertation, Duke University, 1969), p. 162; Gary J. Shandroff, "The Evolution of Area Bombing in American Doctrine and Practice" (Ph.D. dissertation in history, New York University, 1972), p. 131.

176–31   Shinmyō Takeo, "Hondo kūshū" [Mainland air raids], in *Nihon kūshū* [Air raids on Japan], ed. Okumura Yoshitarō (Tokyo: Mainichi Shinbunsha, 1971), pp. 1975–76; Fujiwara Akira, ed., *Nihon minshū no rekishi*, vol. 9, *sensō to minshū* [History of the Japanese people, vol. 9, War and the people] (Tokyo: Sanseidō, 1975), pp. 305–07; Akimoto Ritsuo, *Sensō to minshū: Taiheiyō sensōka no toshi seikatsu* [War and the people: City life during the Pacific war] (Tokyo: Gakuyō Shobō, 1974), pp. 189–96; U.S. Strategic Bombing Survey, Morale Division, *The Effects of Strategic Bombing on German Morale* (Washington, D.C., 1947), 1:2–9; MacIsaac, "Bombing Survey," pp. 161–62; Shandroff, "Area Bombing," p. 131; Cohen, *Japan's Economy*, p. 407.

177–6   Keizai Antei Honbu Sōsai Kanbō Kikakubu Chōsaka, *Taiheiyō sensō ni yoru waga kuni no higai sōgō hōkokusho* [General report on damage to our country as a result of the Pacific war] (Tokyo, 1949), pp. 30–31.

177–22   Shandroff, "Area Bombing," p. 145; Akimoto, *Sensō to minshū*, p. 191; Masuo Kato, *The Lost War: A Japanese Reporter's Inside Story* (New York: Alfred A. Knopf, 1946), pp. 197–200. See U.S. Army Air Forces, Intelligence Headquarters, Assistant Chief of Staff, *Mission Accomplished: Interrogations of Japanese Industrial, Military, and Civil Leaders of World War II* (Washington, D.C., 1946), p. 23.

178–2   Chitoshi Yanaga, *Japan Since Perry* (New York: McGraw-Hill Book Co., 1949), p. 615; Shandroff, "Area Bombing," pp. 130–32; Gene Gurney, *Journey of the Giants* (New York: Coward-McCann, Inc., 1961), pp. 214–16, 223; William Craig, *The Fall of*

Japan (New York: Dell Publishing Co., Inc., 1967), pp. 15–18; Daniels, "Tokyo Air Raid," pp. 116–19.

179–3   Matsumura Hidetoshi, *Daihon'ei happyō* [Imperial general headquarters announcements], p. 257, quoted in Akimoto, *Sensō to minshū*, p. 245; Kurashi no Techōsha, *Tokushū* Kurashi no techō, no. 96, *sensōchū no kurashi no kiroku* [Special issue of *Notebook on Daily Living*, no. 96, Record of daily living during the war] (Tokyo: Kurashi no Techōsha, 1969), pp. 64, 75; Shandroff, "Area Bombing," pp. 138–41; Kato, *Lost War*, p. 213; Craig, *Fall of Japan*, pp. 20–21.

179–20   Yamamoto Katsuko, quoted in Kubota Shigenori, *Tōkyō daikūshū—kyūgotaichō no kiroku* [The great Tokyo air raids—Record of a rescue squad chieftain] (Tokyo: Ushio Shuppansha, 1973), p. 83; Craig, *Fall of Japan*, p. 21; Kao, *Lost War*, p. 211.

179–34   Kubota, *Tōkyō daikūshū*, p. 78; Kato, *Lost War*, p. 212.

180–10   Kubota, *Tōkyō daikūshū*, pp. 75, 78, 84, 91.

180–31   Kurashi no Techōsha, *Sensōchū no kurashi no kiroku*, pp. 66–67. See also ibid., p. 103.

181–5   Lars Tillitse, "When Bombs Rained on Us in Tokyo," *Saturday Evening Post*, January 12, 1946, p. 85; Kubota, *Tōkyō daikūshū*, p. 79; Kato, *Lost War*, p. 215; David H. James, *The Rise and Fall of the Japanese Empire* (New York: Macmillan, 1951), p. 293; Tōkyō Kūshū o Kirokusuru Kai, *Tōkyō daikūshū—sensaishi* [The great Tokyo air raids—Record of war damage] (Tokyo: Tōkyō Kūshū o Kirokusuru Kai, 1973), 1:1013–35.

181–21   Bunkyōku, *Bunkyōkushi* [History of Bunkyōku] (Tokyo: Bunkyōku, 1969), 4:824; MacIsaac, "Bombing Survey," p. 160; Shandroff, "Area Bombing," p. 141; Craig, *Fall of Japan*, p. 22; Daniels, "Tokyo Air Raid," p. 129.

181–31   MacIsaac, "Bombing Survey," p. 160; Shandroff, "Area Bombing," pp. 141, 152–53, 158.

182–11   Yoshizawa Hisako, "Shūsen made" [To the end of the war], in Shōwa Sensō Bungaku Zenshū Henshū Iinkai, *Shōwa sensō bungaku zenshū*, vol. 14, *shimin no nikki* [Complete wartime literary works of the Shōwa era, vol. 14, City residents' diaries] (Tokyo: Shūeisha, 1965), pp. 369, 373; Dennis Wenger, "DRC Studies of Community Functioning," *Proceedings of the Japan–United States Disaster Research Seminar: Organizational and Community Responses to Disasters* (Columbus: Disaster Research Center, The Ohio State University, 1972), pp. 30–34; Tōkyō Kūshū o Kirokusuru

Kai, *Tōkyō daikūshū* (1974), 5:31; *Nippon Times*, March 17, 1945, morning ed., p. 3; ibid., March 24, 1945, morning ed., p. 3; Daniels, "Tokyo Air Raid," pp. 128–29.

182–30   Gurney, *Journey*, pp. 228–30; Shandroff, "Area Bombing," pp. 142–43; James, *Rise and Fall*, p. 295; Kōbeshi, *Kōbeshishi*, vol. 3, pt. 2, *shakai bunkahen* [History of Kobe, vol. 3, pt. 2, Society and culture] (Kobe: Kōbeshi, 1965), p. 421; *Nippon Times*, April 26, 1945, morning ed., p. 1.

183–24   Sutō Ryōsaku, *Tonarigumichō no shuki* [A neighborhood captain's notes] (Tokyo: privately printed, 1970), pp. 1, 5–7; *Nippon Times*, May 10, 1945, morning ed., p. 3; Bruno Bitters, quoted in U.S. Army Air Forces, *Mission Accomplished*, p. 100.

183–37   James, *Rise and Fall*, p. 307; Sutō, *Tonarigumichō no shuki*, pp. 8–9.

184–24   Sutō, *Tonarigumichō no shuki*, pp. 9–12. See Wenger, "DRC Studies," pp. 30–34; Robert J. Lifton, *Death in Life: Survivors of Hiroshima* (New York: Random House, 1967), pp. 31–34, 82–102.

185–11   James, *Rise and Fall*, pp. 307–09, 316–17; Kato, *Lost War*, p. 200.

185–31   Takaaki Aikawa, *Unwilling Patriot* (Tokyo: The Jordan Press, 1960), p. 91; Ikeuchi Hajime, "Taiheiyō sensōchū no senji ryūgen" [Wartime rumors during the Pacific war], *Shakaigaku hyōron* [Sociology review] 2, no. 2 (August 1951): 30–42. See Wenger, "DRC Studies," pp. 36–39, 67; Fred C. Iklé, *The Social Impact of Bomb Destruction* (Norman: University of Oklahoma Press, 1958), p. 186.

187–2   Alexander H. Leighton, *Human Relations in a Changing World* (New York: E. P. Dutton and Company, Inc., 1949), pp. 9, 58–59; U.S. Army Air Forces, *Mission Accomplished*, pp. 26, 74, 76; Gordon Wright, *The Ordeal of Total War, 1939–1945* (New York: Harper & Row, 1968), pp. 174–82; Iklé, *Social Impact*, p. 198.

187–13   U.S. Strategic Bombing Survey, Morale Division, *The Effects of Strategic Bombing on Japanese Morale* (Washington, D.C., 1947), pp. 83–84, 224–25.

187–17   See Iklé, *Social Impact*, pp. 31, 198.

188–23   Hashimoto Denzaemon et al., eds., *Ishiguro Tadaatsu den* [Biography of Ishiguro Tadaatsu] (Tokyo: Iwanami Shoten, 1969), p. 353; Kisaka Jun'ichirō, "Nihon fuashizumu to jinmin shihai no tokushitsu" [Japanese fascism and special features of leading the people], *Rekishigaku kenkyū* [Historiographical studies], special number (October 1970): 126–27; Kyōto Daigaku Bungakubu Koku-shi Kenkyūshitsu, *Nihon kindaishi jiten* [Dictionary of modern Japanese history] (Tokyo: Tōyō Keizai Shinpōsha, 1958), p. 188; Fukuiken, *Taishō Shōwa Fukuikenshi* [History of Fukui prefecture in the Taishō and Shōwa periods] (Fukui: Fukuiken, 1956), 1:214.

189–5   Araki Sadao, quoted in Aikawa, *Unwilling Patriot,* p. 46; see also ibid., p. 41; Isoko Hatano and Ichiro Hatano, *Mother and Son: The Wartime Correspondence of Isoko and Ichiro Hatano* (Boston: Houghton Mifflin, 1962), p. 114; Kato, *Lost War,* pp. 16–17; Tōkyō Kūshū o Kirokusuru Kai, *Tōkyō daikūshū,* 5:115–21.

190–2   Rekishigaku Kenkyūkai, *Taiheiyō sensōshi* [History of the Pacific war], (Tokyo: Aoki Shoten, 1973), 5:101; Aikawa, *Unwilling Patriot,* p. 95; Gwen Terasaki, *Bridge to the Sun* (Chapel Hill: University of North Carolina Press, 1957), p. 168.

190–12   Kurashi no Techōsha, *Sensōchū no kurashi no kiroku,* pp. 137–38.

190–27   "Kokuryoku no genjō" [The present state of national power], June 8, 1945, in Hara Shobō Henshūbu, *Haisen no kiroku—sanbō honbu shozō* [Record of defeat—General staff documents] (Tokyo: Hara Shobō, 1967), p. 268; Ichikawa Ryōichi, "Senjika minshū ishiki kenkyū nōto" [Research notes on people's outlooks in wartime], *Hitotsubashi ronsō* [Hitotsubashi collection], 70, no. 6 (1973): 74–75; Tōkyō Kūshū o Kirokusuru Kai, *Tōkyō daikūshū,* 5:115.

191–5   Ezaki Tsuneko, quoted in Ienaga Saburō, *Taiheiyō sensō* [The Pacific war] (Tokyo: Iwanami Shoten, 1968), p. 154; U.S. Army Air Forces, *Mission Accomplished,* p. 26; Toshikazu Kase, *Journey to the Missouri,* ed. David N. Rowe (New Haven: Yale University Press, 1950), p. 207; *Nippon Times,* August 8, 1945, morning ed., p. 1; army announcement, quoted in Sutō, *Tonarigumichō no shuki,* pp. 24–25.

191–25   Yoshizawa, "Shūsen made," p. 361; U.S. Strategic Bombing Survey, *Japanese Morale,* pp. 83–84, 224–25; Ōto Sueko, quoted in *Nigai hibi—senchū, sengo* [Bitter days—Wartime, postwar], ed. Satō Suzuko (Tokyo: Kusa no·Mi Kai, 1972), p. 19; Ichikawa, "Senjika minshū," pp. 75–76.

193–24   Sutō, *Tonarigumichō no shuki,* pp. 26–27.

CHAPTER 11

194–7   Yoshizawa Hisako, "Shūsen Hisako, [To the end of the war], in Shōwa Sensō Bungaku Zenshū Henshū Iinkai,

Shōwa sensō bungaku zenshū, vol. 14, *shimin no nikki* [Complete war-time literary works of the Shōwa era, vol. 14, City residents' diaries] (Tokyo: Shūeisha, 1965), p. 370. See Michael Howard, *Studies in War and Peace* (New York: The Viking Press, 1970), pp. 184–97.

195–20   Arthur Marwick, *War and Social Change in the Twentieth Century* (London: Macmillan, 1974), p. 109; Gordon Wright, *The Ordeal of Total War, 1939–1945* (New York: Harper & Row, 1968), pp. 44–47, 61–65.

195–25   Francis E. Merrill, *Social Problems on the Home Front: A Study of War-time Influences* (New York: Harper Brothers, 1948), pp. 10–11.

196–6   Jerome B. Cohen, *Japan's Economy in War and Reconstruction* (Minneapolis: University of Minnesota Press, 1949), pp. 53–54.

196–21   See Walter Millis, *Arms and Men* (New York: G. P. Putnam's Sons, 1956), pp. 264–71. I am grateful to Bernard S. Silberman for advice on this point.

196–30   Fujiwara Akira, *Kokumin no rekishi,* vol. 23, *taiheiyō sensō* [National history, vol. 23, The Pacific war] (Tokyo: Bun'eidō, 1970), p. 285; Fujiwara Akira, "Taiheiyō sensō to Nihon teikokushugi no hōkai" [The Pacific war and the collapse of Japanese imperialsim], in Rekishigaku Kenkyūkai and Nihonshi Kenkyūkai, *Kōza Nihonshi,* vol. 7, *Nihon teikokushugi no hōkai* [Colloquium on Japanese history, vol. 7, The collapse of Japanese imperialism] (Tokyo: Tōkyō Daigaku Shuppankai, 1971), p. 320.

197–6   See Merrill, *Social Problems,* pp. ix, 230–35; Marwick, *War and Social Change,* p. 13.

197–24   See Fujiwara, *Taiheiyō sensō,* p. 298.

198–14   Cohen, *Japan's Economy,* p. 288; Irene B. Taeuber, *The Population of Japan* (Princeton: Princeton University Press, 1958), p. 385. See also ibid., pp. 96, 117, 384.

198–26   Marwick, *War and Social Change,* p. 98, suggests that political structures change more slowly than social ones, but presumably he refers to postwar changes in victorious states.

199–15   Cohen, *Japan's Economy,* p. 7; Karl D. Hartzell, *The Empire State at War: World War II* (Albany: The State of New York, 1949), p. 379; Richard R. Lingeman, *Don't You Know There's a War On?* (New York: Paperback Library, 1971), pp. 136–50.

200–2   See Thomas E. Drabek and William H. Key, "Meeting the Challenge of Disaster: Family responses and Long-term Consequences," *Proceedings of the Japan–United States Disaster Research Seminar: Organizational and Community Responses to Disasters* (Columbus: Disaster Research Center, The Ohio State University, 1972), p. 102; Merrill, *Social Problems*, p. 20; Arthur Marwick, *The Deluge: British Society and the First World War* (New York: W. W. Norton & Company, Inc., 1970), pp. 105–13; Richard Polenberg, *War and Society: The United States, 1941–1945* (Philadelphia: J. B. Lippincott Company, 1972), pp. 138–53; Paul W. Tappan, *Crime, Justice, and Correction* (New York: McGraw-Hill Book Co., 1960), pp. 183–87.

200–8   Minoguchi Tokijirō, "Joshi dōinron" [On mobilizing women], *Kaizō* [Reconstruction] (March 1943): 42.

202–5   See Lingeman, *Don't You Know?*, pp. 249–83, 330–94; Angus Calder, *The People's War: Britain—1939–1945* (New York: Pantheon Books, 1969), pp. 514–23; Marwick, *The Deluge,* pp. 140–48.

202–21   Marwick, *The Deluge*, p. 313.

202–25   Keizai Antei Honbu Sōsai Kanbō Kikakubu Chōsaka, *Taiheiyō sensō ni yoru waga kuni no higai sōgō hōkokusho* [General report on damage to our country as a result of the Pacific war] (Tokyo, 1949), quoted in Akimoto Ritsuo, *Sensō to minshū: Taiheiyō sensōka no toshi seikatsu* [War and the people: City life during the Pacific war] (Tokyo: Gakuyō Shobō, 1974), pp. 190–91, 196.

203–3   See Marwick, *The Deluge*, pp. 289–90.

203–24   See Fujiwara, *Taiheiyō sensō*, pp. 296–97; Wright, *Total War*, pp. 249–63.

204–36   Merrill, *Social Problems*, p. 22.

Bibliography

Abend, Hallett. *Japan Unmasked*. New York: Ives, Washburn, Inc., 1941.

Aikawa, Takaaki. *Unwilling Patriot*. Tokyo: The Jordan Press, 1960.

Akimoto Ritsuo. "Senjika no toshi ni okeru chiiki jūmin soshiki" [Local organization of city residents in wartime]. *Shakai kagaku tōkyū* [Social Science Review] 18, no. 2, consecutive no. 51 (February 1973): 63–95.

————. *Sensō to minshū: Taiheiyō sensōka no toshi seikatsu* [War and the people: City life during the Pacific war]. Tokyo: Gakuyō Shobō, 1974.

Amagasakishi. *Amagasakishishi* [History of Amagasaki]. 3 vols. and supplement. Amagasaki: Amagasakishi, 1966–1970.

Anderson, Joseph L., and Richie, Donald. *The Japanese Film: Art and Industry*. New York: Grove Press, Inc., 1966.

Anderson, Ronald S. *Japan: Three Epochs of Modern Education*. Washington, D.C.: U.S. Department of Health, Education, and Welfare, 1959.

————. "Nishi Honganji and Japanese Buddhist Nationalism, 1862–1945." Ph.D. dissertation in history, University of California, Berkeley, 1956.

Andō Masako. "Kinrō dōin no akekure" [Labor mobilization day and night]. In Kusa no Mi Kai Daishichi Gurūpu, *Sensō to watakushi* [The War and I], pp. 17–19. Tokyo: Kusa no Mi Kai, 1963.

Aragaki, Hideo. "Japan's Home Front." *Contemporary Japan* 7, no. 2 (1938): 288–96.

Araishishi Henshū Iinkai. *Araishishi* [History of Arai]. 2 vols. Niigataken, Araishi: Araishishi Henshū Iinkai, 1971.

Ari Bokuji. "Chihō seido—burakukai chōnaikai seido" [Local institutions—The community council system]. In *Kōza Nihon kindaihō hattatsushi* [Colloquium on the development of modern Japanese law], edited by Ukai Nobushige et al., 6:163–208. Tokyo: Keisō Shobō, 1959.

Armstrong, John A. et al. *Soviet Partisans in World War II*. Madison: University of Wisconsin Press, 1964.

Asahi jānaru. *Shōwashi no shunkan* [Moments in Shōwa History]. 2 vols. Tokyo: Asahi Shinbunsha, 1966.

Asanuma Kazunori. "Nihon fuashizumu no seiji katei" [The political process of Japanese fascism]. *Takushoku Daigaku ronshū* [Takushoku University reports], no. 79 (1971), pp. 15–34; no. 80 (1971), pp. 79–100.

Aso, Makoto, and Amano, Ikuo. *Education and Japan's Modernization.* Tokyo: Ministry of Foreign Affairs, 1972.

Ayusawa, Iwao F. *A History of Labor in Modern Japan.* Honolulu: East-West Center Press, 1966.

Bakufū to danpen [Bomb blasts and shell fragments], shown at National Film Center, Kyōbashi, Tokyo, March 28, 1973 (first released February 10, 1944).

Bettelheim, Bruno. *The Informed Heart: Autonomy in a Mass Age.* Glencoe, Ill.: The Free Press, 1960.

Bisson, T. A. *Japan's War Economy.* New York: International Secretariat, Institute of Pacific Relations, 1945.

Braibanti, Ralph J. D. "Neighborhood Associations in Japan and Their Democratic Potentialities." *Far Eastern Quarterly* 7, no. 2 (February 1948): 136–64.

Brown, Delmer M. *Nationalism in Japan: An Introductory Historical Analysis.* Berkeley and Los Angeles: University of California Press, 1955.

Brown, Penelope D. "The Thought Control Program of Japan's Military Leaders 1931–1941." B.A. thesis in history, Connecticut College, 1972.

Bunkyōku. *Bunkyōkushi* [History of Bunkyōku]. 4 vols. Tokyo: Bunkyōku, 1969.

Buss, Claude A. "Inside Wartime Japan." *Life,* January 24, 1944, pp. 84–86, 88, 90, 93.

Caiger, John G. "Education, Values, and Japan's National Identity: A Study of the Aims and Contents of Courses in Japanese History, 1872–1963." Ph.D. dissertation, Australian National University, 1966.

Calder, Angus. *The People's War: Britain—1939–1945.* New York: Pantheon Books, 1969.

Calvocoressi, Peter, and Wint, Guy. *Total War.* New York: Ballantine Books, 1973. Vol. 1, *The War in the West.*

Chaen Yoshio. *Gakuto kinrō dōin* [Student labor mobilization]. Tokushima: Tokushimaken Kyōikukai, 1969.

Chafe, William H. *The American Woman: Her Changing Social, Economic, and Political Role, 1920–1970.* New York: Oxford University Press, 1972.

Cohen, Jerome B. *Japan's Economy in War and Reconstruction.* Minneapolis: University of Minnesota Press, 1949.

Coyne, Fumiko H. "Censorship of Publishing in Japan: 1868–1945." M.A. thesis, Graduate Library School, University of Chicago, 1967.

Craig, William. *The Fall of Japan.* New York: Dell Publishing Co., Inc., 1967.

Dai Nihon Seinendan Honbu. *Seinendan nenkan, 1941* [Youth group annual, 1941]. Tokyo: Dai Nihon Seinendan Honbu, 1940.

————. *Seishōnendan nenkan, 1943* [Youth group annual, 1943]. Tokyo: Dai Nihon Seinendan Honbu, 1943.

————. *Seishōnendan nenkan, 1944* [Youth group annual, 1944]. Tokyo: Dai Nihon Seinendan Honbu, 1944.

Daniels, Gordon. "The Great Tokyo Air Raid, 9–10 March 1945." In *Modern Japan: Aspects of History, Literature and Society,* edited by W. G. Beasley, pp. 113–31. Berkeley and Los Angeles: University of California Press, 1975.

Dejima Motoko. "Gakuto dōin" [Student mobilization]. In *Hikisa-karete—haha no sensō taiken* [Separated—Mothers' war experiences], edited by Tsurumi Kazuko and Makise Kikue, pp. 96–109. Tokyo: Chikuma Shobō, 1959.

De Mendelssohn, Peter. *Japan's Political Warfare.* London: George Allen & Unwin, Ltd., 1944.

De Vos, George A. *Socialization for Achievement: Essays on the Cultural Psychology of the Japanese.* Berkeley and Los Angeles: University of California Press, 1973.

Dore, Ronald P. *Land Reform in Japan.* London: Oxford University Press, 1959.

Drabek, Thomas E., and Key, William H. "Meeting the Challenge of Disaster: Family Responses and Long-term Consequences." In *Proceedings of the Japan–United States Disaster Research Seminar: Organizational and Community Responses to Disasters,* pp. 89–107. Columbus: Disaster Research Center, The Ohio State University, 1972.

Dumas, Samuel, and Vedel-Petersen, K. O. *Losses of Life Caused by War.* Oxford: Clarendon Press, 1923.

Ebihara Haruyoshi. "Sensō no shinkō to kyōiku" [Progress of the war and education]. In *Nihon kindai kyōikushi* [History of Modern Japanese Education], edited by Kaigo Muneomi, pp. 284–305. Tokyo: Iwanami Shoten, 1962.

Embree, John F. "Japanese Administration at the Local Level." *Applied Anthropology* 3, no. 4 (1944): 11–18.

————. *The Japanese Nation: A Social Survey.* New York: Rinehart & Co., 1945.

Fahs, Charles B. *Government in Japan: Recent Trends in Its Scope and Operation.* New York: International Secretariat, Institute of Pacific Relations, 1940.

Fleisher, Wilfrid. *Volcanic Isle.* New York: Doubleday, Doran and Company, Inc., 1941.

Foreign Affairs Association of Japan. *The Japan Year Book, 1946–48.* Tokyo: Foreign Affairs Association of Japan, 1948.

Fortune, April 1944.

Fujiwara Akira, ed. *Nihon minshū no rekishi,* vol. 9, *sensō to minshū* [History of the Japanese people, vol. 9, War and the people]. Tokyo: Sanseidō, 1975.

————. *Kokumin no rekishi*, vol. 23, *Taiheiyō senso* [National history, vol. 23, The Pacific war]. Tokyo: Bun'eidō, 1970.

————. "Taiheiyō senso to Nihon teikokushugi no hōkai" [The Pacific war and the collapse of Japanese imperialism]. In Rekishigaku Kenkyūkai and Nihonshi Kenkyūkai, *Kōza Nihonshi*, vol. 7, *Nihon teikokushigi no hōkai* [Colloquium on Japanese history, vol. 7, The collapse of Japanese imperialism], pp. 311–28. Tokyo: Tōkyō Daigaku Shuppankai, 1971.

————, Imai Seiichi, and Ōe Shinobu, eds. *Kindai Nihonshi no kisō chishiki* [Basic knowledge about modern Japanese history]. Tokyo: Yūhikaku, 1972.

Fukawa Kakuzaemon. "Senji no shuppan tōsei" [Wartime publishing controls]. *Bungaku* [Literature] 29, no. 5 (May 1961): 137–51.

Fukawa, Stanley T. "Neighbourhood Associations in Japanese Cities and Their Political Implications." M.A. thesis in sociology, London University, 1964.

Fukuda Bunji. *Waga machi no senki—chōchō memo* [Our towns's war records—Mayor's memo]. Gunmaken, Ojimamachi: privately printed; 1970.

Fukuiken. *Taishō Shōwa Fukuikenshi* [History of Fukui prefecture in the Taishō and Shōwa periods]. 2 vols. Fukui: Fukuiken, 1956–1957.

Funabashi Seibu Fujinkai kaihō, no. 10, *tokushū—kurushikatta senso no omoide* [Memoirs of the Funabashi Seibu Fujinkai, no. 10, special issue—Memories of the difficult war], March 1967.

Futagawa Yoshifumi. *Genron no dan'atsu* [Suppression of discussion]. Tokyo: Hōsei Daigaku Shuppanbu, 1959.

Gekkōhara Shōgakkō. *Gakudō sokai no kiroku* [Record of student evacuation]. Tokyo: Miraisha, 1960.

Gibney, Frank. *Five Gentlemen of Japan*. New York: Farrar, Straus and Young, 1953.

Glines, Carroll V. *Doolittle's Tokyo Raiders*. Princeton: D. Van Nostrand Company, Inc., 1964.

Gosden, Eric W. *Night Came to Japan*. London: Marshall, Morgan and Scott, 1951.

Guillain, Robert. *Le peuple japonais et la guerre: choses vues, 1939–1946*. Paris: R. Julliard, 1947.

Gunmaken. *Gunmaken hyakunenshi* [Hundred-year history of Gunma prefecture]. 2 vols. Maebashi: Gunmaken, 1971.

Gurney, Gene. *Journey of the Giants*. New York: Coward-McCann, Inc., 1961.

Hadley, Eleanor M. *Antitrust in Japan*. Princeton: Princeton University Press, 1970.

Hall, Robert K. *Education for a New Japan*. New Haven: Yale University Press, 1949.

Hamadate Kikuo. *Gakudō shūdan sokai* [Student group evacuation]. Tokyo: Taihei Shuppansha, 1971.

Hani, Setsuko. *The Japanese Family System, As Seen from the Standpoint of Japanese Women*. Tokyo: Japan Institute of Pacific Studies, 1948.

Hartzell, Karl D. *The Empire State at War: World War II*. Albany: The State of New York, 1949.

Hashikawa Bunzō, ed. *Nihon no hyakunen*, vol. 3, *hateshinaki sensen* Japan's hundred years, vol. 3, The endless war front]. Tokyo: Chikuma Shobō, 1962.

———, Kano Masanao, and Hiraoka Toshio, eds. *Kindai Nihon shisōshi no kiso chishiki* [Basic knowledge about the history of modern Japanese thought]. Tokyo: Yūhikaku, 1971.

Hashimoto Denzaemon et al., eds. *Ishiguro Tadaatsu den* [Biography of Ishiguro Tadaatsu]. Tokyo: Iwanami Shoten, 1969.

Hatanaka Shigeo, "Shuppan dan'atsu" [Repression of the press]. In Nihon Janārisuto Renmei, *Genron dan'atsushi* [History of repression of the press], pp. 75–138. Tokyo: Ginkyō Shobō, 1949.

Hatano, Isoko, and Hatano, Ichiro. *Mother and Son: The Wartime Correspondence of Isoko and Ichiro Hatano*. Boston: Houghton Mifflin, 1962.

Hauser, William B. *Economic Institutional Change in Tokugawa Japan*. Cambridge: Cambridge University Press, 1974.

Hayashi, Saburō, and Coox, Alvin D. *Kōgun: The Japanese Army in the Pacific War*. Quantico, Va.: Marine Corps Association, 1959.

Hayashi Toshikazu. *Nōson igaku josetsu* [Introduction to rural medicine]. Tokyo: Itō Shoten, 1944.

Hiraide Hiizu. *Senjika no genron tōsei* [Press controls in wartime]. 2nd ed. Tokyo: Kashiwaba Shoin, 1944.

Hirano Ken. "Nihon Bungaku Hōkokukai no seiritsu" [Founding of the Japan Patriotic Literary Association]. *Bungaku* [Literature] 29, no. 5 (May 1961): 1–8.

Hokkaidō Keisatsu Honbu. *Hokkaidō keisatsushi* [History of the Hokkaido police]. 2 vols. Sapporo: Hokkaidō Keisatsu Honbu, 1968.

Hori Shichizō, ed. *Tōkyō Joshi Kōtō Shihan Gakkō gakudō no sokai* [Student evacuation from Tokyo Women's Higher Normal School]. Tokyo: privately printed, 1965.

Hoshi Imae. "Sensō makki no shōgakkō" [Grade school at the end of the war]. In Iida Bunkazai no Kai, *Dainiji taisen no koro* [The World War Two period], pp. 25–27. Iida: Minami Shinshū Shinbunsha, 1972.

Howard, Michael. *Studies in War and Peace*. New York: The Viking Press, 1970.

Hrdlicka, Ales. "The Effects of the War on the American People." *Scientific Monthly* 8 (1919): 542–45.

Ichikawa Ryōichi. "Senjika minshū ishiki kenkyū nōto" [Research notes on people's outlooks in wartime]. *Hitotsubashi ronsō* [Hitotsubashi collection] 70, no. 6 (1973): 71–77.

Ienaga Saburō. *Kindai Nihon no shisōka* [Modern Japanese thinkers]. New ed. Tokyo: Yūshindō, 1970.

———. *Taiheiyō sensō* [The Pacific war]. Tokyo: Iwanami Shoten, 1968.

Ikeuchi Hajime. "Taiheiyō sensōchū no senji ryūgen" [Wartime rumors during the Pacific war]. *Shakaigaku hyōron* [Sociology review] 2, no. 2 (August 1951): 30–42.

Iklé, Fred C. *The Social Impact of Bomb Destruction*. Norman: University of Oklahoma Press, 1958.

Inoue Kiyoshi. *Gendai Nihon joseishi* [History of modern Japanese women]. Tokyo: San'ichi Shobō, 1962.

———. *Nihon joseishi* [History of Japanese women]. Rev. ed. Tokyo: San'ichi Shobō, 1967.

International Labor Organization. "A Survey of Economic and Social Conditions in Japan." *International Labor Review* 60, no. 1 (July 1949): 1–27.

Inumaru Giichi and Nakamura Shintarō. *Monogatari Nihon kindaishi* [The story of modern Japanese history]. 3 vols. Tokyo: Shin Nihon Shuppansha, 1971.

Ishida Takeshi. *Nihon kindaishi taikei*, vol. 8, *hakyoku to heiwa* [Series on modern Japanese history, vol. 8, Cataclysm and peace]. Tokyo: Tōkyō Daigaku Shuppankai, 1968.

Ishii Kin'ichirō. "Nihon fuashizumu to chihō seido" [Japanese fascism and local institutions]. *Rekishigaku kenkyū* [Historiographical studies], no. 307 (December 1965): 1–12.

Ishii Tominosuke. "Taiheihō sensōka no 'kessen' shokuseikatsu" [Eating habits during the "decisive battle" of the Pacific war]. *Kanagawakenshi kenkyū* [Studies in the history of Kanagawa prefecture], no. 23 (February 1974): 29–35.

Ishizuka Rui. "Hokkaidō Uragawa ni sokaishite" [Evacuating to Uragawa in Hokkaido]. In Kusa no Mi Kai Daishichi Gurūpu, *Sensō to watakushi* [The war and I], pp. 54–57. Tokyo: Kusa no Mi Kai, 1963.

Iwasaki Akira. "Tōsei teikō tōhi—senji no Nihon eiga" [Control, resistance, flight—Wartime Japanese movies]. *Bungaku* [Literature] 29, no. 5 (May 1961): 66–75.

Iwateken Ichinoseki Kokumin Kyōiku Kenkyūkai. *Kyōshi no sensō taiken no kiroku* [Record of teachers' war experiences]. Tokyo: Rōdō Junpōsha, 1969.

James, David H. *The Rise and Fall of the Japanese Empire*. New York: Macmillan, 1951.

Japan Times Advertiser.

Japan Times & Advertiser.

Jichi Daigakkō. *Sengo jichishi,* vol. 1, *tonarigumi oyobi chōnaikai bura-kukaitō no haishi* [History of postwar self-rule, vol. 1, The abolition of neighborhood associations and community councils]. Tokyo: Jichi Daigakkō, 1960.

Johnson, Anne S. "The Emperor and the Imperial Institution in Modern Japan: A Study of Symbolism." Manuscript, Connecticut College, 1976.

Johnson, Chalmers A. *An Instance of Treason: Ozaki Hotsumi and the Sorge Spy Ring.* Stanford: Stanford University Press, 1964.

Johnston, Bruce F., with Mosaburo Hosoda and Yoshio Kusumi. *Japanese Food Management in World War II.* Stanford: Stanford University Press, 1953.

Jōhōkyoku. *Shūhō* [Weekly Report].

Kagawa Tetsuo. *Jōketsu kenmin—sei no kyōiku* [Pure-blooded public health—Sex education]. Tokyo: Hokkō Shobō, 1943.

Kagoshimashishi Hensan Iinkai. *Kagoshimashishi* [History of Kago-shima]. 3 vols. Kagoshima: Kagoshimashishi Hensan Iinkai, 1969–1971.

Kajinishi Mitsuhaya et al. *Nihon shihonshugi no botsuraku* [The collapse of Japanese capitalism]. 4 vols. Tokyo: Tōkyō Daigaku Shup-pankai, 1964.

Kamiyama Shigeo. "Gokuchū Taiheiyō sensōshi" [Prison history of the Pacific war]. In *Jitsuroku Taiheiyō sensō* [True record of the Pacific war], edited by Itō Masanori et al., 7:257–75. Tokyo: Chūō Kōronsha, 1960.

Kasahara Yoshimitsu. "Kojin Kirisutosha no teikō" [Resistance by individual Christians]. In Dōshisha Daigaku Jinbun Kagaku Ken-kyūjo, *Senjika teikō no kenkyū* [Studies of Wartime Resistance], pp. 41–99. Tokyo: Misuzu Shobō, 1969.

Kase, Toshizaku. *Journey to the Missouri,* edited by David N. Rowe, New Haven: Yale University Press, 1950.

Katō Hidetoshi et al. *Meiji Taishō Shōwa sesōshi* [History of social conditions in the Meiji, Taishō, and Shōwa eras]. Tokyo: Shakai Shisōsha, 1967.

Kato, Masuo. *The Lost War: A Japanese Reporter's Inside Story.* New York: Alfred A. Knopf, 1946.

Kawahara Hiroshi. "Senjika ni okeru kagaku gijutsuron" [On science and technology in wartime]. In Waseda Daigaku Shakai Kagaku Kenkyūjo Fuashizumu Kenkyū Bukai, *Nihon no fuashizumu,* vol. 2, *sensō to kokumin* [Japanese fascism, vol. 2, War and the people], pp. 45–84. Tokyo: Waseda Daigaku Shuppanbu, 1974.

Kawakami Hajime. *Jijoden* [Autobiography]. 5 vols. Tokyo: Iwanami Shoten, 1952.

Kawasakishi. *Kawasakishishi* [History of Kawasaki]. 2 vols. Kawasaki: Kawasakishi, 1968.

Kawazu Katsu, ed. *Sagamiharashishi* [History of Sagamihara]. 4 vols. Yokohama: Kanagawa Shinbunsha, 1971.

Keene, Donald. "Japanese Writers and the Greater East Asia War." In *Landscapes and Portraits: Appreciations of Japanese Culture,* pp. 300–21. Tokyo: Kodansha International, Ltd., 1971.

————. "The Sino-Japanese War of 1894–95 and Its Cultural Effects in Japan." In *Landscapes and Portraits: Appreciations of Japanese Culture,* Tokyo: Kodansha International, Ltd., 1971.

Keimu Kyōkai Shihō Hogo Jigyō Kenkyūjo. *Senjika no shōnen hanzai to sono bōshi* [Juvenile crime in wartime and its prevention]. Tokyo: Daidō Shobō, 1942.

Keizai Antei Honbu Sōsai Kanbō Kikakubu Chōsaka. *Taiheiyō sensō ni yoru waga kuni no higai sōgō hōkokusho* [General report on damage to our country as a result of the Pacific war]. Tokyo, 1949.

Kinoshita Uji. "Senjichū no gakkō kyōiku no ichijirei" [One example of wartime school education]. In Iida Bunkazai no Kai, *Dainiji taisen no koro* [The World War Two period], pp. 158–63. Iida: Minami Shinshū Shinbunsha, 1972.

Kisaka Jun'ichirō. "Nihon fuashizumu to jinmin shihai no tokushitsu" [Japanese fascism and special features of leading the people]. *Rekishigaku kenkyū* [Historiographical studies], special number (October 1970): 117–28.

————. "Taisei Yokusankai no seiritsu" [Establishment of the Imperial Rule Assistance Association]. In *Iwanami Kōza Nihon rekishi,* vol. 20, *kindai,* pt. 7 [Iwanami colloquium on Japanese History, vol. 20, Modern, pt. 7], pp. 269–314. Tokyo: Iwanami Shoten, 1976.

Kitayama Mine. "Ningen no tama wa horobimai" [The spirit of mankind will not be destroyed]. In Asahi Shinbunsha, *Tōkyō hibakuki* [Tokyo bombing victims' record], p. 214. Tokyo: Asahi Shinbunsha, 1971.

Kiyosawa Kiyoshi. *Ankoku nikki* [Diary of darkness]. Tokyo: Tōyō Keizai Shinpōsha, 1954.

Kobayashi Keizaburō, ed. *Kikigaki: senka ni ikita fubotachi* [Transcript: Parents who lived during the war flames]. Tokyo: Taihei Shuppansha, 1972.

Kōbe Kūshū o Kirokusuru Kai. *Kōbe daikūshū* [The great Kobe air raids]. Kobe: Nojigiku Bunko, 1972.

Kōbeshi. *Kōbeshishi,* vol. 3, pt. 2, *shakai bunkahen* [History of Kobe, vol. 3, pt. 2, Society and culture]. Kobe: Kōbeshi, 1965.

Kodama Yukita et al., eds. *Zusetsu Nihon bunkashi taikei,* vol. 12, *Taishō Shōwa jidai* [Illustrated series on the history of Japanese culture, vol. 12, The Taishō and Shōwa periods]. Rev. ed. Tokyo: Shōgakukan, 1967.

Kokumin Seishin Sōdōin Honbu. *Kokumin seishin sōdōin chihō taikei narabi jissenmō seibi jōkyō chōsa* [Investigation of the local system of the national spiritual mobilization and current conditions of provisions for practical implementation]. Tokyo: Kokumin Seishin Sōdōin Honbu, 1940.

———. *Kokumin seishin sōdōin undō* [The national spiritual mobilization movement]. Tokyo: Kokumin Seishin Sōdōin Honbu, 1940.

"Kokuryoku no genjō" [The present state of national power], June 8, 1945. In Hara Shobō Henshūbu, *Haisen no kiroku—sanbō honbu shozō* [Record of defeat—General staff documents], pp. 268–70. Tokyo: Hara Shobō, 1967.

Komori Ryūkichi. "Tōkyō ni okeru chōnaikai no hensen ni tsuite" [Changes in community councils in Tokyo]. *Nihon rekishi* [Japanese history], no. 297 (February 1973): 81–96.

Konishi Shirō. "Senjika no kokumin seikatsu" [People's livelihoods in wartime]. In *Taikei Nihonshi sōsho*, vol. 17, *seikatsushi*, pt. 3 [Series of works on Japanese history, vol. 17, History of daily life, pt. 3], edited by Morimatsu Yoshiaki et al., pp. 389–462. Tokyo: Yamakawa Shuppansha, 1969.

Kōriyamashi. *Kōriyamashishi*, vol. 5, *kindai*, pt. 2 [History of Kōriyama, vol. 5, Modern, pt. 2]. Kōriyama: Kōriyamashi, 1971.

Kubota Ai. "Sensō tōji no fujin dantai no ugoki" [Movements of wartime women's groups]. In Iida Bunkazai no Kai, *Dainiji taisen no koro* [The World War Two period], pp. 46–50. Iida: Minami Shinshū Shinbunsha, 1972.

Kubota Shigenori. *Tōkyō daikūshū—kyūgotaichō no kiroku* [The great Tokyo air raids—Record of a rescue squad chieftain]. Tokyo: Ushio Shuppansha, 1973.

Kulischer, Eugene M. *Europe on the Move: War and Population Changes, 1917–1947*. New York: Columbia University Press, 1948.

Kumagai Jirō, ed. *Tonarigumi tokuhon* [A reader for neighborhood associations]. Tokyo: Hibonkaku, 1940.

Kumagai Sonoko. "Senji tōsei to sonraku shakai" [Wartime controls and village society]. *Shakaigaku hyōron* [Sociology review] 20, no. 3 (January 1970): 38–54.

Kurashi no Techōsha. *Tokushū* Kurashi no techō, no. 96, *sensōchū no kurashi no kiroku* [Special issue of *Notebook on Daily Living*, no. 96, Record of daily living during the war]. Tokyo: Kurashi no Techōsha, 1969.

Kuroda Hidetoshi. *Chi nurareta genron* [Bloodied free speech]. Tokyo: Gakufū Shoin, 1951.

Kyōchōkai Chōsabu. *Senji rōdō jijō* [Wartime labor conditions]. Tokyo: Kyōchōkai, 1944.

Kyōto Daigaku Bungakubu Kokushi Kenkyūshitsu. *Nihon kindaishi jiten* [Dictionary of modern Japanese history]. Tokyo: Tōyō Keizai Shinpōsha, 1958.

Lamott, Willis. *Nippon: The Crime and Punishment of Japan*. New York: John Day Company, 1944.

Larson, T. A. *Wyoming's War Years, 1941–1945*. Laramie: The University of Wyoming, 1954.

Leighton, Alexander H. *Human Relations in a Changing World*. New York: E. P. Dutton and Company, Inc., 1949.

Lifton, Robert J. *Death in Life: Survivors of Hiroshima*. New York: Random House, 1967.

Lingeman, Richard R. *Don't You Know There's a War On?* New York: Paperback Library, 1971.

Lory, Hillis. *Japan's Military Masters: The Army in Japanese Life*. New York: Viking Press, 1943.

MacIsaac, David. "The United States Strategic Bombing Survey, 1944–1947." Ph.D. dissertation, Duke University, 1969.

Maejima Tadao. "Senchū sengo no iryō" [Medicine during and after the war]. In Iida Bunkazai no Kai, *Dainiji taisen no koro* [The World War Two period], pp. 33–39. Iida: Minami Shinshū Shinbunsha, 1972.

Mainichi Newspapers. *Fifty Years of Light and Dark: The Hirohito Era*. 2nd ed. Tokyo: Mainichi Newspapers, 1976.

Marwick, Arthur. *The Deluge: British Society and the First World War*. New York: W. W. Norton & Company, Inc., 1970.

——. *War and Social Change in the Twentieth Century*. London: Macmillan, 1974.

Matsuoka, Yoko. *Daughter of the Pacific*. New York: Harper and Brothers, 1952.

McGlauflin, Deborah A. "Minority Status in Japan: The Koreans and the Burakumin." B.A. thesis in Asian studies, Connecticut College, 1975.

Meo, Lucy D. *Japan's Radio War on Australia, 1941–1945*. Carlton: Melbourne University Press, 1968.

Merrill, Francis E. *Social Problems on the Home Front: A Study of Wartime Influences*. New York: Harper & Brothers, 1948.

Merrill, Frederick T. *Japan and the Opium Menace*. New York: Institute of Pacific Relations and Foreign Policy Association, 1942.

Millis, Walter. *Arms and Men*. New York: G. P. Putnam's Sons, 1956.

Milward, Alan S. *The German Economy at War*. London: University of London, 1965.

Mimisaka Tarō, Fujita Chikamasa, and Watanabe Kiyoshi. *Genron no haiboku* [Collapse of free speech]. Tokyo: San'ichi Shobō, 1959.

Minatokuritsu Mita Toshokan. *Senran to Minatoku* [War and Minatoku]. Tokyo: Minatokuritsu Mita Toshokan, 1969.

Minoguchi Tokijirō. "Joshi dōinron" [On mobilizing women]. *Kaizō* [Reconstruction] (March 1943): 37–43.

Mishima, Sumie S. *The Broader Way*. London: Victor Gollancz, 1954.

Mitchell, Richard H. *Thought Control in Prewar Japan*. Ithaca: Cornell University Press, 1976.

Miura Tōsaku, ed. *Kokumin seishin sōdōin gengi* [Basic principles of the national spiritual mobilization]. Toyko: Tōyō Tosho, 1937.

Monbushō. *Gakusei hachijūenshi* [Eighty-year history of the education system]. Tokyo: Ōkurashō Insatsukyoku, 1954.

Mori Takemaro. "Senjika nōson no kōzō henka" [Changes in the structure of wartime villages]. In *Iwanami kōza Nihon rekishi*, vol. 20, *kindai*, pt. 7 [Iwanami colloquium on Japanese history, vol. 20, Modern, pt. 7], pp. 315–65. Tokyo: Iwanami Shoten, 1976.

Mori Teru. *Kaze wa sugiyuku—watakushi no senchū nōto* [The passing wind—My wartime notes]. Tokyo: Rinjinsha, 1967.

Morris, John. *Traveler from Tokyo*. New York: Sheridan House, 1944.

Nagai Kenji. *Aa kokumin gakkō* [National schools]. Tokyo: Asahi Shinbunsha, 1972.

Naikaku, Naimushō, Monbushō. *Kokumin seishin sōdōin shiryō* [Materials on the national spiritual mobilization]. 10 vols. Tokyo: Naikaku, 1937–1938.

Naimushō. "Burakukai chōnaikaitō seibi yōryo" [Essentials of providing for community councils], September 11, 1940. In Jichi Daigakkō, *Sengo jichishi*, vol. 1, *tonarigumi oyobi chōnaikai burakukaitō no haishi* [History of postwar self-rule, vol. 1, The abolition of neighborhood associations and community councils], pp. 2–3. Tokyo: Jichi Daigakkō, 1960.

Naimushō Keihokyoku Hoanka. *Tokkō geppō* [Special Higher Police Monthly Reports]. 4 vols. Tokyo: Seikei Shuppansha, 1972.

Naimushō, Nōrinshō, Shōkōshō, Kōseishō. "Chōnaikai shōhi keizai shisetsu seibi ni kansuru ken" [Regulations concerning providing consumer economy facilities in community councils], October 29, 1942. In Jichi Daigakkō, *Sengo jichishi*, vol. 1, *tonarigumi oyobi chōnaikai burakukaitō no haishi* [History of postwar self-rule, vol. 1, The abolition of neighborhood associations and community councils], pp. 14–16. Tokyo: Jichi Daigakkō, 1960.

Nakajima Kenzō. *Shōwa jidai* [The Shōwa period]. Tokyo: Iwanami Shoten, 1957.

Nakamoto, Hiroko, as told to Mildred Mastin Pace. *My Japan, 1930–1951*. New York: McGraw-Hill Book Co., 1970.

Nakanishi San'yō. "Senjika no higōhō katsudō" [Illegal wartime activity]. *Rekishi hyōron* [History Review], no. 269 (November 1972): 80–89.

Nakanoku. *Nakanokushi*, vol. 1, *Shōwahen* [History of Nakanoku, vol. 1, Shōwa era]. Tokyo: Nakanoku, 1971.

Newman, Joseph. *Goodbye Japan*. New York: L. B. Fischer, 1942.

Nihon Igaku Hyakunenshi Kankōkai. *Nihon igaku hyakunenshi* [Hundred-year history of Japanese medicine]. Tokyo: Rinshō Igakusha, 1957.

Nihon Kindaishi Kenkyūkai. *Zusetsu kokumin no rekishi,* vol. 17, *kokumin seishin sōdōin* [Illustrated national history, vol. 17, The national spiritual mobilization]. Tokyo: Kokubunsha, 1965.

Nihon Seinenkan. *Dai Nihon Seishōnendanshi* [History of the greater Japan youth association]. Tokyo: Nihon Seinenkan, 1970.

Niigataken. *Niigataken hyakunen no ayumi* [Hundred-year history of Niigataken]. Niigata: Niigataken, 1971.

Nippon Times.

Nishimoto, Mitoji. *The Development of Educational Broadcasting in Japan.* Tokyo: Sophia University and Charles E. Tuttle Company, 1969.

Ogura, Takekazu, ed. *Agricultural Development in Modern Japan.* Rev. ed. Tokyo: Fuji Publishing Co., Ltd., 1967.

Ōhara Shakai Mondai Kenkyūjo. *Taiheiyō sensōka no rōdōsha jōtai* [Workers' circumstances during the Pacific war]. Tokyo: Tōyō Keizai Shinpōsha, 1964.

Ohta, Hideaki. "Evacuating Characteristics of Tokyo Citizens." In *Proceedings of the Japan–United States Disaster Research Seminar: Organizational and Community Responses to Disasters,* pp. 175–82. Columbus: Disaster Research Center, The Ohio State University, 1972.

Ohtani, F., ed. *One Hundred Years of Health Progress in Japan,* Tokyo: International Medical Foundation of Japan, 1971.

Okayamashishi Henshū Iinkai. *Okayamashishi, sensai fukkōhen* [History of Okayama, volume on recovery from war damage], Okayama: Okayama Shiyakusho, 1960.

Okochi, Kazuo. *Labor in Modern Japan.* Tokyo: The Science Council of Japan, 1958.

Ōmutashishi Henshū Iinkai. *Ōmutashishi* [History of Ōmuta]. 3 vols. and supplement. Omuta: Ōmutashishi Henshū Iinkai, 1965–1969.

Ōsaka Shiyakusho. *Ōsaka sensai fukkōshi* [History of Ōsaka's recovery from war damage]. Osaka: Ōsaka Shiyakusho, 1958.

Ōya Akiko. "Binbō monogatari" [Tale of poverty]. In Izumi no Kai, *Shufu no sensō taikenki* [Record of housewives' war experiences], pp. 162–68. Nagoya: Fūbaisha, 1965.

Pempel, T. J. "The Politics of Enrollment Expansion in Japanese Universities." *Journal of Asian Studies* 33, no. 1 (November 1973): 67–86.

Perkin, Harold. *The Origins of Modern English Society, 1780–1880.* London: Routledge and Kegan Paul, 1969.

Plath, David W. *The After Hours.* Berkeley and Los Angeles: University of California Press, 1964.

Polenberg, Richard. *War and Society: The United States, 1941–1945*. Philadelphia: J. B. Lippincott Company, 1972.

Randau, Carl, and Zugsmith, Leane. *The Setting Sun of Japan*. New York: Random House, 1942.

Rekishigaku Kenkyūkai. *Taiheiyō sensōshi* [History of the Pacific war]. 6 vols. Tokyo: Aoki Shoten, 1971–1973.

Roth, Andrew. *Dilemma in Japan*. Boston: Little, Brown, 1945.

Saitō Hideo. "Kūshū to minshū" [Air raids and the people]. *Rekishi hyōron* [History review], no. 268 (October 1972): 1–16, 45.

Saitō Isamu. "Shōgatsu o mukaete" [Greeting the new year]. In Gakuto Kinrō Dōin no Kiroku Henshūkai, *Kurenai no chi wa moyuru* [Crimson blood on fire], pp. 203–13. Tokyo: Yomiuri Shinbunsha, 1971.

Sakuraba Hiroshi. "Dainiji taisenka no sensō dōin soshiki o megutte" [Outline of mobilization organizations during World War Two]. *Kanagawakenshi kenkyū* [Studies in the history of Kanagawa prefecture], no. 23 (February 1974): 20–28.

Sato, Kennosuke. "How the Tonarigumi Operates." *Contemporary Japan* 13, nos. 7–9 (July–September 1944): 779–87.

Satō Suzuko, ed. *Nigai hibi—senchū, sengo* [Bitter days—Wartime, postwar]. Tokyo: Kusa no Mi Kai, 1972.

Scalapino, Robert A. "Labor and Politics in Postwar Japan." In *The State and Economic Enterprise in Japan*, edited by William W. Lockwood, pp. 669–720. Princeton: Princeton University Press, 1965.

Seidensticker, Edward. *Kafū the Scribbler: The Life and Writings of Nagai Kafu, 1879–1959*. Stanford: Stanford University Press, 1965.

"Senchū sengo tonarigumi nikki" [Wartime and postwar neighborhood association diary]. In Hirosakishishi Hensan Iinkai, *Hirosakishishi, Meiji Taishō Shōwahen* [History of Hirosaki, volume on the Meiji, Taishō, and Shōwa eras], pp. 645–96. Hirosaki: Hirosakishishi Hensan Iinkai, 1964.

Shandroff, Gary J. "The Evolution of Area Bombing in American Doctrine and Practice." Ph.D. dissertation in history, New York University, 1972.

Shima Tameo. *Meiji hyakunen kyōikushi* [Hundred-year history of education since Meiji]. 2 vols. Tokyo: Nihon Kyōto, 1968.

Shimonaka Yasaburō, ed. *Yokusan kokumin undōshi* [History of the national imperial rule assistance movement]. Tokyo: Yokusan Undōshi Kankōkai, 1954.

Shinmyō Takeo. "Hondo kūshū" [Mainland air raids]. In *Nihon kūshū* [Air Raids on Japan], edited by Okumura Yoshitarō, pp. 172–77. Tokyo: Mainichi Shinbunsha, 1971.

Shiomi, Saburo. *Japan's Finance and Taxation, 1940–1956*. Translated by Shotaro Hasegawa. New York: Columbia University Press, 1957.

Sokai [Evacuation]. Shown at National Film Center, Kyōbashi, Tokyo, March 26, 1973 (first released July 1944).

Sōrifu Kokuritsu Seron Chōsajo. *Chihō jichi seron chōsa—chōnaikai, burakukai, tonarigumi ni tsuite* [Opinion survey of local self-rule— Concerning community councils and neighborhood associations]. Tokyo: Sōrifu, 1952.

Sōrifu Tōkeikyoku. *Nihon tōkei nenkan* [Japan statistical yearbook]. Vol. 1. Tokyo, 1949; vol. 3. Tokyo, 1951.

————. *Nihon tōkei nenkan, tekiyōhan* [Japan statistical yearbook, summary]. Tokyo, 1950.

Steinhoff, Patricia G. "*Tenkō:* Ideology and Societal Integration in Prewar Japan," Ph.D. dissertation in social relations, Harvard University, 1969.

Sukagawashi Kyōiku Iinkai. *Sukagawashishi, gendai,* vol. 2 [History of Sukagawa, modern, vol. 2]. Fukushimaken, Sukagawashi: Sukagawashi Kyōiku Iinkai, 1972.

Sukekawa Hiroshi, ed. *Sōdōinhō taisei* [Administration of the general mobilization law]. Tokyo: Yūhikaku, 1940.

"Supottoraito" [Spotlight]. NHK, channel 1, Tokyo, September 16, 1976.

Sutō Ryōsaku. *Tonarigumichō no shuki* [A neighborhood captain's notes]. Tokyo: privately printed, 1970.

Suzuki Yoshiko. "Kiga no omoi" [Thoughts about hunger]. In Izumi no Kai, *Shufu no sensō taikenki* [Record of housewives' war experiences], pp. 154–61. Nagoya: Fūbaisha, 1965.

Taeuber, Irene B. *The Population of Japan.* Princeton: Princeton University Press, 1958.

Taikakai. *Naimushōshi* [History of the home ministry]. 4 vols. Tokyo: Chihō Zaimu Kyōkai, 1970–1971.

Taisei Yokusankai. *Kokumin sōjōkaishi—daisankai chūō kyōryoku kaigi sōjōkai kaigiroku (zen)* [Record of national general meeting— Record of discussions at the third general meeting of the central cooperation conference (complete)]. Tokyo: Taisei Yokusankai, 1942.

Takahashi Aiko. "Sensō kara no nikki" [Diary from the war]. In Shōwa Sensō Bungaku Zenshū Henshū Iinkai, *Shōwa sensō bungaku zenshū,* vol. 14, *shimin no nikki* [Complete wartime literary works of the Shōwa era, vol. 14, City residents' diaries], pp. 322–57. Tokyo: Shūeisha, 1965.

Takahashi Ichiharu. "Senjika no kokutetsu" [The national railways in wartime]. In Chibaken Sensō Taiken Kiroku Undō Susumeru Kai, *Sensō taiken no kiroku* [Record of war experiences], no. 1,

p. 63. Chiba: Chibaken Sensō Taiken Kiroku Undō Susumeru Kai, 1972.

Takahashi Saburō. "Shūmatsuki no kokumin shisō" [People's thought at the end]. In *Kindai Nihon seiji shisōshi* [History of modern Japanese political thought], edited by Hashikawa Bunzō and Matsumoto Sannosuke, 2:415–34. Tokyo: Yūhikaku, 1970.

Takasuka Kōsei. "Taiheiyō sensōka no gakudō sokai to bunsan jugyō" [Student evacuation and dispersed teaching during the Pacific war]. *Iyo shidan* [Iyo Historical Discussions], no. 200 (January 1971): 79–86.

Takeda Hikozaemon. "Sokai gakudō no ukeire" [The reception of student evacuees]. In Iida Bunkazai no Kai, *Dainiji taisen no koro* [The World War Two period], pp. 117–21. Iida: Minami Shinshū Shinbunsha, 1972.

Tanaka Ningo. "Hyakushō nikki" [Farmer's diary]. In Kurashi no Techōsha, *Tokushū* Kurashi no techō, no. 96, *sensōchū no kurashi no kiroku* [Special issue of *Notebook on Daily Living,* no. 96, Record of daily living during the war], pp. 220–50. Tokyo: Kurashi no Techōsha, 1969.

Tappan, Paul W. *Crime, Justice, and Correction.* New York: McGraw-Hill Book Co., 1960.

Tatakau shōkokumin [Fighting young citizens]. Shown at National Film Center, Kyōbashi, Tokyo, March 26, 1973 (first released September 28, 1944).

Teikoku kokuryoku no genjō [Current condition of the empire's strength], August 11, 1944. In Hara Shobō Henshūbu, *Haisen no kiroku—sanbō honbu shozō* [Record of defeat—General staff documents], pp. 57–162. Tokyo: Hara Shobō, 1967.

Terasaki, Gwen. *Bridge to the Sun.* Chapel Hill: University of North Carolina Press, 1957.

Tillitse, Lars. "When Bombs Rained on Us in Tokyo." *Saturday Evening Post,* January 12, 1946, pp. 34, 82, 85.

Titmuss, Richard M. *Problems of Social Policy.* London: Longmans, Green and Co., 1950.

Tocqueville, Alexis de. *Democracy in America.* In *War: Studies from Psychology, Sociology, and Anthropology,* edited by L. Bramson and G. W. Goethals, pp. 332–44. New York: Basic Books, 1964.

Tōdai Jūhachi Shikai. *Gakuto shutsujin no kiroku* [Record of student mobilization]. Tokyo: Chūō Kōronsha, 1968.

Tōkyōfu Sōmubu Shinkōka. *Tonarigumi fujin tokuhon* [A reader for neighborhood association women]. Tokyo: Tōkyōfu Sōmubu Shinkōka, 1941.

Tōkyō Kokuritsu Kindai Bijutsukan Fuirumu Sentā. *FC fuirumu sentā* [FC Film Center].

Tōkyō Kūshū o Kirokusuru Kai. *Tōkyō daikūshū—sensaishi*

[The great Tokyo air raids—Record of war damage]. 5 vols. Tokyo: Tōkyō Kūshū o Kirokusuru Kai, 1973–1974.

Tōkyō Shisei Chōsakai. *Godai toshi chōnaikai ni kansuru chōsa* [Investigation of community councils in five large cities]. Tokyo: Tōkyō Shisei Chōsakai, 1944.

———. *Nihon toshi nenkan, Shōwa jūgonen'yō* [Japan city annual, 1940]. Tokyo: Tōkyō Shisei Chōsakai, 1940.

———. *Nihon toshi nenkan, Shōwa jūhachinen'yō* [Japan city annual, 1943]. Tokyo: Tōkyō Shisei Chōsakai, 1943.

———. *Tōkyōshi chōnaikai ni kansuru chōsa* [Investigation of community councils in the city of Tokyo]. Tokyo: Tōkyō Shisei Chōsakai, 1925.

Tōkyō Shisei Kakushin Dōmei. *Tōkyōshi no chōkai* [Community councils in the city of Tokyo]. Tokyo: Tōkyō Shisei Kakushin Dōmei, 1938.

Tōkyō Shiyakusho. *Tōkyōshi chōnaikai no chōsa* [Investigation of community councils in the city of Tokyo]. Tokyo: Tōkyō Shiyakusho, 1934.

Tōkyō Teikoku Daigaku Shakai Kagaku Kenkyūkai. *Tachiagaru hitobito* [People who are springing back]. Tokyo: Gakusei Shobō, 1946.

Toland, John. *The Rising Sun.* New York: Random House, 1970.

Tolischus, Otto D. *Tokyo Record.* New York: Reynal & Hitchcock, 1943.

Tomita Kimiko. "Kokubōshoku no seishun" [Youth in khaki]. In Izumi no Kai, *Shufu no sensō taikenki* [Record of housewives' war experiences], pp. 127–32. Nagoya: Fūbaisha, 1965.

Torinoumi Shigeko. "Shōidan o abite" [In the midst of incendiary bombs]. In Kusa no Mi Kai Daishichi Gurūpu, *Sensō to watakushi* [The war and I], pp. 33–36. Tokyo: Kusa no Mi Kai, 1963.

Totsuka, Hideo. "Korean Immigration in Prewar Japan." *Annals of the Institute of Social Sciences*, no. 17 (1976): 89–110.

Tottoriken. *Tottorikenshi, kindai*, vol. 4, *shakai bunkahen* [History of Tottori prefecture, modern, vol. 4, Society and culture]. Tottori: Tottoriken, 1969.

Tōyama Shigeki, Imai Seiichi, and Fujiwara Akira. *Shōwashi* [History of the Shōwa era]. Rev. ed. Tokyo: Iwanami Shoten, 1959.

Tsuji Toyoji, ed. *Aa Toyokawa joshi teishintai* [The Toyokawa women's volunteer corps]. Tokyo: Kōyō Shobō, 1963.

Tsurumi, Kazuko. *Social Change and the Individual: Japan Before and After Defeat in World War II.* Princeton: Princeton University Press, 1970.

U.S. Army Air Forces, Intelligence Headquarters, Assistant Chief of Staff. *Mission Accomplished: Interrogations of Japanese Industrial, Military, and Civil Leaders of World War II,* Washington, D.C., 1946.

U.S. Bureau of the Budget, War Records Section. *The United States at War: Development and Administration of the War Program by the Federal Government*. Bureau of the Budget, Historical Reports on War Administration, no. 1. Washington, D.C.: U.S. Government Printing Office, 1946.

U.S. Strategic Bombing Survey, Morale Division. *The Effects of Strategic Bombing on German Morale*. 2 vols. Washington, D.C., 1946–1947.

———. *The Effects of Strategic Bombing on Japanese Morale*. Washington, D.C., 1947.

U.S. Strategic Bombing Survey, Over-all Economic Effects Division. *The Effects of Strategic Bombing on Japan's War Economy*. Washington, D.C., 1946.

Urabe Takeyo. "Shirami" [Lice]. In Izumi no Kai, *Shufu no sensō taikenki* [Record of housewives' war experiences], pp. 144–51. Nagoya: Fūbaisha, 1965.

Vasiljevová, Zdenka. "The Industrial Patriotic Movement—A Study on the Structure of Fascist Dictatorship in War-Time Japan." In Vlasta Hilská and Zdenka Vasiljevová, *Problems of Modern Japanese Society*, pp. 65–157. Prague: Charles University, 1971.

Wagner, Edward W. *The Korean Minority in Japan, 1904–1950*. Vancouver: University of British Columbia Publications Centre, 1951.

Wenger, Dennis. "DRC Studies of Community Functioning." In *Proceedings of the Japan–United States Disaster Research Seminar: Organizational and Community Responses to Disasters*, pp. 29–72. Columbus: Disaster Research Center, The Ohio State University, 1972.

Wray, Harold J. "Changes and Continuity in Japanese Images of the *Kokutai* and Attitudes and Roles Toward the Outside World, A Content Analysis of Japanese Textbooks, 1903–1945." Ph.D. dissertation in history, University of Hawaii, 1971.

Wright, Gordon. *The Ordeal of Total War, 1939–1945*. New York: Harper & Row, 1968.

Yabashi Yasuko. "Musume ni kataru" [Telling my daughter]. In Izumi no Kai, *Shufu no sensō taikenki* [Record of housewives' war experiences], pp. 133–36. Nagoya: Fūbaisha, 1965.

Yanaga, Chitoshi. *Japan Since Perry*. New York: McGraw-Hill Book Co., 1949.

Yasko, Richard. "Hiranuma Kiichiro and the New Structure Movement 1940–1941." *Asian Forum* 5, no. 2 (April–June 1973): 121–29.

Yoneda Sayoko. *Kindai Nihon joseishi* [History of modern Japanese women]. 2 vols. Tokyo: Shin Nihon Shuppansha, 1972.

Yoshizawa Hisako. "Shūsen made" [To the end of the war]. In Shōwa Sensō Bungaku Zenshū Henshū Iinkai, *Shōwa sensō bungaku zenshū*, vol. 14, *shimin no nikki* [Complete wartime liter-

ary works of the Shōwa era, vol. 14, City residents' diaries],
pp. 358–88. Tokyo: Shūeisha, 1965.

Young, James R. *Behind the Rising Sun*. New York: Doubleday, Doran
and Company, Inc., 1941.

Zenkoku Nōgyōkai Chōsabu. *Sokaisha ni kansuru chōsa* [Inquiry concerning evacuees]. N.p.: Zenkoku Nōgyōkai, 1946.

Index

France, 54; movies, 24; mobilization, 14
Free Artists' Association (Jiyū Bijutsuka Kyōkai, 1937), 68
Fujihara Genjirō, 117
Fujita Tsuguji, 68
Fukui pref., 48, 60, 144
Fulbright, J. William, 5
Funabashi, 124
Furui Yoshimi, 71
Futabayama, 2

Gallant Death of Attu, 68
geisha, 150–51
Germany, 3, 41, 53; air raids, 176, 181, 186–87; evacuation, 167–68; inflation, 35; labor, 104; music, 149; nutrition, 130; press, 66; propaganda, 20; Tripartite Alliance, 54; wages, 93; women workers, 107
Gilbert Islands (11/43), 155
Ginza, 15, 17–18, 40, 156, 162
"Going to the Sea" (Umi Yukaba), 85
golf, 51–52
Great Britain, 6; divorces, 137; evacuation, 167–68; inflation, 35; mobilization, 14; movies, 24; nutrition, 130; propaganda, 20; surrenders Singapore, 148; wages, 93; women workers, 107, 109
Greater East Asia Co-Prosperity Sphere (Dai Tōa Kyōeiken, 9/40), 28, 55, 202
Greater Japan Assistance Adult Association (Dai Nihon Yokusan Sōnendan, 1/16/42), 59–60
Greater Japan Patriotic Industrial Association (Dai Nihon Sangyō Hōkokukai, 11/23/40), 56–58
Greater Japan Women's Association (Dai Nihon Fujinkai, 2/2/42), 58–59
Greater Japan Youth Association (Dai Nihon Seishōnendan, 1/16/41), 57–59
Guadalcanal (2/43), 155, 175
Guidebook for Neighborhood Association Meetings, 77
Guillain, Robert, 118, 148
Gunma pref., 94, 170

Hamada girls' high school (Shimane pref.), 133
Hamadate Kikuo, 165–66
Han, 167
Hanaoka (Akita pref.), 106
Hatano Isoko, 71, 124, 171, 188–89
Hayashi Fumiko, 23
health, 46–49, 96, 111, 142–47, 165–66
health centers, *see* public health centers
Hegel, 64
Herodotus, 9

Hesse, 64
Hiraide Hiizu, 65
Hiranuma Kiichirō, 56, 59
Hiroshima, 102, 111, 176–77, 190–91, 205
History of Japanese Thought, 65
History of the Japanese Spirit, 65
Hitler, 34, 107, 195
hodgepodge dining halls (Zōsui Shokudō), 126, 129
Hokkaido, 67, 102, 139
home ministry (Naimushō), 53, 56–58; air defense and, 158–59; censorship by, 25; community councils, neighborhood associations, and, 36–39, 42–43, 75, 78–83, 86; evacuation and, 162–66; health and, 47–49, 143; labor and, 44–46, 95; spiritual mobilization and, 13, 37; thought police (Tokkō), 22, 69–71, 95–96, 100
Honjo national school (Tokyo), 179
"honor home" (*meiyo no ie*), 33
Hoshi Imae, 141
Hosokawa Karoku, 66
"Hotaru no hikari," 149
housing, 121–22, 159, 167–68, 176–77

Ichikawa Fusae, 78
ideology, 14, 195–97
Ienaga Saburō, 71
Iida (Nagano pref.), 48, 99, 141, 163
Ikenoue national school (Tokyo), 164
illness, *see* health
Imperial Edict Day (Taishō Hōtaibi, 2/8/42f), 17
imperial education rescript, *see* education rescript
Imperial Hotel, 122
Imperial Rule Assistance Association (Taisei Yokusankai, 9/27/40), 45, 55–61, 108, 188, 199, 204; community councils, neighborhood associations, and, 77–83
Indochina, 54; *see also* Vietnam
inflation, *see* prices
Inoue Kiyoshi, 107, 132
Isetan, 121
Ishii Tominosuke, 128, 131
Ishizuka Rui, 171
Italy, 3; Tripartite Alliance, 54; music, 149
Itō Gorō, 184
Itō Ryōichi, 122
Iwase Tatsuko, 111
Iwo Jima, 175, 183

James, David H., 180
Japan Communist party, 66
Japan Patriotic Literary Association (Nihon Bungaku Hōkokukai, 5/42), 65

INDEX : 275